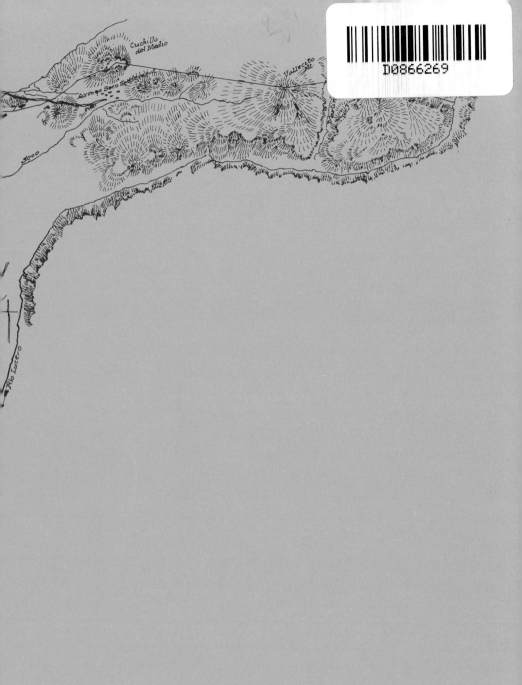

Cuchillo
del Medio

Arroyo Seco Sevilleta

Seco

Vallecito

Rio Lucero

To Possess the Land

A Biography of
Arthur Rochford Manby

To Possess the Land

A Biography of
Arthur Rochford Manby

Frank Waters

SAGE BOOKS

THE SWALLOW PRESS INC.
CHICAGO

First Edition
First Printing

Sage Books are published by
The Swallow Press Incorporated
1139 South Wabash Avenue
Chicago, Illinois 60605

This Book is printed on 100% recycled paper

ISBN 0-8040-0647-4
LIBRARY OF CONGRESS CATALOG CARD NUMBER 73-13210.

Contents

Illustrations

Introduction

The story of Arthur Manby's incredible life and mysterious death or disappearance can be recounted from three widely divergent viewpoints.

From one, it is a story of violent action and events that exceed the wildest imaginations of Hollywood producers of Western thrillers and mystery horror-films. In approved tradition, it opens on the frontier of the Wild West with a cowboy feud and a shoot-out. Fantastic incidents, unequalled in pure fiction, mark the career of this brilliant promoter, ruthless land grabber, and art connoisseur—a legal contract drawn for the disposal of $827,000,000; a forged U.S. government gold certificate for $1,000,000; a secret society terrorizing towns and villages. And the story ends with Manby's horrible murder or mysterious disappearance, which, with its international complications, remains the greatest unsolved mystery of the West.

From a second viewpoint it is a detailed, documented history of the devious methods by which one of the numerous Spanish land grants was individually acquired during the era of American occupation of New Mexico following the Mexican War. The United States government made no effort to observe the provision in the Treaty of Guadalupe Hidalgo insuring the preservation of the rights of the conquered people. Greedy promoters, land grabbers, lawyers and politicians, corporations and railroads, moved in swiftly to take possession of the newly

acquired territory. Their virtual theft of the land and its vast
natural resources from the commonwealth and public domain
is an aspect of history not yet thoroughly documented and made
public. Recently it has emerged to national prominence through
the issue of the ownership of the vast Tierra Amarilla Land
Grant: the storming of the courthouse in the village of Tierra
Amarilla, the arrest and conviction of Tijerina, and the formation of his *Alianza* to assert the rights of Spanish Americans.
Hence this account of Manby's acquisition of the Antonio Martinez or Lucero de Godoi Land Grant is a significant part of
the overall political, economic, and social picture and of historical importance.

The third approach differs greatly from its extroverted
Western-mystery aspect, and its impersonal and historical
aspect. The story of Manby can be recounted from a wholly
introverted, psychological viewpoint. No antecedents in the
genealogy of his distinguished English family can account for
his deviation as a curious blacksheep. Even to the members
of his immediate family he was a mystery. His life might well
constitute a psychological case history: apparently that of a
man finally and completely possessed by his "shadow," that
negative and usually repressed aspect of the dual nature of
each of us.

It is obviously impossible to narrate Manby's story on all
three of these widely different levels in a book that is required
by usual literary standards to adhere strictly to one point of
view. Yet each approach is essential. To solve this dilemma
without subterfuge, I have deliberately ignored all literary pre-
tenses to form, letting the chips fall where they may. I have
simply presented here, for the first time, all the facts known
about him, the conjectures, the tantalizing clues to his enigmatic
character. From this primary source material can be developed
later fiction, historical papers, and psychological studies.

FRANK WATERS
TAOS, NEW MEXICO

Epilogue

On a hot morning in the summer of 1929 United States Deputy Marshal Jim Martinez from Santa Fe, driving a dust-covered jalopy, crawled out of the dark gorge of the Rio Grande. Taos Valley spreading out before him was a long-familiar scene. His historic family had lived in northern New Mexico for generations. It included the famous Padre Antonio Martinez who had helped to organize a bloody revolt against American occupation in 1847, probably for the very good reason that in 1716 a preceding Antonio Martinez had been awarded a large land grant below the shoulder of the lofty peak ahead and saw no reason why it and the rest of the country should be taken over by gringos. Now, two centuries later, the marshal's brother Malaquias was still living on a piece of the grant although the rest had been stolen by the old man the marshal now had been sent to see.

He was in fact carrying papers to serve on A. R. Manby in renewal of a suit brought against him by a woman in 1922. The court had awarded her a judgment, but it had not been paid. Now after seven years the suit would expire unless it was renewed, and Marshal Jim Martinez had been instructed to serve the papers without fail.

He puttered through the familiar straggle of small adobes which surrounded the massive, buttressed Mission Church of San Francisco at Ranchos de Taos, and rumbled into the town of Don Fernando de Taos. Old Manby's large hacienda-style home was only a few buildings away from the central plaza and surrounded by a high adobe wall. The front gate was locked and several people stood uneasily in front of it.

"*Que pasó?*" he asked.

A bystander shrugged—an eloquent answer.

It was the sweltering noon of July 3; and fearing that the old man might have gone off for a Fourth of July celebration before he could serve his papers, the marshal returned to the plaza. The sidewalks were jammed with a holiday crowd: Spanish villagers, Anglo merchants, cowpokes, farmers, gamblers, Indians wrapped in their white sheets despite the heat, a few artists, loafers of all kinds. The marshal went inside the courthouse. His brother Malaquias, the deputy sheriff, was talking to another idle group in the hall. The marshal explained his errand.

"Something must be wrong," answered Malaquias. "George Ferguson here tells me he thinks Manby is dead."

Ferguson nodded assent. "Flies are swarming all over the back screen door."

How Ferguson could have looked through two high walls and seen flies on the back door, the marshal didn't know or ask. He simply accompanied both men back to Manby's house.

A crowd was beginning to gather at the front gate by now, probably drawn by rumors spreading from Ferguson's assertions. Several people the marshal knew; others Malaquias identified in a low voice. They included Doc Martin who lived next door; big-boned Milton A. Spotts, a county commissioner; Teracita Ferguson, George's aunt; Carmen Duran, with whom Teracita was now living; her friend, a large woman named Mrs. Felix Archuleta who operated a restaurant in town; a *politico* by the name of Des Georges; and several others.

Led by Carmen Duran, the group walked around the high adobe wall to the far side, climbed over it, and walked through the back patio to the back of the front wing of the house. Here Duran discovered that he had a key to the door. Unlocking it, he led the group inside.

Following a terrible stench and the swarm of blue bottle-flies, Marshal Martinez entered one of the front bedrooms. There on a cot beside the wall, he confronted an unpleasant sight: the decapitated body of a man dressed in heavy underwear, a red sweater, and a khaki coat. The body was swollen in the July heat but not decomposed, and maggots were crawling around it. Beside the cot lay Manby's large German police dog.

"Here Lobo!" Carmen Duran, taking the dog by the collar, led him out into the patio where Malaquias shot him. Another dog was howling and jerking at his tether, and this one Malaquias tied up to take home later.

When the men returned to the house, the group was standing in the adjoining bedroom where Deputy Marshal Martinez had discovered the decapitated head, the right side of the face obliterated.

A coroner's jury was formed immediately, with Des Georges as foreman. Without hesitation it pronounced that Manby had died from natural causes and that Lobo had then gnawed off his master's head.

"That's that!" grunted Doc Martin. "The crazy old coot's dead. Let's git him under!"

Within an hour the group had placed the old man's head and torso in a wooden box and buried it on the back of his property which adjoined the small cemetery in which the famous scout Kit Carson was buried.

For Deputy Marshal Martinez the matter was ended; he got into his car and drove back to Santa Fe.

For the town it was just beginning. A few persons confidently asserted that the old man had been murdered, and darkly hinted that they could offer proof. This was vociferously denied by others who claimed the decapitated body found was not Manby's. Still others swore they had seen Manby the day after his alleged body had been buried. All agreed there was something strange about the whole business, and their wild conjectures, allegations, and suspicions were echoed by the press.

So there began to mushroom one of the greatest unsolved mysteries of the Southwest, and of America, with international complications. Yet the manner of Manby's passing did not equal the mystery of his long life. Who he was, what manner of man he was—this disreputable old recluse in his enormous, nineteen-room Spanish hacienda who had been taken for granted for so many years—no one knew. They only knew that from the day of his mysterious death or disappearance, his squat, wide-shouldered figure cast a shadow long in time and substance. Like a headless body, it stretched from the somber black gorge of the Rio Grande, over the corn *milpas* around the little adobe town, to the blood-red peaks of the Sangre de Cristos. For more than forty years it had lain dark and heavy upon them all. The poor Spanish folk seeking relief in the charms of native *brujas* from the evil he cast upon them. The Indians lifting their hairless eyebrows and growing elaborately dumb at the mention of his name. And the Anglo artists and newcomers volubly probing the undying speculations about him.

No one, perhaps, ever really knew him. Always unpredictable, he exceeded everything told about him. Yet, image and shadow, all that he was and did reflected the monstrous immensities of the land that had been his one great passion—the great bulks of the heaving mountains, the grassy *vegas* sere under drought, the flat-topped mesas and the buttes weirdly carven as his own fantastic dreams and schemes, all the richness and poverty, the beauty and cruelty of the land that was at once his great dream and his folly. The mystery of Manby, if one would seek its ultimate meaning, is still embodied within the mountain below which lies his alleged grave.

The Dream

1

A rthur Rochford[1] Manby. This was the apple-cheeked young
Englishman who on the afternoon of September 12, 1883
was walking down the boardwalk street of frontier Raton.
There was no mistaking his casual but expensive worsted
jacket, sturdy body, and big head with its noble brow; but the
undeniable stamp of his personality was that intangible aura
which, even then, was gathering like a coming storm about him.
Just twenty-four years old, he had arrived in the Territory of
New Mexico three months before and already had made up
his mind to stay. Entering the court house, he filed with O. M.
Phillips, District Court Clerk of Colfax County, his declaration
to become a citizen of the United States.

The few terse facts with which he filled out his papers did
not sufficiently outline his impressive background. The family
tree could be traced back to 1656, extending branches into
government, law, army, navy, and the church. His great-grandfather, Dr. Edward Manby of Buckinghamshire, was a surgeon
in the Royal Navy and an aide to Captain James Cook during
his third voyage to Australia in 1776. Manby Point in southern
Alaska was named in his honor. His grandfather, the Reverend
John Manby, first served as secretary to the Duke of Sussex,
the third son of King George III, and was then ordained as
Vicar of Lancashire, his position being affirmed by the King.

Both his father, the Reverend Edward Francis Manby, and

his mother, Emily Norton, granddaughter of Sir John Blois, were natives of Southwold parish in Suffolk. Soon after their marriage on September 30, 1848[2] they too moved to the prosperous borough of Lancashire, about fifty miles north of Liverpool. Lancaster, the county seat, was a small river port on the banks of the Lune. On a nearby hill stood the ruins of a thirteenth century castle with a Norman tower built on the site of a Roman *castrum* or military post, and the fifteenth century church of St. Mary. A few miles downstream lay the village of Morecambe which overlooked the bay. Here in Poulton parish the couple established residence in the comfortable circumstances permitted by Edward's secure position as clerk in Holy Orders and elder of the Established Church of England. As the rector of Morecambe, Reverend Edward Francis Manby was not obliged to live in a small vicarage. From his father he had inherited Poulton Hall, a large, ivy-covered, two-story manor set on a small estate. Here he lived like a country squire, a sporting and hunting parson.

Regularly, almost every year from 1849 to 1862, Emily Norton Manby gave birth and the family grew to nine children, three girls and six boys.[3] Arthur Rochford Manby, born on July 14, 1859, was the next to the last child, Jocelyn.

Manby's childhood must have been pleasant but dull. His mother's favorite child, he accompanied her whenever she could escape the demands of the other children. On the hill he played among the stones of the ruined castle while she set up an easel and painted the old church and the docile landscape. The bay may have been more interesting, for the little village of Morecambe, already becoming popular as a seaside resort, boasted two piers, a quay, and a long promenade. Here his mother painted delicate watercolors of the piers jutting out into the bay. They were small pictures, painted broadly, but with a sure touch that reflected her mild, pleasant nature and love of the land.

Yet the sea never appealed to Manby, as it did later to his sea-going younger brother Jocelyn. He felt cramped in the little river valley, dreaming of farther, wider shores. Roaming up and down the long promenade and the beach, he was forever building castles in the sand. From his mother he inherited not only a taste for art, but a feeling for the land. His was not

Poulton Hall, the Manby family home in Morecambe, England.

the feeling of a peasant, but of an imperialist. There were always those castles he was building of stones, sand, and clouds.

His oldest brother Eardley years later recalled that Manby when young had fallen from their two-story balcony, injuring his head; this had made him "peculiar," unable to get along with the family and neighbors.[4] Spoiled and willful he may have been, but certainly the injury did not retard Manby's rapid mental development.

As a youth he was sent to Belfast, Ireland for schooling. A talented watercolorist, he first was engrossed in art, then took up the study of architecture, later developing an avid interest in mineralogy. At this time he first read in a British newspaper of the fabulously rich natural resources and opportunities for exploitation in the backward Territory of New Mexico, exemplified by the massive Maxwell Grant, the largest land-holding in America.

No one needs to question further what brought Manby to America. Its untouched wilderness had aroused from the start a greedy passion in the breasts of colonists from all Europe: Spanish, Portuguese, French, Dutch, and especially the English, so constricted on their tiny islands. Of all these freebooters in the era of worldwide colonialism, the English were as distinguished for their mist-cold and shrewd mercenary greed to wring commercial profit of all kinds from the land, as the Spanish were for their hot-blooded and naive rapaciousness for gold.

Manby's rector father died in 1876 and some four years later disposition of his estate was made. The bulk of the assets was invested undivided by all his children, the interest by their common assent going to one of Manby's married sisters, Mrs. Clara Athill, who was in financial difficulties due to her husband's crippling heart attack. One can question whether Manby's full share of the estate was invested with those of his brothers and sisters. With an irascible disposition that caused him to be regarded as the black sheep of the family, he was itching to go to America and clamoring for money. Moreover his mother would never have permitted her favorite son to sail in steerage to a strange country where as a penniless immigrant he would have to grub for a living as best he might. It seems probable that he was given about 2,000 pounds sterling out of the estate.[5] So late in May 1883 Manby, with ample funds, set sail for

New York where he boarded a train to the New Mexico wilderness.

Despite his wildest imaginings, Manby must have been unprepared for its majestic immensity when he first saw the high blue wall of the Sangre de Cristos rising abruptly from the short-grass buffalo plains as his train climbed steadily westward; and he glimpsed from the summit of Raton Pass wave upon wave of forested ranges emerging from the lifting mists, and far beyond, the cloud-capped twin Spanish Peaks, *Wah-to-Yah*, those rounded "Breasts of the World" as the Indians called them. Tidy and cramped little England had not prepared him for this! Yet something within him rose to meet its challenge. Already he was caught by the impalpable mystery of the mountains which were to hold him for the rest of his life.

Raton at the bottom of Raton Pass in northern New Mexico where he and two companions got off the train, like its counterpart, Trinidad, Colorado at the northern foot of the pass, was strategically located on the old Santa Fe Trail. To this high rocky barrier for a half-century the great wagon caravans had rolled their way across the baking plains, crawled laboriously over its summit, and snaked on to Santa Fe. Neither of the settlements were held to be much shakes as towns, yet they were beginning to grow. The Santa Fe Railroad had replaced the Santa Fe Trail only three years before. Now to the small but tough population of bullwhackers, teamsters, cartwrights, ranchers, cowpokes, and gamblers, were being added railroad workers, settlers, merchants, saloon keepers, confidence men, and land speculators.

The *Raton Comet* of June 8, 1883 announced Manby's arrival with A. H. Hartley and E. Winter, describing all three men as gentlemen of large means from Belfast, Ireland who were seeking ranches, ranges, and cattle to invest in. They were reported to be the guests of Albert Shaw of Belmont Ranch. Nothing more was known of Hartley and Winter who probably bought no property and left New Mexico. Nor was anything heard of Shaw of the Belmont Ranch. Evidently Manby's stay with him was short, for he moved into the Moulton Hotel.

It was a big country for a stranger to survey, and Manby took his time. He was particularly interested in the Maxwell Grant of which he had heard so much. Learning that several

officers of the company which controlled it were meeting some
forty miles away in Cimarron, he inquired about stage accommodations from the hotel clerk. He was promptly offered a ride
by a lanky cowpoke who was lounging at the desk.

The clerk introduced him. "Mr. Manby, this is Mr. Jesse
Lee, the deputy sheriff from Springer. You'll be quite all right."

Lee flung back his vest to reveal a tin star. "Yep. Come along.
You won't mind stopping with a rancher I've got to see. He'll
bed us down for the night."

Riding in a buckboard next day, they drove south and then
turned west toward the base of the mountains. The long-grass
country was darkly splotched with herds of cattle among which
grazed bands of delicate quick-stepping antelopes. Occasionally
they glimpsed clumps of squat adobes around which played
naked mud-brown children.

"Goddamned squatters!" said Lee. "That's what's worryin'
the company. See what I mean?"

This was the rambling topic of conversation that night between
Lee and their rancher host as they sat over a bottle of bourbon.
The ranch house was small and tawdry; and Manby, wrapped
in a blanket on the floor, ignored it as he tried to sleep.

Next day he and Lee followed Cimarron Creek up toward the
mountains. Manby felt a twinge of excitement as the canyons
of that dark blue wall began to reach out like fingers to enclose
him, the great hulks to heave up around him. He could en-
vision the high mountain meadows teeming with deer and elk
and the little mountain sheep called *cimarrones* jumping from
crag to crag; feel the wind from forests of spruce and pine cooling his armpits; hear the arpeggio of trout streams playing over
the rocks; and glimpse from ridgetop to ridgetop a panorama
of wilderness without end. Manby had imagination, though not
wholly of the poetic kind. He knew right then he was where
he belonged and what he wanted.

That afternoon Lee drew up his team in front of a huge
adobe in the small town of Cimarron. "This was Maxwell's old
rancho. Who you figurin' on seein'?"

Manby did not reply as he looked over the famous old manor
with the interest of an architect. It was indeed a great mansion
of twenty-two rooms, built of sun-dried adobe bricks as was
the custom here, but two stories high, with a pitched roof and

dormer windows that reminded him of an English country house. A queer anomaly built by a man part French, part Irish, and married to a Spanish woman! Still it had been the seat of a wilderness empire, and tales of its fabulous hospitality still entranced him.

"Wait here," he said curtly, climbing out of the buckboard.

"I ain't sittin' on my behind for nobody! You come over to the hotel!" Lee whipped up his mares and rolled away in a cloud of dust.

Late that afternoon Manby came out of the old mansion and trudged down the road to the hotel. The St. James was also an oddity to the young Englishman. Built by a young French cook named Henri Lambert who had straggled across the buffalo plains, it had been opened a decade before but had just been replastered and modernized. Serving excellent French cuisine and decorated with great heads of grizzly bear, elk, deer, and antelope mounted on the walls, it was acclaimed one of the finest hotels in New Mexico. It certainly must be one of the rowdiest too, thought Manby as he glimpsed the bullet holes attesting to the first dozen of the twenty-six men to be killed here. After registering, Manby walked into the bar and found Lee sitting in a corner with a big-boned man wearing a gun on his hip.

"Manby. The furriner I was tellin' you about," said Lee. "This here's my pal, Jim Masterson."

Manby sat down with them and ordered a bottle brought over. "Help yourselves. I don't drink bourbon."

Lee warmed up enough to ask, "Well, how'd you come out on your business, whatever it was?"

"I'm staying here tonight so we can talk more about it tomorrow," he said cautiously. "About my taking up some land and raising cattle."

A quick sharp look passed between Masterson and Lee. The deputy sheriff was not one to control his astonishment. "The company's tryin' to run all settlers and squatters off the grant! How come you're movin' in?"

"Maybe there's a reason for it," Masterson said, carefully appraising Manby's worsted coat and well-groomed hands, his air of cold determination and aloof superiority. "English, eh? And hankerin' to pitch hay and herd cows?" He shrugged, then asked suddenly, "You got enough money to get started?"

"I have ample funds to defray all expenses. Perhaps you can help me."

"Buy yourself a gun first off, and learn how to shoot it," said Masterson tersely. "We can talk about cows later."

Manby's negotiations with the Maxwell Land Grant Company finally concluded with his purchase of four sections of land in Vermejo Park, a remote area of the grant. He sent to England for two of his brothers, Alfred and Jocelyn. Meanwhile he bought a rifle and a revolver, and practiced shooting every day, also spending several hours in the saddle. Masterson and Lee were a great help. The vulgarity of these Westerners impressed Manby; yet their practical appraisals of the company's feud with the settlers embroidered the legal history of the Maxwell Grant which he studied every night. If there was something incongruous about a young Englishman learning to ride a horse and shoot a gun by day, and reading law by night, Manby did not know it. He knew only that he was beginning his career on the vast wilderness empire known as the Maxwell Land Grant, and that he must learn every ramification of its involved history.

The Maxwell Grant, he found, was a Mexican grant of fairly recent origin.[6] Early in 1841, when Nuevo Mexico was still a province of Mexico, Guadalupe Miranda and Carlos Beaubien were given upon petition a huge land grant of 2,680 square miles or 1,714,764 acres extending along the eastern slope of the Sangre de Cristo mountains north into Colorado. Desirous of still more land, Beaubien petitioned for another grant in the name of his fourteen-year-old son Narciso, and his brother-in-law Stephen Luis Lee. The petition was duly approved, giving them the Sangre de Cristo Grant of 1,622 square miles or 1,038,195 acres on the western slope and extending north of Taos into the great San Luis Valley of Colorado.

There now happened in swift succession a series of complicated events that brought all this domain under the control of Lucien Bonaparte Maxwell, an energetic trader and trapper who had married Beaubien's fourteen-year-old daughter Luz. In 1846, upon the outbreak of the American-Mexican War, General Kearny marched to Santa Fe and annexed all the northern province of Nuevo Mexico to the United States.

Miranda fled to Mexico. In the bloody Taos revolt against American occupation the following year both Narciso and Lee were massacred as well as Charles Bent to whom Beaubien had secretly sold one-fourth interest in the Beaubien-Miranda Grant. Beaubien inherited his son's share of the Sangre de Cristo Grant and bought Lee's share for $100.

When the country quieted down, Miranda returned on a brief visit to sell his half of the Beaubien-Miranda Grant to Maxwell for $2,745. In 1864 Beaubien died, leaving his one-half share of the grant to his six children, and Maxwell promptly bought five of the six legacies for $14,500. Two years later he bought the remaining one-fourth interest from Charles Bent's heirs for $18,000. He thus became owner, for a total expenditure of $35,245, of what was now known as the Maxwell Land Grant, making him the largest landholder in the United States.

Maxwell was a man simple enough to take pleasure walking barefoot through a lush meadow and cooling his feet in a ditch of cold mountain water. Yet he was shrewd enough to manage his empire with the iron hand of a benevolent despot. Each of the five hundred or more men who lived on his land was a virtual peon living a feudal life according to the traditional Spanish pattern. Still, as a good patron, Maxwell demanded of them only the labor required to keep up his fields and herds. Freighters over the Santa Fe Trail between Raton Pass and Fort Union were seldom out of sight of his herds of 100,000 sheep, cattle, and horses. The ruling seat of his back-country empire was the huge, two-story, adobe manor house on the Cimarron that Manby had seen. His hospitality was legendary; any traveler passing by was welcome—honored guest or stray *vacquero* alike.

It was a good life until 1866 when gold was discovered in Moreno Valley, a high mountain meadow on Maxwell's grant. There was no damming the flood of prospectors and miners sweeping across his land to the mountains above. What Maxwell's income was now from his stock, produce, and mines no one knew. Money was coming in too fast for him to spend with his comparatively simple tastes, but the feudal, pastoral life on his grant was being swept away by forces over which he had no control. There seemed no way out until in 1869 the dexterous hands of General William J. Palmer and Dr. William Bell reached out to succor him.

Palmer was a proud and aristocratic Philadelphian born with the strange compulsion to ape English life and manners; a man who dressed all his life in an English tweed coat, riding breeches, and boots. Attaining the rank of general in the Civil War, he had made a railroad survey to the West Coast for the Kansas Pacific. Palmer then conceived a north-south line of his own to run from Denver south through the valley of the Rio Grande into Mexico—the Denver and Rio Grande. His key problem was to acquire a great tract of land along the right-of-way which could be bought cheaply and sold at a profit high enough to finance construction of the line.

Young Dr. Bell supplied a helpful idea. The son of one of England's most fashionable doctors, Bell was a medical graduate who, loving adventure, had joined Palmer's surveying crew. He recalled to Palmer that half of the immense Sangre de Cristo Grant on the other side of the mountains had been sold to a group of influential Englishmen including William Blackmore, a barrister, promoter, and friend of Bell's. Blackmore had promptly issued in London a privately printed land prospectus seeking British investments in the grant. One of Blackmore's brothers was R. D. Blackmore, author of the immensely popular novel *Lorna Doone*. The other two brothers were alcoholics whom William had brought to the grant in hopes the outdoor life would cure them. The country then, insisted Bell, was known to other affluent English friends who would be eager to invest in other valuable property. That property, the astute General Palmer recognized at once, was the more immense Maxwell Land Grant which lay along the route of his projected railroad.

Backstage manipulations began at once when four offstage speculators offered to relieve Maxwell of his great burden. One of them was Wilson Waddingham, a wealthy Englishman. Maxwell accepted their terms: $12,000 for an option on his grant at a purchase price of $650,000.

Evidently the promoters already had been dickering through Bell with a syndicate of English speculators headed by John Collinson of London who offered $1,350,000 for the grant. Six months later, in 1870, Maxwell released his entire grant save for his home ranch of 1,000 acres.

As American laws did not permit foreigners to hold real estate, the English syndicate filed for incorporation in New

Mexico under the name of the Maxwell Land Grant and Railroad Company, with General Palmer as president. The company
was capitalized at $5,000,000 and four men owned most of the
stock: Collinson, Waddingham, Bell, and Palmer. That June
they mortgaged the grant to a new group of English and Dutch
speculators for 700,000 pounds sterling (about $3,500,000,)
payable in London or Amsterdam to avoid United States taxes.
This was followed two years later by a second mortgage given
to the Farmers Loan and Trust Company in New York for
275,000 pounds sterling.

Even Maxwell must have realized that he had been made
the victim of a colossal stock and bond swindle. In August he
relinquished his last holdings and drove off in a carriage from
his great empire. Nettled by his loss, he invested heavily in
a paper railroad, the Texas Pacific, and then established the
First National Bank in Santa Fe. Both were failures. In despair
he turned back to the only thing he knew—the land—purchas-
ing in southern New Mexico the deserted buildings of Fort
Sumner and the military reservation on which the Navajo tribe
had been imprisoned for a time. The flat, alkalai-bitter, and
sunstruck land worked on his nerves. He kept pining for the
mountain forests, green meadows, and cold streams of his grant.
Five years were enough. He died in 1875.

His virtual successor, English-style, was the astute and ruthless General Palmer. Having milked the Maxwell Land Grant,
he diverted his railroad west to tap the fabulous ore strikes
in the Colorado Rockies around Leadville. Then by more
shrewd manipulations he secured another great tract of land
at the base of Pike's Peak, on which he was now developing
the new town of Colorado Springs.

This then, as Manby sat studying maps, titles, and legal
briefs, was the place and time for him to make a start. The
American government made no effort to back up its promises
in the Treaty of Guadalupe Hidalgo to preserve the rights of
the conquered people. It required all claimants of land in
Spanish and Mexican grants to pay for their own surveys and
legal procedures to perfect their titles—expenses which few of
them could afford. Government officials, lawyers, railroads, corporations, and Anglo promoters were now moving in, taking
possession of tracts large and small. There was little to stop

them in a backwoods territory whose population was preponderantly Spanish and uneducated, and whose laws were few and not enforced.

In what way, Manby wondered, could he take advantage of this confusing situation? To be sure, he had secured a foothold by his purchase of land in a remote part of the Maxwell Grant itself. But this was not enough. He had no intention of spending the rest of his life recuperating his investment by raising cattle. He wanted to expand. How? Again he devoted himself to the study of the current problems of the grant itself, with the help of the vulgar and vociferous Masterson and Lee.

2

Manby was not only appalled by the size of the Maxwell Grant, but by the ease with which his countrymen had grabbed it. The process was so simple if one knew how! The new Maxwell Land Grant Company, although partly capitalized by British investors and organized under the laws of the Kingdom of the Netherlands, was nominally operated by a local New Mexico board of trustees. It was faced with one major problem —the five hundred or more settlers living on the land. Spanish and Spanish-Indian families who had worked all their lives under their patron Maxwell, and a number of new dirt-poor American settlers, they considered the land theirs and refused to be driven off as unwelcome squatters. The stakes were high, Manby found; they were grazing some 65,000 cattle, 16,000 sheep, 3,600 horses, and 2,000 goats. In the past year alone there had been eight murders and sixteen deaths resulting from brawls during efforts to drive them off.[1]

"Maybe you know what you're doin', movin' up there in the Park," Masterson told him late that fall. "But if you don't, you better polish up that shootin' iron of yours some more. Griffin ain't goin' to like your company."

"Who's Griffin?" demanded Manby.

"The richest man up along the Vermejo." Masterson explained why. The Park lay in the northwest corner of Maxwell's immense grant, just below the Colorado line and flanked by the eastward wall of the Sangre de Cristos. It was a choice range watered by the Vermejo River, but, as it was too remote, Maxwell had never bothered to develop it. So a few years ago Dan Griffin, George Brackett, and a few other settlers had moved in and built up a small community. Griffin opened a general merchandising store which was now doing a thriving business. Also he took up land, asserting in the *Raton Comet* that it would be the finest farm and stock range in the country when the patent to the Maxwell Land Grant was put aside.

Manby nodded. Griffin's outspoken condemnation of the English company which claimed the grant evidently echoed the feelings of all his neighbors. But it also focused upon them the company's growing impatience with all settlers. Such a thriving community was setting a dangerous precedent that was a menace to the whole grant.

"Griffin's a popular fellow," Masterson went on. "At the Fourth of July celebration up there last summer he made the big speech, and he won the Fat Man's Race just before the barbecue."

"Very interesting," said Manby. "But what does Griffin have to do with me?"

Masterson grinned. "He's your next door neighbor, so's to speak. What'cha goin' to do about that?"

"We'll see," replied Manby shortly.

Alfred and Jocelyn, Manby's brothers, arrived from England. Alfred, a year older than Manby, was simple, quiet, and reserved. Jocelyn, the youngest brother, just turned twenty-one, was his exact antithesis, outgoing, resolute, and adventurous. Following the precedent of his sea-going great-grandfather, he had joined the British Merchant Marine, shipping out on a vessel transporting wheat from Oregon to England by way of Cape Horn. During a storm off the coast of Chile he was washed overboard, but managed to grab a line and was hoisted back aboard. The vessel returned to San Francisco for repairs, where Jocelyn jumped ship. Voluntarily returning to England, he stood court-martial and was exonerated. He had then sailed for America to join his two brothers in their ranching venture in the wilds of New Mexico.[2]

Loaded with supplies, Manby took them on the long trek to their new home. Vermejo Park seemed indeed the heart of the wilderness, a majestic immensity of mountain grasslands cut by ramparts of rock eroded into fantastic shapes. The area in which their own land lay took its name from a rugged crag shaped like a castle.[3]

"Castle Rock! Of course!" laughed Alfred when he first saw it rising on the horizon. "Arthur's Castle!" Always those castles.

The house prepared to quarter the three Englishmen, however, was far from comprising a Camelot. It consisted only of a small log and adobe hut of three rooms. In the traditional Spanish arrangement, the room on the left was a kitchen containing a wood-stove, shelves, and table and chairs; the room on the right a bedroom; and the middle room a common utility room.

"It's awfully small, really," protested Alfred, envisioning a huge ranch house.

"Range quarters!" snorted Manby, "Only a place to eat and sleep. We'll be out all day!"

Jocelyn walked over to a similar adobe-plastered log house about twenty yards east. His two brothers followed him. The door was open; and looking inside, they saw the same arrangement of rooms. A sleeping room containing cots with grimy blankets, on the right; to the left a kitchen holding a grain storage bin; and in the center a tack room.

"Whose house is this?" Jocelyn asked sharply.

"Griffin's and his two cronies, Abe Howe and Garnett Lee," exclaimed Manby irritably. "You'll learn about them soon enough."

There was a great deal to learn about Griffin in Castle Rock. Daniel B. Griffin, like George Brackett farther down the Vermejo, had been born in Alabama. Admitted to the bar in 1874 at the age of twenty-five, he had gone to California, then sailed for the Sandwich Islands. In Honolulu three years later he had married his present wife, Jennie, and returned to San Francisco where he engaged in the wholesale millinery business. In 1881 the couple came to New Mexico, opening the first store in Blossburg, near Raton. Shortly afterward they moved to Vermejo Park, establishing their present successful store and large ranch. Now thirty-four years old, Griffin was a large, well-built man, educated, ambitious, and immensely popular in Castle Rock.

It might have seemed that he and the Manbys, near neigh-

Manby ranch house at Castle Rock, 1884.

bors, would have become close friends with much in common. Instead, from the start, they manifested a deep-rooted antipathy. The three Englishmen, in short, did not mix well with their American neighbors. Perhaps because they seemed too aloof, too superior. But Griffin voiced other suspicions to his companions. "What're these Britishers up here for?" he demanded. "They're fresh over the water. Tenderfeet. Don't know a bull from a cow. They're not here to run cattle."

"They bought the land," Brackett said quietly in his Southern drawl.

"The company sent 'em up here to help run us out with every settler on the whole damned grant! That's why!"

"Calm down, Dan," Brackett remonstrated. "We don't want trouble."

Griffin's suspicions may have been unfounded, but they reflected the fears of all the settlers at Castle Rock at being dispossessed of their land. Another rumor spread that Manby, in an attempt to increase his land holdings, was selling bogus quit claim deeds.[4]

The winter dragged past. Dissension increased. An uneasy feeling crept over Castle Rock.

Spring came early, hot and dry, bringing another cause for trouble. By May the runoff from the mountains had begun to dwindle until the streams were mere trickles. Abe Howe and Garnett Lee took up quarters in the Griffin house next to the Manby house in order to water their cattle. Griffin then came down, apparently to request access to water. Manby may not have known the ranching ethics that a man whose stock needed water was permitted to drive his herd across his neighbor's land to a spring or waterhole. Perhaps he deliberately ignored the ranching code because of his ill-feeling toward Griffin. Whatever the reason, he refused Griffin's request.

Matters came to a head on Sunday morning, May 11. Abe Howe and Garnett Lee had been joined by Dan Griffin who had spent the night with them. About ten o'clock Griffin walked over to the Manby house. Manby met him outside. Alfred and Jocelyn inside the house could hear their angry voices. At the sound of a shot, Jocelyn grabbed up his pistol and rushed outside. Alfred behind him heard more shots as he reached the door. On the ground before him lay Griffin, with Manby and

Jocelyn bending over him. A few yards beyond them Howe and
Lee, who had been eating breakfast in their own house, were
rushing out at the sound of the shots. Silently all the men surrounded the still body of Griffin.

"What happened?" asked Alfred, dazed by the unbelievable
swiftness of the tragedy.

No one answered.

Manby rode to Trinidad, Colorado immediately and secured
an attorney, John M. Johns, to represent him at a hearing
before Justice of the Peace Hunt in Raton next morning.

In his lengthy testimony Manby related in detail what had
happened during the shooting affair. After a heated conversation he had ordered Griffin off his property. Griffin pulled out
a .38 caliber pistol, aiming it at Manby's head. Manby ducked
and rushed forward. As the two men clinched and struggled, the
pistol was discharged, the bullet lodging in Manby's clothes.
At this moment Jocelyn rushed out of the Manby house, firing
his own gun. The sound of the shot startled Griffin so much
that he relaxed his hold on the pistol. Manby wrested it from
him and shot him in the breast. Then, seeing Griffin still standing, Manby shot him again in the head as Howe and Lee came
running out from their house a few yards away.[5]

At the conclusion of the hearing Justice Hunt stated that
he was "compelled to believe that he (Manby) had fought for
self-protection. Just what any man would do, and therefore he
(Hunt) should discharge the accused."

The Daily Optic of Las Vegas on Wednesday, following the
reportage of the case in the *Raton Register* on Monday evening, lamented that during the past year no less than a dozen
persons had been killed in the area.

Manby's discharge was protested at Castle Rock by Griffin's
widow, Jennie, his family and close friends. His testimony
seemed too pat. He gave no reason for the quarrel save that
he had ordered Griffin off his property "by the right each man
has to choose and select his own friends and have them about
him." Detailed as his account of the killing had been, it was
not altogether accurate. He had not shot Griffin in the breast
and left temple, as reported. An examination of the body showed
that one bullet had torn into his left side below the ribs. The
other shot had struck him squarely in the head a little above

the ears, finally killing him.

After frantic appeals for justice by Jennie Griffin all summer, a court bill was drawn up on September 20 charging that Manby "feloniously, willfully, from a premeditated design to effect death," had shot and killed Daniel B. Griffin with a pistol in his right hand.

On the following day a warrant for the arrest of Manby on indictment for murder was issued to Sheriff W. J. Parker. Subpoenas were also issued for Jocelyn and Alfred Manby, Abe Howe, Garnett Lee, William Hoffman, and Jeff Anderson at Castle Rock. Manby, taken into custody, was then released on a $10,000 bond to await trial.

He moved back into his room at the Moulton Hotel in Raton, leaving Jocelyn and Alfred to weather the high feeling at Castle Rock. Masterson had a room down the hall and spent much time with him. What his relationship with the Maxwell Land Grant Company was, Manby didn't know, but he seemed on intimate terms with its officers and the territorial officials in Santa Fe. Uncouth, vulgar, condescending—and useful—he would strut into Manby's room with the latest news.

"There won't be no trial for a long time. The company'll see to that. Who gives a damn about a killin' way up the Vermejo anyway, with the whole pot boilin' over! Them goddamned Democrats are raisin' hell everywhere."

The election of 1884 was coming up and the Maxwell Land Grant situation had become the main political issue. Manby, sitting in his stiff, cold room, was fascinated by its legal aspects. The company's claim did indeed have a solid basis; its title to the Maxwell Grant had been recognized by the Supreme Court. The doubtful issue was how much land, for the boundaries were still uncertain. The Secretary of the Interior had granted the company a patent for 96,000 acres. Stephen B. Elkins, a delegate to Congress, then had authorized his brother to make a survey which fixed the boundaries to include 2,000,000 acres. This done, he induced Congress to pass an act approving the boundaries. With this encouragement, the company now claimed all of Colfax County and parts of Taos and Las Animas counties, and was preparing a concerted drive to evict all settlers as trespassers.[6]

The Griffin killing in remote Castle Rock was but one of

many taking place. Manby felt that it would be to the company's interests if he were not put on trial. For now, weeks before election, a swell of opinion against the company was gathering force. Apparently, even out here in this sparsely populated land, there were two political factions, Democrats and Republicans. The Republican party, now in power, backed the Maxwell Land Grant Company. The Democratic party opposed it with an anti-Grant ticket. In the hotel, on the streets, no one talked of anything else. Manby's trial, as he had hoped, was postponed in the mounting excitement.

For the son of a church rector who had been in America just a year it was an auspicious beginning.

3

Manby was surprised at the election returns. The Democratic anti-grant ticket swept the field. If its surprising victory also alarmed the long-entrenched Republican directors of the company, Masterson at least was confident a way could be found to stem the turn of the tide against them. That way led through a maze of local politics and bloody riots which took Manby's mind off his impending trial for murder.

Raton was wracked that fall by a factional fight for power between two political bosses, Charles Wheeler and John Lysitt, both saloon owners. Wheeler enlisted the gun arm of a Texas cowboy, Dick Rogers, who had shot and killed a man named Miller on October 13, and who lived in "Chihuahua," the disreputable quarter of town. The Redoubtable Rogers, as he was called, was generally believed to be an outlaw and desperado, although little was known about him. The Lysitt faction in turn managed to have its man, John Hixenbaugh, elected as sheriff. In an attempt to arrest Rogers, Hixenbaugh, had been shot in the leg. Whereupon he appointed, on January 23, 1885, James H. Masterson as his deputy sheriff.[1]

A week later, on the night of January 31, the second annual reunion and ball of the Colfax County Cowboys was held in Raton's beautiful new skating rink. Hundreds of people poured into town to make it a notable social affair. The cattle brands of ranches for miles around decorated the walls of the great hall, and the gowns and costumes of the ladies were dutifully described in detail by reporters from the *Raton Comet* and *Livestock Journal*. Following the ball, the guests adjourned to the Raton House for a late supper. The formidable menu covered two full pages. It included iced oysters and clams, broiled lobsters, and a confusing array of entrees spelled in French, as well as smoked buffalo tongue, venison haunch, and antelope cutlets, all accompanied by imported wines, and followed by pastries and ices.

For this gala occasion Rogers and his companions took over Williams and Sargents Dance Hall for their own entertainment. Masterson, as a week-old deputy sheriff, felt it incumbent to discourage his participation in the celebration. The Redoubtable Rogers was not a man to be intimidated. The instant Masterson entered the dance hall, he was confronted by a six-shooter and escorted to a corner. Here Rogers gave him a pistol beating that left him cowering on the floor, his head covered with blood.

The *Comet* a few days later reported that Masterson had not been seriously injured in the affray and was fast recovering from his wounds. It added that Jesse Lee, deputy sheriff at Springer, had ridden into town to render what assistance he could against the Rogers gang.

That night the ranch house of Garnett Lee—a close friend of Rogers and of the murdered Griffin—was burned to the ground with its caretakers, a Mexican named Joe and an old woman.

Manby, sitting in his room with the two deputies, may have been surprised how quickly Masterson had recovered his health and spirits. "Yes, sir!" declared Masterson. "That little business last Friday night was just what me and the company needed. We're goin' straight to the governor about it." He winked at Manby. "You just wait and see what happens!"

Manby did not have long to wait. Masterson returned from Santa Fe to announce jubilantly, "We done it! Now we're all set to go! From now on just call me Captain!"

In Santa Fe, he explained, he and the officials of the Maxwell Land Grant Company had persuaded Governor Lionel A. Sheldon of New Mexico that an armed force was needed to dispossess the settlers who were usurping land on the company's grant. The governor, due to the recent Democratic landslide, hesitated to issue the territorial ejection orders necessary to make the action legal. Hence the company directors urged him to organize a militia armed with federal ejection orders. Only one last argument was needed to convince the easily influenced governor. Masterson pulled out of his pocket a number of statements from citizens of Raton saying that the notorious Dick Rogers was terrorizing the town, and that it needed military protection. He suggested that Rogers' gang included many disgruntled settlers.

This was the excuse Governor Sheldon needed. On February 16 he posted a reward of $1,000 for the capture of Dick Rogers —$500 for the murder of Miller, and $500 for the attempted murder of Sheriff Hixenbaugh. Two days later he organized a militia whose ostensible purpose was to hunt down Rogers and curb Raton's lawlessness. This new Territorial Militia, designated "Company H" of the 2nd Infantry, was to consist of three commissioned officers, three non-commissioned officers, and thirty-five privates under the command of James H. Masterson, Captain, and Jesse W. Lee, 2nd Lieutenant.[2]

"See? It's all legal now to move in on Rogers and them squatters," continued Masterson. "I'm goin' to send back to Kansas for a few boys from Dodge. But I'm goin' to count on you too, Manby, hey?"

His coarse-featured, swarthy face wore a fatuous grin that betrayed the curious respect he had held for Manby since the Griffin killing. He was a bully, of course, and Manby detested him. He had found out that Jim Masterson was the brother of the already infamous Bat Masterson, former sheriff and gunman of rip-roaring Dodge City. There Bat had been a trigger-happy crony of Wyatt and Morgan Earp who had been run out of town to become still more notorious killers in Tombstone, Arizona.[3] He had then served as city marshall in Trinidad while running a gambling hall. Bat's last stint as a gunman before joining the Earps was no more savory. A few years before, when the Santa Fe and Palmer's Denver and Rio Grande railroads were battling in Colorado for the right-of-way through the stupendous Royal Gorge of the Arkansas, he had been recruited by the Santa Fe to bring a hundred gunmen from Dodge City to help expedite construction. Jim was now eager to make an equal name for himself out of similar employment by the Maxwell Land Grant Company.

Still, as Manby was learning, that was how business was conducted out here in the crude West of America.

"Why not?" he shrugged in answer to Masterson's question.

No, not for a minute did he hesitate to ally himself with the entrenched powers of the company. This was where money, influence, and power lay. He had not come from England to grub a meager living from a few acres. Too, he knew of his affluent countrymen and their audacious pattern of success. He was twenty-five, ambitious and impressed by the comparative ease with which wealth could be obtained by one given the talent of possessiveness. That Masterson had a shady reputation was inconsequential.

There arrived from Dodge City several men, gunned and ready for fun, to be sworn in as members of Masterson's militia. They were followed by two cases of arms and ammunition from Santa Fe which Masterson distributed to the members of his militia.

But that weekend J. C. Holmes, an influential Raton resident, hurried to Santa Fe to interview Governor Sheldon. With him he took a petition signed by some eighty businessmen, giving "the true state of affairs and asking that our town be relieved of the odium of the militia company." The *Comet*, tongue in cheek, dutifully reported the outcome of their talk. Holmes admitted Rogers had caused a little trouble, but asserted that he was no menace to town. Moreover he had promised to give himself up. The governor admitted he had formed the militia company primarily to give the owners of the Maxwell Land Grant protection and to enforce the decrees of the court in the company's suit against the settlers. At this, the *Comet* reporter interjected a loud horse laugh, writing that the claim of the Maxwell Land Grant Company was one of the pet schemes of Steve Elkins, and that the grant occupied many thousands of acres illegally obtained. Moreover, he alleged that the militia company had been fraudulently organized. It was proved that many of its enlisted men were only "paper members," Masterson having inscribed the names of citizens without their knowledge or consent. The easily influenced governor, confronted with this opposite view of the "true state of affairs," immediately issued special orders suspending the commissioned officers and disbanding the militia.

Rogers, true to his promise, gave himself up and was taken to a preliminary hearing of the three charges against him: the killing of Miller, the shooting of Hixenbaugh, and the assault upon Masterson. Rogers admitted killing Miller but pleaded self-defense, proving that Miller twice had threatened his life. He was promptly released on $1,000 bail.[4]

Masterson, aghast at the turn of affairs, was not a man to be betrayed behind his back by town and governor, deprived of his captaincy, and thwarted in taking revenge upon Rogers for his public beating. He promptly called a meeting of his militia on the outskirts of Raton. Standing before them, he talked, he yelled, he swore. He flung the orders disbanding them on the ground, and stamped on them with his boots. "Are we goin' to be made fun of in town, laughed at by Rogers and his gang? Or are we goin' to show these double-crossing businessmen we mean business too? Don't forget the company's behind us! What do you say we have a little fun?"

A single roar of acclaim was answer enough. Behind him, the gang swarmed into downtown Raton.

"Jesse, you take the other side of the street! I'll take this one!" Masterson shouted. "Come on! Let's tear it up!"

The men rioted down the street amid the crash of store windows, men's shouts, a woman's shrill scream. Just ahead of them D. W. Stevens, a prominent wholesale and retail merchant, ran out of his large store on the corner of Saunders Avenue and Second Street.

"Here's the way to do it!" yelled Masterson, jerking out his gun and buffaloing Stevens over the head with its long barrel. Jumping over his fallen body, he and the rest of his gang swarmed on down the street.

Stevens' young clerk, George Curry, saw the incident through the window and ran out to where his employer lay unconscious. Picking up Stevens' limp body, he carried it inside the store.

Curry was an unusually resolute and competent young man of twenty-four, a year younger than Manby. He had been a member of the Colfax County delegation sent to the Democratic Territorial Convention just before the election, and in due time he was to be elected governor of New Mexico. Having lived in Dodge City as a boy, he knew the reputation of the Mastersons and recognized Jim Masterson.

He immediately began to round up the terrified Raton citizens, calling a meeting in the skating rink. Several hundred men answered his call, and these he organized into a force of vigilantes. To lead them as captain they selected the so-called outlaw, Dick Rogers. Arming themselves with every available rifle in town, they closed all the saloons and locked the stores. Then they began to patrol the streets, hunting out Masterson's gang.

It was one thing for the bullies to assault unarmed and surprised men, terrify women and children, and knock in store windows, but something else to look into the end of a rifle barrel backed by a pair of sharp, determined eyes. Pursued into corners, confronted on the streets, the men were captured one by one.

Early next morning nearly six hundred people assembled at the skating rink with the prisoners. J. Osfield called the meeting to order, with Dick Rogers, captain of the vigilantes, and George Curry beside him. It was decided that Masterson, his imported gunmen from Dodge City, and all non-resident members of his defunct militia, were to be ejected from New Mexico. Three men on the roster of the militia were excepted on the grounds that they were bona fide residents: Arthur Manby, Jesse Lee, and another man.

Accordingly, the men were then marched over Raton Pass to the Colorado line and released with orders never to come back.[5]

The status of Manby during these riotous events is uncertain.

In a "Card from Arthur Manby" to the *Raton Comet*, he asserted that he had declined to have anything to do with the militia, Masterson having put his and his brother Jocelyn's names on the roster without authority. During the riot he had been in Santa Fe, trying to find an attorney to represent him in his coming trial for the murder of Griffin. Upon returning to Raton he had learned that Dick Rogers had threatened to kill him. Manby was now trying to meet Rogers for an amicable settlement of their differences, but couldn't find him.

These assertions were greeted with many loud guffaws. Rogers proclaimed that his whereabouts were always known and that he was available at any time. George Curry was positive he had seen Manby during the rioting. Others were certain both Manby and Lee had taken part in the rioting but fled town when Rogers and his vigilantes had organized to hunt them down.

The trouble now seemed over, however, and the *Comet* saluted the Redoubtable Rogers with a long and glowing editorial. "Dick Rogers," it proclaimed, "has been commonly called an outlaw, a desperado, and other unsavory names. Our citizens, however, have come to believe that Mr. Rogers is a young man of more than average education, widely traveled, and who possesses an abundance of that valuable commodity known as good, hard, common sense. He took a prominent part in the affair of last Thursday. Under his care and vigilance the town was rid of its disreputable characters—cleansed of its filth, as it were, without bodily injury to anyone."

The trouble was not yet over, however, for the reprieve of Manby and Jesse Lee did not prevent Lee from settling the score with Rogers. A short time later in Springer he arrested a vigilante named John Dodds who had driven into town with a load of corn and got drunk. Deputy Jesse Lee promptly arrested him. Dick Rogers, sensing more trouble, rushed down from Raton. After talking things over with several eyewitnesses, he walked toward the courthouse where Lee and his deputies had taken refuge, to inform Lee that as Dodds had been at fault it was proper for the justice of peace to fine him $6.50 plus costs. With Rogers were Red River Tom Wheaton, George Curry's nineteen-year-old brother John, and Marshall Williams.

Lee, Kimberly, and his other deputies saw them coming. As the group neared the courthouse, they opened fire with their rifles from the window. Dick Rogers and young John Curry were killed in the first volley, then Tom Wheaton who had stopped to pick up Rogers' body. Williams fled for his life.

A troop of soldiers from Fort Union was immediately called to prevent rioting and to escort Lee and Kimberly to jail in Las Vegas. No witnesses appeared at their trial and both men were released.

Lee fled to Oklahoma where he was killed. Kimberly moved to Arizona, reportedly being killed while attempting to hold up a store. Jim Masterson went to Oklahoma where he became involved in the Gray County Seat War, and finally died in Guthrie at the age of forty.[6]

Whether or not it could be proved that Manby was a willing

Dick ("The Redoubtable") Rogers, photographed in Raton.

member of Masterson's fraudulent militia and participated in its riotous assault, these were the men with whom he was undeniably associated. If there had been something "peculiar" about him as a child which prevented him from getting along with his family and neighbors, the same peculiarity set him apart from his more respectable American neighbors. It could not be rationally explained. He simply seemed to be a man whom no one knew or would ever know. Nor did Manby know himself any better; often it must have seemed to him, as it does to every man, that a nebulous shadow hovered about him, never visibly apparent but always present, as if it were a part of his own nature. If most men by childhood training and the pressures of society are taught to repress this shadow self as embodying the secret instincts and forces regarded as evil, Manby was under no such restrictions. Members of his family attest their tribulations in trying to control his willful impulses. But in New Mexico there were few restrictions of any kind. Manby found himself in a lawless land where men seemed free of all restraints and could give vent to their greed and violence. And here Manby's shadow self came into full bloom with his association with Masterson and Lee, and his killing of Griffin. How exhilarating it may have felt, this complete release into uninhibited freedom of action, this giving way to the dominance of his darker self! That there was in him another conflicting self, he probably was not then aware. One only knows today that these first experiences in New Mexico impressed upon him a pattern of behavior that was never to be eradicated.

4

Meanwhile the district court in Raton resumed its tardy interest in the killing of Daniel B. Griffin. It decided now that Jocelyn Manby had fired the shot which had torn into Griffin's left side below the short ribs. So on September 1, 1885 a new bill was drawn to this effect, and he too was arrested and put under bond.

On September 29 a final bill was drawn indicting both Arthur and Jocelyn Manby for killing Griffin, and a grand jury was formed under E. L. Hubbard as foreman.

Again Manby's apparent or imagined association with the Maxwell Land Grant Company presented itself as a possible bulwark against disaster. In Santa Fe he had requested that one of its two lawyers defend them.

"Which one would be best?" asked Jocelyn while they were awaiting the answer. "Springer?"

Frank W. Springer, for whom the settlement of Springer had been named, was certainly influential. He was not only president of the company's board of trustees, but one of the original four members of the Santa Fe Ring which cracked the whip over the territory's dominant Republican organization. It controlled all local offices, the sheriff, assessor, treasurer, probate judge, representative to the legislature, and even the delegate to the Congress.

Manby shrugged. "Why not Catron?"

"He's had a county named after him," agreed Jocelyn.

Manby laughed. "Jocelyn, you've never bothered to understand what's going on in this backwoods territory or informed yourself about the men who are running it. Let me tell you what I've found out about Catron who's head of that ring you mentioned."

Thomas Benton Catron was born in Lexington, Missouri and attended the University of Missouri. His classmate had the same middle name—Stephen Benton Elkins. They had much more in common. Moving to New Mexico, Elkins served in the territorial legislature and as district attorney and attorney general. Catron, who had served in the Confederate Army after graduating from the university, was afraid that he would not be permitted to practice law in a country against which he had taken up arms. Hence Elkins persuaded him to emigrate to New Mexico where he was admitted to the bar on the motion of Elkins. Switching his political affiliation from the Democratic party to the Republican party, Catron climbed quickly up the ladder behind Elkins. He too was appointed a district attorney general upon Elkins' recommendation, and then United States Attorney General for New Mexico. In Santa Fe he and Elkins formed a law partnership, and soon controlled the stock of the First National Bank. Soon he became the nominal head of the Santa Fe Ring which exercised political domination over all New Mexico, and one of the two lawyers for the Maxwell Land Grant Company.[1]

When the Supreme Court recognized title to the Maxwell Grant, the company was granted a patent to 96,000 acres. But Elkins, as a delegate to Congress, authorized his brother to make a survey which fixed the boundaries to include 2,000,000 acres. Then he induced Congress to pass an act approving the boundaries.

Manby paused, then continued. "Elkins has moved to West Virginia and Washington, marrying the daughter of Senator Davis of West Virginia, and becoming chairman of the Republican National Committee. Right now he's organizing a campaign to put Benjamin Harrison into office at the next election. He's done all right. Now let's get back to Catron—who's doing better."

Catron, remaining in New Mexico, had become its most

powerful figure simply by dealing in land, vast expanses of almost virginal land. He was acquiring, if he didn't already own, the Tierra Amarilla Land Grant of 584,515 acres, 240,000 acres of the Mora Grant, the Espiritu Santo Grant of 113,141 acres, the Mesita de Juan Lopez Grant of 42,022 acres, half-interest in the San Cristobal Grant of 91,032 acres—interests in thirty-one land grants.

"Land grants, Jocelyn! Land! The one basic source of wealth of this country, of all the world. That's where influence and power come from. Not from a few cows and sheep as you and Alfred think. But land! Lots of land, Jocelyn!"

"Right now you're indicted for murder and so am I," grumbled Jocelyn.

"Oh, stop worrying! Do you think for one minute that a local jury of small potatoes would bring in a verdict against either one of the most powerful figures in New Mexico?"

A week or two later Manby was imperiously summoned to Santa Fe, and was ushered into the imposing presence of a giant of a man attired in a long frock coat, a hard-boiled shirt and collar, and a black cravat that showed a spot of grease. His massive bulldog face showed heavy jowls, a double chin, bristly mustache, and narrowed glinting eyes. He looked like a man ready to fight at the drop of a hat with words, fists, a cane, or a pistol.

"Catron's the name!" he boomed out in a resonant, authoritative voice. "Your counsel for defense against preposterous charges! What in the name of God is all this monkey business anyway?"

Taking over the case, he promptly obtained another postponement of the trial until the grand jury under Hubbard had been dismissed and a more favorable one formed with Ed Clouthier, a prominent banker and commission merchant of Springer, as foreman. Finally on September 28, 1886 the case came up for trial.

Griffin had been killed two years and two months before. The high feeling in Castle Rock had subsided. Catron and his two defendants, pleading not guilty, faced the jury with complete confidence.

The trial was over quickly. Clouthier brought in the verdict: "We the jury find the defendants Arthur Manby and Jocelyn

Manby not guilty." No one was surprised. The Griffin killing was but one of the many that had taken place during the Maxwell Grant battles.[2]

Manby by now had learned how easily the laws in this backward territory could be circumvented by a smart and resolute man, and did not bother to pay taxes. That April the territory had brought suit against him and Jocelyn, "doing business as the Manby brothers," for unpaid property taxes amounting to $191.60. The following year a similar suit was brought for $400. Manby contested it, bringing the amount down to $378.75.[3]

Relieved by his acquittal, Jocelyn made a trip to England in 1887. Another maritime adventure befell him when he was returning with an English friend, Norman Raynor. Approaching New York through a thick fog their ship, the *Celtic*, rammed the outgoing *Britannic*, her bow driving ten feet into its side. Several passengers were killed and injured. In the confusion the passengers of the *Britannic* were transferred to the *Celtic* by lifeboats. These included a child who was the future Eleanor Roosevelt and her father, to whom Jocelyn Manby and Raynor volunteered the use of their stateroom.[4]

This same year Jocelyn married Louella Young, took out citizenship papers, and with Raynor as a partner resumed ranching in New Mexico.

Manby now took a bite at the hand that had fed him. He began to run cattle over the Maxwell Land Grant Company's beef range. In January 1889 the trustees filed suit against the three Manby brothers and Raynor, and in June issued an injunction against them. Manby, tongue in cheek and well-grounded in legal technicalities, tartly asserted the company's title to the Grant was still in question. Finally on November 10 the trustees dismissed their suit.[5]

The writing was on the wall, however. As the *Comet* observed, "The scheme of the Maxwell Land Grant Company from the beginning has been to bulldoze, to terrorize the settler. The greatness of the corporation and their enormous wealth enables them to employ the best talent in the world, men who are thoroughly posted in all the intricacies of the law, and who have influence in the courts, so that on technical points they always win their cases and preponderate over the little settler; but the fact that the so-called Maxwell Grant is a great fraud,

Alfred Manby's ranch house. Seated on top step is Alfred, his wife and two children seated behind.

an enormous steal, still remains as it was twenty years ago."

So one by one all the settlers were made to come to terms with the company; or lacking money, forced to leave their land. The eviction orders included Manby, whose land, being in the Elkins area, had always been in dispute.

In 1891 Jocelyn and Raynor moved the last of their cattle up to Moreno Valley, high in the mountains. Here, with Manby, they jointly filed on four mining claims. Jocelyn and Raynor then moved north into Colorado, Jocelyn locating on the Mount Massive Ranch near Malta. Eventually he settled in Denver, becoming a livestock dealer and real estate agent.

Simple Alfred returned to England to marry Rita Robinson whom he brought back to New Mexico. He may have lived for a short time on the Sugarite, north of Raton, then at the 47 Ranch on the Mora River, and on the Watrous Ranch. Records show that he picked up a little piece of forty acres for $168. He then settled on some land at the eastern boundary of the Maxwell Grant and marked by the rimrock of the Eagle Tail Mesa. Where he raised the money to purchase it, is not known. But the trustees of the company sold him the large tract of 9,247 acres for $8,135, reserving all coal and mineral deposits, access, and other rights. Six months later he added to this another eighty acres bought from the trustees for $320. Finally giving up ranching, he and his wife moved to Canada.[6]

Manby remained for a time in the colorful mining district of Moreno Valley. It was the turning point of his career. He was done with ranching and, for a time, with mining explorations. His unrestrained ambition encompassed an empire like Maxwell's. But where and how he was to find it, he did not yet know.

5

Manby had a nose for land, an instinct that never failed him. If it had led him from England to the Maxwell Land Grant, it now led him from Moreno Valley, over the Palo Flechado pass and down the western slope of the Sangre de Cristos to another old grant that embraced his wildest ambitions.

Travel accommodations in this direction were sparse and primitive. The four-horse Concord stage was no longer running. Mail was carried by a wagon whose driver sat hunched up in a blanket on the plank seat. Manby, his only passenger, sat beside him. Neither spoke.

It was early March. The snow pack was still deep on the summits of the peaks, but under a warm chinook water was pouring down the walls of the steep canyons and flooding the stream they followed down into the valley of Taos. Manby's first glimpse of its great sweep, as the driver reined up his team on the last pine-covered ridge, embraced a country big enough to fulfill any dream. A vast, high, level plateau enclosed by smoke-blue mountains on every horizon, and split from north to south by the razor-cut of the Rio Grande. A land that had been known and loved for centuries, but which still seemed lost in space and undeveloped. That it seemed a pastoral land of rough sagebrush, arid and uncut by the plow save for a few straggly corn *milpas*, did not concern him. He saw the extent of the landscape, not its texture.

That afternoon the driver pulled up at the mouth of the canyon and pointed toward the three mud clumps that comprised Taos. "That 'un to the left's Ranchos—Ranchos de Taos, where the big church is." He waved his whip vaguely toward the right. "Mebbe you can see it and mebbe you can't. But there's the old Indian mud pile, five stories she is. San Geronimo de Taos."

"And where are we going?" asked Manby curtly.

"We're already there," the driver answered, whipping up his team. "Don Fernando de Taos, the one in the middle. The real one, you might say, where most everybody lives 'cept the Indians."

The town was not impressive. The squat adobes they passed seemed ready to return to the earth from which they had sprung, especially now when the melting snows were clawing off patches of mud from the walls. Even the larger buildings enclosing the square central plaza seemed rooted to the land. Manby could see at once that Taos, unlike Raton and Trinidad, was not a new Americanized frontier town. An ancient Indian homeland, one of the first Spanish settlements in this northern province, and then a rendezvous for Kit Carson and other early mountain men, it still defied growth and progress as a remote and forgotten outpost of civilization. It looked old. He recognized its peculiar mellow charm at once, yet also felt underneath it an inimical hardness.

Getting out of the mail wagon at the livery stable, and washing up at Aloysius Liebert's hotel next door, he then walked stiffly across the plaza to stretch his legs: a squat, wide-shouldered man wearing muddy leather boots, splashed riding trousers, and a flowing kerchief around the neck of his plaid wool shirt.

In the courthouse a large group of *políticos* and loafers were carrying on a spirited discussion. Down in Santa Fe, Manby heard, the Court of Private Land Claims was getting ready to conduct a hearing on an old land grant near Taos.

"It is March, *no es verdad?*" asserted one without conviction.

A minute later another replied, "The fifth day it will begin, as was said."

After another few minutes one in the group listlessly voiced the sentiments of all. "*Mucho negócio.* For what?"

Funeral procession through north side of Taos Plaza, 1897. *Courtesy Kit Carson Memorial Foundation.*

They were not concerned about it, nor anyone else in town except four men who had said they were going down to see if they could claim the grant.

"What's the name of it?" asked Manby at last.

"What is that which does not have a name?"

"*Burro!* He asked what is the name of that grant! What else have you been talking about all this time?"

"That old piece of land? *Pues*. The Antonio Martinez Grant it is called. Or perhaps the Lucero de Godoi. Who is to know such things?"

"And where is it, if I may beg your gracious pardon for my ignorance?" asked Manby again in excellent Spanish.

The first speaker replied with a wave of his hand that swept the horizon from the mountains westward to the river. *"Quien sabe?"*

Manby shook his hand formally and strolled back across the plaza. Antonio Martinez. Lucero de Godoi. Manby had never heard the names before, but deep within him a little bell tinkled at their sound.

On a sudden impulse he turned into the livery stable, hired a horse, and rode north out of town. Jogging past the last straggle of adobes, he turned toward the jutting range of mountains. Across the flat and empty *vega* he could glimpse a high, weathered, and terraced adobe cliff: the Indian pueblo his driver had pointed out. San Geronimo de Taos. Manby had no curiosity about it nor the Indians it housed. But as he stared at it, the setting sun flooded the summit of the high mountain rising directly above it with a blood-red glow that slowly ate down its slopes to color the terraced walls of the pueblo. Sangre de Cristo. The Blood of Christ. A strange warm effulgence, as if from a fire lit deep within, that made the peak seem suddenly and curiously alive. Then just as abruptly the life, the fire, died out; and he was staring at a mountain black, somber, and inimical—a little frightening, really. With its sudden change of mood and aspect, Manby felt it was a mysterious mountain in a way he could not define.

Turning his back on it, he rode on a piece. For westward from the mountain lay somewhere the old, unclaimed land grant he had heard about. The Antonio Martinez or Lucero de Godoi. Again the little bell inside him rang for the words. Just where

was it? Or was it everywhere he looked? From the summit of
the mysterious mountain sloping down through forested slopes,
open vegas, and across the empty sagebrush to the Rio Grande
—there it must be, an almost forgotten and ignored land grant
with uncounted acres of virgin land waiting to be claimed.

Elated, he rode back to the Liebert Hotel. He had completely
forgotten the man he had come to see in hopes of selling one
of his unworked mining claims.

Early next morning he engaged a man to drive him downriver to Santa Fe. The tortuous dirt road wound down through
the sunless gorge of the Rio Grande. It was still iced over. The
horses slipped, the wheels slid, the driver swore. Manby got
out and walked around the sharpest turns, expecting any minute
to see the conveyance hurtle off the precipice into the frothing
white rapids below. The rest of the way was little better.
Tumbled boulders required arduous detours. The buckboard
was mired in mud, then whipped with blowing sand. The
seventy-mile trip took almost ten hours.

Manby had been in Santa Fe before; yet late that afternoon
when he arrived it struck him again how strangely foreign this
ancient capital of a remote province was, with its narrow cobble-
stoned streets, its mud-walled Palace of the Governors, and its
posted signs and public notices in Spanish. A woodcutter was
whacking a burro loaded with firewood across the central plaza.
The wood was piñon; Manby could smell the fragrance in the
smoke rising lazily from the chimneys. A ragged *chamaco*, his
bare feet blue in the cold, stuck out a grimy hand for a penny.
Two fat Indian women, shrouded in blankets against the wind,
squatted on the *portal* with a display of pottery.

Entering the old inn at the corner of the plaza, Manby went
directly to his room. It was small, bare and clean, but icy cold.
There was no wood in the fireplace and no water in the white
porcelain pitcher and basin on the dresser. He lay down on
the bed to read a heavy volume of mining laws printed in Spanish
while awaiting time for supper. There would be no beef, of
course. In New Mexico it was always lamb or chicken. And the
chicken always had a distinctive taste because it was the custom
here to douse the hen into the pot immediately after wringing
its neck, without waiting to properly cool it.

Next morning he walked to the courthouse to attend the

hearing. The courtroom was big enough to hold more than the scatter of people sitting stiffly on the wooden benches. An iron woodstove in the corner smoked with piñon. There were five judges on the bench representing the defendant, the United States. Contrary to the white-wigged and black-robed figures who presided in England, they wore wrinkled business suits. Without dignity, they looked like jaded American travelers who had been stranded overnight in Spanish New Mexico. Of the five, the big man in the center was the most impressive but Manby dismissed him with a glance. Anyone could sell him anything. It was the scrawny little man on the left who held his attention. He kept trying to pluck an invisible hair off the tip of his nose as if unconcerned with the whole proceedings. Yet over his knuckles, his sharp shoe-botton eyes darted glances about the room as quick and furtive as marmots scurrying about the rocks on Mount Baldy.

After due time the U.S. Court of Private Land Claims came to order. The clerk began to read. The facts he brought out were few but pertinent. Nearly two centuries before, on October 26, 1716, one Antonio Martinez, a resident of the Province of Sonora and a citizen of the Kingdom of New Mexico, had petitioned Captain Felix Martinez, governor and captain-general of New Mexico at the royal garrison in Santa Fe, for a grant described as "a tract of land situated in the Valley of Taos, and formerly belonging to Sergeant-Major Diego Lucero de Godoi."

Captain Felix Martinez promptly granted the petition in accordance with the will of his Majesty, the King of Spain, that the province of New Mexico be settled up. He made one provision: that the Indians of the Pueblo of Taos be notified in case they wanted to make any objections to the grant.

Accordingly, three days later Captain Felix Martinez, his officials, and Antonio Martinez assembled at the "Pueblo of San Geronimo de Taos, in the Royal Houses, with the Cacique and other aged Indians." As the Indians offered no objections, they all went to the tract. It was described as being bounded on the east by the nearest arroyo to the pueblo; on the west by the Rio del Norte; on the north by the mountains which were the source of the Rio Lucero; and on the south by the junction of the Taos and Del Norte rivers. Taking Antonio Martinez by the hand, the governor and captain-general led him over the tract, "and he plucked up grass, cast stones, and shouted aloud, entering upon the Royal Possession which I gave him in the name of his Majesty."[1]

This much was clear to Manby and everybody else; the judges looked sleepy. Since then the matter had been clouded. In 1821 Mexico, upon achieving independence from Spain, confirmed all land grants in its northern province. She was then obliged in 1848, by the Treaty of Guadalupe Hildalgo, to cede all of New Mexico to the United States. Its Surveyor General in turn began studies in 1854 to determine the validity of the grants. Congress confirmed some thirty of sixty grants, but work progressed slowly under difficult conditions. To expedite it, Congress established on March 3, 1891 a Court of Private Land Claims to conduct hearings.

So here they were, a year later, assembled to confirm or deny that tract known as the Antonio Martinez or Lucero de Godoi Land Grant. Manby sat up stiffly on his wooden bench. The scrawny little judge resumed plucking at the hair on his nose.

Apparently the old Spanish grant had been forgotten and would have been ignored had not a few people, four years before, showed up to claim it for some sixty-eight heirs. The clerk read off their names: Daniel Martinez and wife, Francisco Martinez y Martinez and wife, Maria Encarnacion Martinez and husband, Maria Andrea Martinez and husband, Maria Juliana Martinez and husband, and Maria Filomena Martinez. They all had agreed jointly to pay for redemption of the grant and its confirmation by the court.

So now to the hearing had come from Taos four men to claim it. The clerk read off these plaintiffs' names: Francisco Martinez y Martinez, Juan G. Martinez, Antonio T. Gallegos, and Bernabe Garcia. Manby looked them over carefully; so did the five judges. They were strong, simple men with unruly hair and weatherbeaten faces, dressed in ragged trousers, frayed shirts, and hand-sewn leather vests. Duly they avowed ownership of the grant as rightful heirs of Antonio Martinez. As they were sworn in, the scrawny little judge on the left stopped plucking at his nose.

"What proof have you that you are the direct descendants and rightful heirs of Antonio Martinez?" he asked sharply.

The interpreter translated.

One of the men answered simply and proudly. "What man needs proof? I have my name. It is a good name. I have my land. It is not so good, lacking water. But I have lived on it as my father and my grandfather before me, and his father and his father's father before that. The land is ours."

"This court needs proof," the little judge said drily.

At last it was over, the interminable talk, the everlasting recesses. The United States as the defendant could only assert through its five judges that the plaintiffs had no definite proof they were the rightful heirs of Antonio Martinez. The land lay to the north and west of Taos, between the Sangre de Cristo mountains and the Rio Grande, but its boundaries were indefinite and no one knew how much acreage it comprised. Still other questions were involved. Hence all these questions should be answered and due consideration be given to all factors before the court could confirm the title. With this, court adjourned.

The nebulous and confused situation caught Manby's fancy. His imagination was still leaping toward its possibilities a few days later when he boarded the toy train at the station. It was General William J. Palmer's Denver and Rio Grande narrow-gauge to Antonito, Colorado where it connected with the main line running west through the mountains. Giving an amused look at the small locomotive with its square headlight box and its straight stack spouting smoke and cinders, he climbed into the coach and settled down on a sooty red plush seat. In the aisle up front a squat coal stove gave warmth to the few passengers. The doors to the toilets, he noticed, were lettered in Spanish like all signs down here, "Mujeres" and "Hombres."

With the tinkle of a bell that reminded him of the "Muffins All Hot" of his boyhood, the train chugged out of Sante Fe. Manby stared steadily out of the grimy window. For awhile the train crawled alongside the muddy Rio Grande, then swung west to parallel it on the far side of the valley. The frequent stops at the small depots, water tanks, and weed-grown sidings reminded him of the reason for its common name, the "Chile Line"; it had been built to freight out the chiles grown in the river bottoms.

Now, puffing up grades and around curves at fifteen miles an hour, the baby railroad train was crawling steadily northward over a flat and empty plain that broke like a sea against the wall

of the Sangre de Cristos to the east. Behind him he could dimly
make out the shape of the mysterious mountain above Taos,
marking the unclaimed Antonio Martinez Grant. When it passed
from sight he got out a map and unspread it on his knees. This
must be the great San Luis Valley he was entering now, par-
alleling the horseback route of the young English explorer George
Frederick Ruxton some forty years before. The country as he
had described it in his journal had not changed: the mountains
following him on the right, the illimitable expanse of sand and
sage stretching away, an occasional isolated adobe.

This, all this, was the Sangre de Cristo Grant! Manby had
recently come from the Maxwell Land Grant, one-fifth larger
than the state of Delaware. This Sangre de Cristo Grant, which
he was now seeing for the first time, was itself a mammoth
absurdity—only one-fifth smaller than Delaware. Manby was
not interested in its scenery. He had an itch to create an empire
for himself, and he kept tantalizing himself with the methods of
intrigue and exploitation by which all this sand and sage, like the
Maxwell Grant, had been converted into wealth and power.

Half of it had been sold to an English syndicate including
William Blackmore. Within a year of Beaubien's death, all his
heirs—his widow, six children, and two sons-in-law including
Maxwell—had sold their interests for $35,000 to William Gilpin,
the first territorial governor of Colorado, who had been removed
from office for issuing drafts against the government without
authorization. He in turn had sold out for $252,000. A tidy
profit, thought Manby, staring out the window.

But more! The immense grant was now divided into two
sections, the southern portion known as the Costilla Estate, and
the northern portion as the Trinchera Estate. Most of the latter
Gilpin had sold to the omnipotent General William J. Palmer,
and it was being managed by a company whose president was
no less than the familiar Dr. Bell! Of course! And now they held
the whole vast estate in trust to sell for not less than $600,000.[2]

Palmer meanwhile had built this little narrow-gauge down
from his main line in Colorado to Espanola, twenty-five miles
north of Santa Fe. Then he had induced the New Mexico legislature to help finance the rest of the line to Santa Fe. All to
freight out of the valley those abominably hot green chiles so
beloved by the New Mexico natives! The very Chile Line on

which Manby was now riding was adding to his profits.

How shrewd Palmer and Bell had been! They had not only skimmed the cream off the Maxwell Land Grant, but they were milking this Sangre de Cristo Grant too. If anything could have been calculated to rouse Manby's envy, it was this successful history of land speculation and exploitation. His gnawing envy, however, was alleviated by thought of that forgotten grant, 125 years older, which lay between the Maxwell and Sangre de Cristo grants and was claimed only by a handful of Spanish natives wearing leather vests. The Antonio Martinez Grant! He did not know how big it was, but it would be large enough.

At Antonito, just above the border of New Mexico, Manby transferred to the main line of the Denver and Rio Grande. Crossing over La Veta Pass, the train turned north to crawl along the eastern base of the Rockies to Denver. Manby stopped over at the foot of Pike's Peak where that previous young Englishman, Ruxton, had camped for the winter. Here was Palmer's new town of Colorado Springs. Manby, hiring a carriage, took time to appraise it carefully. Despite his prejudices, he fully approved of everything he saw. The new town in its scenic setting on the plain fronting the spectacular rampart of the Rockies, with its many soda and iron springs bubbling out at the entrance to its mountain canyons, was strikingly comparable to the little town of Taos in its great valley below the Sangre de Cristos. It was obvious to him that Palmer and his English associates were taking full advantage of all its possibilities.

Colorado Springs, Manby observed, was aptly nicknamed "Little London" for all the English colonists and visitors it was drawing. Palmer's Antler's Hotel was of English Gothic design, and through his Monument Valley Park Manby saw English nursemaids strolling beside English dogcarts. Dr. Bell, as leader of the social set, had built an English manor house called Briarhurst and a hotel which was being operated for him by the former royal cricket tutor to the Prince of Wales. Blackmore, no less influential, had named the various medicinal springs which were popularizing Little London as a genteel English spa in the crude American West.

If this English-style resort reminded Manby of the tiny seaside resort of Morecambe, it also planted a pattern in his mind for undeveloped Taos. The sight of stiff-necked General Palmer

riding by in English jacket, breeches, and riding boots amply
attested to the Midas touch which had transformed all this
wilderness into a fabulous fortune. Palmer now, Manby heard,
was deriving a net income of $1,000 a day from his vast holdings.
At the mouth of Queen's Canyon he was completing his grand
design, building his manor house Glen Eyrie into a replica of
the Duke of Marlborough's Tudor castle. An immense stone
fortress surrounded by a moat, it would comprise 67 rooms, 20
bathrooms, and a hall big enough to seat 300 people. The green
tile for its roof, Manby was told, was being brought from an old
church in England, as were the stones for its forty fireplaces.
Here, aloof and alone, he could live in the splendor of a man who
had known what he wanted and how to get it.[3]

Continuing on to Denver, Manby was driven from the station
directly to the Brown Palace. The moment he saw its nine-story,
brownstone hulk jutting forth on its triangular, downtown
mooring like the prow of a ship, he liked it. Getting out of his
carriage, he stood peering up with approbation at the frieze of
figures carven in the shapes of bear, wolf, antelope, and buffalo.
Then walking inside to wait his turn to register at the desk, he
stared entranced at the great well-like lobby walled with tiers
of balconies of wrought-iron grillwork, at the panels of onyx—
onyx from Mexico, of course. What a lush and opulent air it
gave forth with its rich appointments and furnishings, its men's
bar, grill and dining room, its small sitting rooms and immense
ballroom. Just opened, it was a palace indeed and Manby felt
fortunate in securing accommodations.

Whizzed up to his room in an elevator, he stepped with delight
on the thick rug, turned on the taps of cold and hot water,
then lifted the coverlet of the bed to feel the texture of the sheets.
He could hardly wait to bathe and go out to buy new clothes,
a suit and all accessories; to return and sit down to civilized
rare roast beef; perhaps to enjoy later the luxury of an opera.
Even out the window he could see in the busy street, filled with
hurrying people and handsome carriages the bustling, prosperous
character of all Denver, of Colorado itself. This was Anglicized
America. There was nothing to remind him of Spanish New
Mexico.

From the instant the narrow-gauge had pulled out of San
Luis Valley, Manby had felt the change. It was as if that

ancient wave of Spanish colonization had washed northward to beat against the wall of the Rocky Mountains and then had slowly receded to lay like a stagnating lake with all its outmoded customs, traditions, poverty, and ignorance. No wonder the rest of the country, vulgar and enterprising as it was, almost completely ignored it. New Mexico was too foreign, too obdurately backward, for the people to understand. It was at best only a stretch of country for them to travel through to better pastures. What was there, a white man would ask, except rattlesnakes, cactus, and Greasers?

Manby as a cultured Englishman could well appreciate the difference between Santa Fe and Denver, Colorado and New Mexico. He had no native love, no emotional bias, for either. He had come to the American West to make money and a name for himself. It was that simple, he thought, stripping off his clothes and settling his muscular body in a hot tub. But how? In the lobby below he had seen men with work-calloused hands who had patiently accumulated little fortunes from timber and cattle, bearded old prospectors who had hit it rich after years of heartbreaking toil. None of that for him! He was an entrepreneur, not a laborer. As a matter of fact, he noticed while soaping his hands, he himself needed a manicure before making appointments with several influential men he had come to see. But still it was the land that held in trust all these fortunes in timber, cattle, silver and gold, wheat and corn, all the potential wealth of the world. Great tracts of unclaimed, virgin land that could be exploited down to a green chile!

Stepping out of his hot tub and rubbing himself down with a thick towel, he envisaged again that old grant marked by the mysterious mountain near Taos. If he was ever to carve out of the wilderness a domain of distinction for his own, that was it. Colorado had nothing to compare with those old Spanish grants, and New Mexico had none so long-ignored as the Antonio Martinez Grant. Yes! He had made up his mind. That was to be his arena, the kingdom he had come to America to win. In high humor he dressed quickly and went out to begin his battle for it.

6

Referred to New York, Manby talked with several capitalists who expressed their willingness to invest in any proposition that looked promising. Manby assured them that he would soon have one. The Court of Private Land Claims had just confirmed the title to the Antonio Martinez Land Grant and ordered a survey to be made, establishing its boundaries.

The decree adjudging the title to be complete and perfect laid to rest Manby's lurking fear that the land might be proclaimed public domain open to homesteaders and settlers. Now there remained to deal with only the few unlettered men who had claimed it in Santa Fe. There was no hurry. Big things took time, and he would have to wait for the survey to be made before taking action.

Manby then sailed for England. His oldest brother Eardley, forty-two and not yet married, met him when he disembarked and took him home to Great Yarmouth, Norfolk for a few days. Eardley Blois Manby was a great pride to the family. Having served with the army in India, he was now home on inactive duty as Lieutenant and Honorable Major of the 52nd Protection Company, Royal Defense Corps of the British Army. Inclining toward stoutness, his erect frame bore his uniform with an air of distinction that seemed reflected in his resolute face. Lounging beside the open fire in his comfortable study on the evening of his brother's arrival, he took his briar out of his mouth

Eardley B. Manby.

and asked casually, "I haven't heard from Jocelyn for some time. What has happened to him?"

"Ranching up in Colorado, north from me. He likes the life, as you know."

"And Alfred?"

"He is still in New Mexico but thinking of moving to Canada." The major chuckled. "Well, that's four of you who emigrated to America. Charles, you know, apprenticed himself as a chemist in a steel mill in Birmingham, Worcester, and became quite respected in his profession. Now he's crossed the Atlantic to live in Pittsburgh, Pennsylvania. Working for the rising steel magnate, Andrew Carnegie, the 'Dread Scot'."[1]

The major observed his younger brother carefully. Arthur here, regarded as the black sheep of the family, had always puzzled him. He had a brilliant mind but a violent temper, a refined taste but a vulgar disposition. He was not one to be questioned too closely, but the major could not forebear asking after a time, "You had a little trouble out there in New Mexico some time ago, did you not?"

Manby carefully flicked a spark from the fire off his well-creased trouser leg. "Not really, Eardley. It's a backward, lawless territory, you know. One has to stand up for one's rights."

Eardley did not press the subject although he had received more illuminating information from Alfred a few years back. Manby's casual reference to it engendered in him a train of conjecture he did not care to follow. What would happen to this strange, violent-natured brother of his in the wilds of New Mexico to which he was returning after his visit here?

Manby, sitting across from him, seemed unafflicted by doubt. His broad-cheeked face with its noble brow was deeply tanned; his heavy-set body was tastefully dressed. Comfortably fortified with excellent roast beef and Yorkshire pudding, he looked like a man who had his future firmly in hand.

"And you, Arthur?" the major finally asked. "You mentioned before dinner that you had something in mind to talk to me about."

Manby decisively leaned forward, his face glowing red in the flamelight. He seemed suddenly like a panther about to leap.

"An empire! A tract of virgin land bigger than the borough of Lancaster, of Morecambe, and the whole valley of the Lune.

Mountains, plateaus, rivers. Gold, timber, grazing and farmlands. Room for a dozen towns. Yes, by Jove! An empire for the taking!"

"Well! Is that so? Well!"

"I'll let you in on it, Eardley. But I need your help."

"Hmm. Is that so?"

"Can we talk? Now? Is this the time?"

The major got up and closed the walnut panelled door. Then he came back, sat down stiff and erect in his chair, and carefully filled his pipe again. "Tell me all about it."

A few days later they went to London. The major was well connected and introduced Manby to several potential investors who also listened attentively. "If you can manage to obtain this grant," they told him, "we will probably be able to help finance its development."

"I'll get it!" said Manby.

Before Eardley left London, he assured his brother that he was delighted with the prospect. "If you really can obtain the grant, I'll do everything over here to help. I might even sail to America to see it."

"I'll get it, Eardley!" replied Manby.

Manby remained in London. A painting in a gallery on Bond Street had caught his attention. Every morning, wearing a fresh carnation in his lapel, he would stroll down the street looking at the showings in every gallery. Inevitably he ended in front of the arresting painting. It was an oil portrait entitled *St. Catherine* that obviously had been painted by an old master in the seventeenth century. Finally he inquired about it.

The proprietor knew only that the painting in his custody, once part of the Threlfall Collection, had been bought by Thomas Agnew and Sons of London at Christies in 1860 and had then been purchased by a Mrs. Bromley at Copes Sale, Manchester. "There is no price on it," the proprietor added, "but I rather think the lady might sell it. Shall I give you her present address?"

Manby promptly went to see Mrs. Bromley, now at Kasal Moor, and induced her to sell it to him. For several weeks he remained in London to make sure the painting was properly cleaned and stored, proud of his acquisition. Old masters were rare, especially in America, and this one would be extremely valuable.[2]

There was no need to visit his old home in Morecombe. His mother and father had died, Poulton Hall had been sold, his brothers and sisters married and scattered. Nor could he get out of his mind the vast wilderness of the Sangre de Cristos, that unknown virgin empire of the Martinez Grant over which he felt himself destined to rule. Through Eardley he obtained a few of his mother's watercolors to take with him, bolstered his finances, and sailed back to America to win the kingdom awaiting him.

Back in Taos, he found the sleepy adobe village stirred with excitement over several gold discoveries which had been made up in the canyon of the Rio Hondo, only seventeen miles away. Manby was born with the faculty of a chameleon to change the color of his skin to fit his surroundings. Dressing in a flannel shirt, riding trousers, boots, and Stetson hat, he rode up the aspen-choked canyon to take a look. A few miles from its mouth a new camp was booming with almost five hundred prospectors, miners, and gamblers crowding its rude plank stores, log cabin saloons, and dancehalls. It had been named Amizette in honor of Amizette Helphstein, the wife of a prospector. Above it at the head of the canyon a still newer camp was growing: Twining, named after the heaviest investor in its largest mine, a banker from Asbury Park, New Jersey.

Manby's cold, steel-gray eyes glowed with enthusiasm. The grant! That was his chief concern, and time and place were coinciding to his advantage. The survey had not been completed yet, but one of the surveyors had told him as he had ridden past that the Rio Hondo had been definitely decided as the northern boundary of the grant. Now Manby could see a never-ending stream of people coming by stage, hack, buckboard, and wagon from Tres Piedras, a stop on the Chile Line sixty miles west, to the tawdry village of Arroyo Hondo and thence up the canyon along the very boundary of the Martinez Grant. These were the settlers he would induce to colonize the new towns and resorts he would build to outdo Little London itself.

There was even better news that night from the strange couple who let him sleep on their cabin floor. The man was a big, raw-boned Scotchman named Columbus Ferguson, and his wife, Juanita, a small Spanish woman. They lived up at Elizabethtown in Moreno Valley where Ferguson owned the Mystic mine, but drawn by the excitement and high wages they had come here to spend the summer. Juanita was tending the toll gate at the mouth of the canyon, and Columbus was hauling clay from a pit near South Fork for two enterprising newcomers to mold and bake into building bricks.

"She's all right, the Mystic is," said Ferguson, drawing out of a sack a few rich specimens of gold. "Of course things are a little mite slow up there now. Me and my partners need somebody with a little money to develop the workings. But look!" He spread out a rude map in the candlelight. "We're right close to the famous Aztec on Mount Baldy. Right on the headwaters of Red River which drains north of us here into the Rio Grande, just like the Rio Hondo. In its canyon there's another new camp, Red River, boomin' from the discovery of some rich gold lodes. You get it, don't you Mister?"

Manby nodded. What a prospectus to present to financiers and promoters in New York and London! That high crest of the Sangre de Cristo range was rich in gold washing down every canyon to the west and east. He had patented four claims with Jocelyn: the Golden Era, Fairfax, Twin, and War Eagle. Here was the means to raise the money to secure and develop the grant.

"I might be able to help you out, if you've got a good thing," said Manby casually. "I've got some undeveloped claims up there myself."

"You come see us, Mr. Manby. We'll be back up there shortly, come fall. Ferguson's the name, mind. And the Mystic. You won't have no trouble finding it. She's got a long history."

Settling in an inconspicuous adobe in Taos to await completion of the Martinez Grant survey, Manby rode up to Elizabethtown often that year to see the Fergusons. From them he learned that the Mystic, as the whole mining district, did indeed have a long and peculiar history.

In the summer of 1866 Captain William Hubert Moore on a reconnaisance from Fort Union—that bastion of military might at the convergence of the two branches of the Santa Fe Trail— had come upon a wounded Ute up in Moreno Valley and had carried him back to the doctor at the fort. When the Indian recovered, he repaid the captain's kindness by leading him to the source of some rich copper float on the slope of Mount Baldy. That fall Moore sent three men back to do assessment work. They discovered traces of gold in Willow Creek and hurried back with news of their discovery.

Early next April when the snows began to melt the gold rush began. Scores of soldiers from Fort Union, hundreds of avid gold-seekers trudged up the trail from Cimarron; more hundreds from Taos and Santa Fe swarmed over Palo Flechado pass to the new diggings. By July four hundred claims had been recorded.

The following year Maxwell joined Captain Moore and a small group of men in organizing the Copper Mining Company to search for the body of copper ore from which had come the original float. Maxwell's luck still held. In November, after tunneling for months after copper, the crew struck three veins of gold only three feet apart, with fibers visible to the naked eye. Named the Aztec, the mine turned out to be the richest gold-bearing quartz mine in New Mexico. By 1870 it had produced $260,000 and was bringing Maxwell $48,000 a year.

The whole district was prospering. More than $2,250,000 in gold had been taken out, the population had increased to almost five thousand, and the main camp was established that year as the first incorporated town in New Mexico. It was named Elizabethtown in honor of Captain Moore's four-year-old daughter at Fort Union.

Several years later Columbus Ferguson of Leavenworth, Kansas arrived. He had previously worked the Copper Hill area near Taos, and during one of his trips to town had met and fallen in love with a Spanish girl. Juanita Medina had been born in Taos, but both her parents had come from Spain. Ferguson admitted his courtship was brief but difficult; he could not speak Spanish, nor could Juanita speak English. Despite this he married her, and after the birth of a son, moved his little family up to the new diggings.[3]

Here he and a Pennsylvania German named William Stone, who had worked in a soap factory in Cincinnati, formed a partnership to develop two claims, the Mystic and the Ajax, near the fabulous Aztec on the shoulder of Mount Baldy. Trouble developed. There was not enough water to work the placer mines. A crude aqueduct known as the Big Ditch was built from the headwaters of Red River, high in the summit of the Sangre de Cristos. Still it looked as if the placers were exhausted. The original mother lode from which the placer gold came, engineers asserted, was still to be found high above on the Red River watershed.

Stone was satisfied to keep taking out small quantities of paying ore from the Mystic and the Ajax. Ferguson also was content with a living wage. His wife Juanita had given birth in 1888 to a daughter named Francisca, and two years later to another whom she named Teracita.

About this time the two men took in a third partner, Wilkerson. Whether his given name was Frank or George, he was generally known as Bill. Wherever he came from, he brought a bad reputation. Old-timers considered him a high-grader: a man who made it his profession to steal out from any mine in which he was working pieces of high-grade ore to dispose of at good profit through dishonest assayers or outside buyers. It was also said he had been implicated in a killing in Kansas.

Shortly after Manby arrived, Wilkerson and Ferguson began to display rich samples of gold, although the Mystic's ore body was known to be neither rich nor extensive. Then the Aztec closed down, its owners protesting that they couldn't make it pay because of high-grading.

Old Stone, a simple man, became disgruntled and kept aloof in his own secluded cabin. One morning his mutilated body was found near the portal of the Mystic. No inquiry was made, and the cause of his death remained unknown.[4]

It was then Wilkerson and Ferguson announced that Stone had been replaced by a new partner—Manby.

Soon afterward Manby left Ferguson and Wilkerson to handle the Mystic according to his instructions and returned to New York. There he proposed to his interested backers that the mine and his own four claims be developed into a great working property. The past history of the Mystic did not warrant the investment Manby asked for, but they put up $85,000 for him to exploit one of his mines in Mexico. This, according to Manby's plans, would do just as well.[5] He went to Mexico, and then hurried back to Taos upon learning that the survey of the Antonio Martinez Land Grant had been completed on February 14, 1895 by the U. S. Surveyor General for New Mexico, Charles

F. Easley, and that a patent had now been granted.

Delineation of its boundaries, as Manby had expected, had been a difficult matter. He had done some probing himself into the musty records. There were few left; Governor William A. Pile during his administration from 1869 to 1871 had sold three-fourths of the state archives to merchants and grocers for wrapping paper. The action amply attested the positive disinterest in New Mexico's over-abundant, if not superfluous, history. Mere chance had saved Antonio Martinez' two-hundred year-old records from being wrapped around a stack of greasy *tortillas* and carried off. But even now, Manby was pleased to observe, no one seemed interested in the old grant whose extent and boundaries were so indefinite.

The land on the slope of the mountains behind the five-storied Pueblo of San Geronimo de Taos comprised the Pueblo Grant originally confirmed to the Indians by King Charles of Spain when the first Spanish conquistadores entered the country. There was no doubt that the Indian title to it far antedated those of all later private land grants. Hence there was a question whether the Antonio Martinez Grant overlapped that of the Pueblo Grant.

There was still another question: whether the Antonio Martinez and Lucero de Godoi were two separate grants, or whether they coincided.

Easley during his survey settled both these questions. Apparently two early grants in the valley had been made to Don Fernando Duran y Chavez and to Sergeant-Major Diego Lucero de Godoi. During the Indian uprising of 1680 all the Spanish settlers in the valley were killed except Don Fernando, his son, and Lucero de Godoi who fled to Mexico with the rest of the Spanish colonists in the territory. Upon De Vargas' reconquest of New Mexico in 1692 neither grantee returned, Don Fernando's grant being issued to a Cristobal de la Serna, and Sergeant-Major Lucero de Godoi's grant to Antonio Martinez.

Hence Easley certified that the Antonio Martinez and Lucero de Godoi grants coincided, being one and the same; that it did not conflict with the Pueblo grant; and that it contained 61,605.48 acres. Accordingly a United States patent was granted on May 8, 1896, the court specifying that the patent should not interfere or overthrow any just unextinguished Indian title or right to any lands within the boundary of the grant.[6]

A patent to 61,605.48 acres! Almost one hundred square miles! Compared to those two enormous land grant empires to the north and east, it was perhaps but a principality. But to Manby who had not known what to expect, it was a vast, ancient, and ignored domain in which a hundred or more other little principalities like Monaco would be lost in its expanse of billowing sage.

Manby could hardly contain his joy. He secured a copy of Walker's plat and a horse at the livery stable to keep overnight. Then with a hearty lunch packed in his saddlebags, he rode out next morning at daybreak to inspect his future kingdom.

7

As he jogged out of town the sun was just clearing the crest of the Sangre de Cristos, crowning its sentinel mountain with a golden aura. The wild plum thickets were white with blossoms. Great cottonwoods were leafing into electric green. Spring was in the air, in the smooth strides of his well coupled roan. Manby settled in his saddle with the assurance of a conqueror.

Guided by the boundary lines marked on the plat, he followed the southwest course of the Rio Lucero from its junction with the Rio Arroyo Seco and Don Fernando creek near Anderson's Mill. The draw it had cut through black volcanic stone was greening with grass and leafing willows. When it pinched out, he found himself crossing a barren plateau of gray-green sage that seemed to sweep unendingly westward under the turquoise sky. Nothing broke the upturned blue horizon. Nothing moved as far as he could see. He might have been alone at sea. Alone in a sea of billowing sage—all his to the wall of mountains looming to the north and east!

Two hours later, like an ancient mariner, he came to world's end. The earth seemed to fall away suddenly, without warning, before him. Manby reined up his horse and stared down with disbelieving eyes. He was standing on the rim of a thousand-foot-deep gorge slashed through volcanic rock by the red-brown Rio Grande below. He had reached the southwest corner of his kingdom.

Now he rode north along the rim of the gorge, the western boundary of the grant, picking his way carefully on the rocky underfooting between knotty clumps of sage. The view was incomparable. The deep chasm on his left; and ahead and to his right the curving blue wall of mountains. How large the grant was when he saw it by horseback! There was room in it for a half-dozen towns!

After perhaps eleven miles he had ridden to within a Spanish league from the northwest corner of the grant. Deciding to study the plat, he dismounted, unsaddled and hobbled the roan to rest and graze among the sage. Then squatting in a cleft of rocks on the rim of the gorge, he unfolded his plat. Here the boundary of the grant swung northeast to avoid the junction of the Rio Hondo with the Rio Grande in a T-shaped canyon. The place had been a noted landmark for years. From the Chile Line stop of Tres Piedras far to the west crawled a rutted wagon road, snaking down the west wall of the Rio Grande, spanning the river over Long John Dunn's wooden toll bridge, then crawling eastward to the old village of Arroyo Hondo. This was the route followed by stage travelers heading up Hondo Canyon to the boom mining camps of Amizette and Twining.

Gobbling a sandwich, Manby stared down into the gorge. A few cliff swallows skittered across the face of the sheer wall opposite him. A hawk floated noiselessly high above the chasm. Down below the river curled white around great boulders, then smoothed out into a stretch of tawny velvet. As he stared at it, mesmerized, he noticed that it was broken near the bank by recurring bubbles. A spring! An underwater spring!

Throwing off his coat, Manby searched along the rim for a way to clamber down the cliff. A few hundred yards south he came upon sheep droppings and the marks of hoofs leading to a rough and steep trail. Evidently this wild and desolate spot was known to sheepherders too. Following its windings down to the bottom of the gorge, he made his great discovery: a pool of hot water among a complex of great boulders. Near it on the sandbank lay the charcoal remnants of a campfire where the sheepherders had camped while bathing in the pool. Nearby, on boulders both to the north and to the south, he now found inscribed ancient Indian markings. Indians too had known of this hot spring centuries before. A strange tingle of excitement

Modern bridge spans the Rio Grande gorge, a few miles below Manby Hot Springs. *Courtesy Taos*

wriggled up his spine.

Taking off his clothes, he waded out into the cold river to the bubbling spot he had noticed from high above. It too was warm, fed by another hot spring seeping up from the rocky bottom. There was no doubt about it. A length of six Spanish leagues along the river spotted with hot springs, all on the east side. What a watering resort, a noted spa, it would make! His muscular body shivering with cold and excitement, he waded back to soak in the hot pool.

It was past noon when he climbed out of the gorge and rode on. He was tired from climbing and he had forgotten to finish his lunch. The roan, an ill-fed livery nag, was tired out too. Also he had short pasterns, making his low trot stiff and uncomfortable. The clear sky had clouded over. A wind was coming up. Looking westward Manby could see a thin, twisting column of dust rising from the sere brown plain miles away. A dust devil. Manby preferred to believe it came from the wheels of another stage loaded with passengers bound up the Hondo Canyon—settlers who would soon be colonizing his grant.

He was close to the mountains now, a forested blue wall curving from east to north in a great sweeping arc broken by three canyons. From the one directly ahead of him the Rio Hondo on its course to the Rio Grande had gouged out the deep arroyo that formed the northern boundary to the grant. Peering down, he could see the tiny village of Valdez and toy horses grazing in the checkerboard fields. Out of the middle canyon to the south trickled a little stream down the Arroyo Seco. This gave its name to a straggle of adobes along it which housed almost all the few people who lived on the entire grant. From a narrow cleft in the mountains still farther south poured the Rio Lucero, marking the southeast boundary of the grant and joining with the Don Fernando creek where Manby had begun his ride that morning.

Here it was, all spread out before him. A great tract of about one hundred square miles, roughly triangular in shape, sloping down from peaks still capped with snow, through glorietas of aspen and cottonwood, open glades and meadows, to the vast and empty sagebrush plateau stretching to the Rio Grande. It had everything, was a pristine world to itself, awaiting a touch to spring to life.

Worn out, he spurred his jaded horse into the upper plaza of the village. A tiny plaza mounting a thick-walled church surrounded by a few old adobes. A village, as villages were out here. Less irritable from fatigue and on a sunny afternoon, Manby might have seen some charm in it—had it been swept of refuse, and the crumbling walls patched up. Now, beclouded with dust from the rising wind, it looked merely squalid. Manby jerked up his horse in ill temper. He had expected to find a cafe of some kind in which he might get a pot of tea and something to eat. There was only an old woman sweeping chicken droppings out of her hut with a broom of *popote*, native grass.

"Mother!" he cried impatiently. "Something hot for a traveler's belly, no? Coffee if you do not have tea. He pays well!"

The old woman gathered her black shawl about her shoulders with hands like the prehensile talons of a hawk, and stared at him with hard black eyes of obsidian. "Who is this traveler in fine clothes who demands food with the voice of a *jéfe*? And in the middle of the afternoon! Mother of God!"

"*Las hojas para el caballo. No hay?*"

"*Sí. Hay.* He pay well too, the horse?"

Manby was in no mood for joking. He dismounted, watched her bring a few of last fall's withered cornstalks for his horse, and then followed her into the hut. In the faint light of a small window the place looked like a cave. Dirt floor. Dirt walls. A chair and an iron bedstead covered with grimy blankets. A few carved and painted Santos hanging on the wall. Nothing more to mark it as the residence of one of Antonio Martinez' illustrious heirs to his vast grant. How easy it would be to get the land from such natives!

The old woman poked up the embers in the corner fireplace and warmed a pot of cooked beans and a few tortillas. There was no coffee, no tea. Manby squatted down on the floor and ate hurriedly with distaste. The beans were lukewarm and sweetened with sugar; the tortillas tasted like worn leather. Then getting to his feet, he dropped a coin on the only chair. "*Bien, Madre! Adios!*"

As he stalked out the door, he heard the ring of the coin on the ground at his heels. Turning around, he saw the old crone standing in the doorway. She gave him one look of inexpressible negation from her black obsidian eyes, spat on the ground, and

went back inside. Manby shrugged, mounted his horse, and
rode on.

The incident, trivial as it was, grated on his nerves. He was
tired from his long ride, still hungry, and a cloud of gritty dust
was sweeping down the draw. To add to his discomfort, his horse
had thrown a shoe and was beginning to stumble. Looking at
the foot, Manby discovered a broken nail he could not draw out.
Wearily he knee-reined the horse toward a squat, solitary adobe
standing off in the vega above.

It looked like a fortress erected against the solitude of earth
and sky, the eternal loneliness of man. Stout walls. No windows.
But an old iron bell mounted above the only door. As he stopped
in front, he realized at once what it was from the strange and
repulsively ominous object drawn up beside the door. It was a
small, dilapidated cart mounted on solid wooden wheels, whose
passenger propped up inside was the black-draped skeleton
of a woman with a white death's head and bony hands holding
a bow and arrow. *Una carreta del muerto.* Beside it lay a huge
wooden cross splashed with black, coagulated spots of blood.
Sangre de Cristo.

The building was a *morada* maintained by that strange sect of
Penitentes—*Los Hermanos Penitentes* or *Hermanos de la Luz*,
Brothers of Light, whose members in this wilderness practiced
self-flagellation with whips of cactus and hung a brother to the
cross on Good Friday of every year in emulation of the Savior.
Easter had come late this year, Manby realized suddenly, and
these gruesome objects used on their march to Calvario had
not yet been dragged inside.

The fading light, the isolate remoteness of the *morada*, and
the sight of these vivid reminders of passion, blood, and death
completely destroyed the lingering vestiges of Manby's daylong
assurance. For the first time he felt like an alien on an earth to
which he was not and never would be attuned. At that moment
the door of the *morada* opened. A man came out quickly and
without a word grasped the bridle of Manby's horse. Manby
was in no mood to permit such an insult. He reined back, lifting
his mount's forefeet off the ground. The man, with a grip of iron,
jerked the horse down again. Quietly, without speaking, he
stared up at Manby with an impenetrable look of negation in
his black, shiny eyes.

It was Manby who spoke first. "My horse. He has a nail in his off forefoot. I stopped but to find somebody to pull it out."

"*Aye de mi! Cómo no, Señor?*"

The man went inside and came back with a pair of rusty pliers. Undoubtedly he was the Hermano Mayor and his back was covered with painful swollen welts, for as he worked on the horse's hoof Manby could see his muscles twitch beneath his thin, dirty shirt.

"*Ah! Qué bueno!*" With his hearty pull and a grunt the nail came out. The man stepped back, warily and silently waiting. His eyes were still like flint, unfriendly, ungiving.

This time Manby did not flip him a coin. "*Muchas gracias, amigo. Muchísimas gracias!*" He wanted to be asked inside. To ask about the strange doings. To engage in a little conversation with this one of his future subjects after his solitary ride. But the Hermano Mayor seemed like the land itself, negative and withdrawn.

"*Por nada, Señor.*"

With a curse under his breath, Manby wheeled his mount and galloped away. These damned, ignorant, unfriendly natives with their queer beliefs and customs! No wonder the grant had been ignored for so many years!

It was dusk now; and as he ruthlessly spurred his jaded nag past the mouth of the Lucero and around the base of the mountain, he felt that even the peak was shadowed by an aura of impalpable malignancy. He suddenly reined up and dismounted, inflamed by a resurgence of savage determination. Hadn't he ridden like Antonio Martinez the boundaries of the grant that was now to be his? He jerked up a handful of weeds. Then grabbing a fistful of dirt, he cast it from him into a dusk that seemed compounded of shadows from an immeasurable past. A gust of wind down the draw flung the dirt back into his face. It was as if the mountain, like the land and its people, were rejecting his presence. Digging out the gritty spume from his mouth and eyes, Manby shouted back his challenge. "Why not!"

As he neared the pueblo, a bloodless white figure stepped forth in the road in front of him. It might have been a pale shadow cast by the thicket of white plum blossoms, but his roan flung up his ears and spooked on quick-stepping feet. Manby pulled up. An Indian, shrouded in a white sheet drawn up to his eyes, stood quietly in the road. Manby stared. The Indian silently stared back from impenetrable eyes. Manby whipped up his horse and galloped on.

Safely past that pale and unmoving but somehow inimical shape that had not drawn aside for him, Manby's assurance returned. A handful of Indians and native Spanish peons! What were they to him? Arriving home, he fell into bed without supper.

Next morning he awoke again confident and secure. The vast plum of an empire to which he had dedicated himself was ripe for the picking. No one was interested in it, and probably for good reason. Both Spain and Mexico had exempted land grants from taxation; their governments needed colonists to support their hold upon the sparsely inhabited wilderness. Now under domination of the United States which would impose taxes the poor grantees would be unable to pay, the land was no longer an asset. It was a liability which Manby was now ready to lift from its burdened owners.

He began buying property in Taos, giving his residence as Elizabethtown in order not to attract attention. By the spring of 1898 his purchases were so numerous they kept the county clerk in the courthouse up nights transcribing his increasing warranty deeds.

In April he bought seven large pieces.[1] Most of them he squeezed out of widows and descendants of old Spanish Colonial families who had come on hard times and needed a few precious American dollars. Their names alone attested the history behind them: Francisca Trujillo de Maxwell, widow; Aloysius Liebert and his wife, Piedad Ledoux de Liebert; Maximiano Romero and his wife, Jacinta Santistevan de Romero; Marina Romero and her aging parents, Santiago Romero and Leonara Martinez de Romero; and the impoverished Lopez heirs.

Most of these pieces of property Manby combined into one large tract in the best location in town. It was within spitting distance of the plaza; a little farther, say a stone's throw, from the adobe house in which Charles Bent, the first American governor of New Mexico, had been scalped and murdered just fifty years before; and adjoining the Kit Carson home in whose garden the famous scout was buried. With frontage on the road leading to the pueblo, it extended west and north to the jutting mountain.

On this large estate he cleared the land of brush and weeds and began building a Spanish hacienda from which to govern his Spanish grant. Huge hand-hewn logs, peeled and seasoned, ready to be hoisted into place as roof-beams or *vigas*, were hauled down from the mountains. In the back pasture barefoot men were making thousands of adobe bricks to be laid into two-foot-thick walls. Manby had taste, was a good architect, and drove a hard bargain. He built slowly but well, driving his workers with an explosive temper.

While the house went up he hired men to bring in trees and shrubs to set out behind the house, creating a large English park with curving walks and sunken pools. He laid it out carefully, with the sure instinct of a gardener, so that he would have an unobstructed view of the mountain. A purple mountain framed by lilacs! Never had it seemed so friendly and looked down upon him so approvingly. How happy he felt!

The town virtually ended at his new house, the dusty road creeping onward through barren, wind-swept fields. Why was it these Spanish people never planted trees along their roads or around their lonely adobes? With a crew digging holes and an irrigation ditch, he now set out a long row of cottonwood seedlings along the public road. Within a few years the trees would link branches overhead, forming a shady lane almost to the little placita far down the road.

He then transplanted a row of young trees to border a dusty lane south of the plaza. Such a hasty manifestation of community pride was too much for at least some townspeople who abhorred progress. Every night they loosed a band of goats to chew the bark off the tender young trees. "The damned rascals! I'll fix them!" Manby one night painted the bark of the trees with poison. Next morning as he strolled by, he was gratified to see a row of dead goats, feet sticking up, strung along the road.[2]

Settling in his large house, he resumed his buying spree. It was not restricted to town lots. He began to pick up from other impoverished Spanish families all the land they owned within the Martinez Grant. The large Sanchez family was among the first to capitulate. Between March and May he acquired the lands of Juanita Abrea de Sanchez, Juan Jose, Jesus Maria, Miguel, Pablo, and Francisquita. Not satisfied with this, Manby traced down Juan Sanchez in Las Animas, Colorado and Encarnaciona

Espinosa de Sanchez in Pueblo, Colorado, to complete the family roster of lawful Antonio Martinez heirs. From each of them he acquired not only the land but all vested rights: timber and grazing rights, and the rights to build dams, reservoirs and ditches to convey water from the Rio Lucero and Rio Seco.[3]

With his plans beginning to take shape, Manby wrote his brother Eardley in England of the immense project under way. The major immediately sailed for America, arriving in New Mexico late that spring.

Manby met him when he stepped off the train in Raton. There was no Spanish *embrazo*—the hug and kiss on each cheek. No American-style slapping on the back. Just a formal, restrained English handshake, both men drawing back then to survey the other. The major was not in uniform but he bore his Army training if not its cloth, giving forth an air of dignity and success. The sight of his brother, dressed in his Western clothes and big Stetson, was not too reassuring. Yet when Manby outlined his great project as they drove over the pass, Eardley's respect for what he regarded as his blacksheep brother took on dimensions.

Arriving in Taos, he saw that Manby's hacienda was large and comfortable. His property looked good. Manby explained that he had picked it up at fairly reasonable prices, but was obliged to spend a great deal of money in a short time, and he needed ready cash.

The stiff-necked major was cautious. He was glad to loan Manby $1,000, but insisted that he sign a promissory note on May 2, payable within five years with five per cent interest to him at the First National Bank of Trinidad, Colorado.[4]

During his visit of almost four months, Eardley spent most of his time going over the Antonio Martinez Grant and his brother's plans for acquiring and developing it. He seemed fully convinced that the project would be successful. "When I get back to England I'll raise investment capital in the venture if you can indeed manage to secure the grant," he promised.

This was reassuring, but not quite enough. Manby needed money to carry him, and struck Eardley for another loan. This one was for a sizable but undisclosed amount; for before he left in August the major took a mortgage on a piece of Manby's land in town.[5]

The following year, on December 4, 1899, Manby was admitted

to United States citizenship by Alfred M. Bergere, the district court clerk of Taos County. For witnesses Manby took with him Smith H. Simpson and Dr. T. Paul Martin, a young country-doctor who had just arrived to begin practice. No one could now question his right to ownership of the grant on the grounds that he was still a citizen of Great Britain.[6]

8

He had a large stable in the courtyard behind his house now, and every morning he would go out and bridle and saddle his big bay gelding. Swinging into the stirrups, he would ride across the Indian Reservation toward the pueblo.

It stood in the middle of a large central plaza—two terraced, five-storied, communal apartment buildings of adobe facing each other across a stream. Indian women in shawls and white deerskin boots would be drawing water from the stream and waddling back across the plaza, their jars balanced on their heads. Men would be working in their fields or cleaning out their irrigation ditches, their blankets or white cotton sheets wrapped around their waists or their heads like burnooses. Others would be standing on the rooftops as if in silent prayer. They were strong, virile men with their black hair worn in two long pigtails hanging down their broad backs or deep chests. There was an Asiatic cast to their dark faces, with their hairless eyebrows and inscrutable black eyes. They moved in a slow rhythm, in a dimension Manby could not fathom, as if they reflected an America that would always be hidden from him. The enigma somehow annoyed him. They were too damned independent, secretive, and aloof!

He hurried on. Turning at the old church blasted into ruins by American howitzers fifty years before, he would ride on to the Antonio Martinez Grant.

Most of the few people on it were concentrated in the little village of Arroyo Seco, a straggle of adobes only ten miles from town but remote and isolated for weeks at a time by an almost impassible road. The village, he had found out, had been established October 7, 1745 on a small grant to Joaquin Codallos y Roybal, but no use of the land had been made until 1815, the hardy settlers living on game and small flocks of sheep they pastured in the mountain meadows. When they did begin to break land with oxen and wooden plows for tiny *milpas* of corn— according to a report of the Ayuntamiento or Town Council of Taos to the Jéfe Político on December 30, 1823—there arose a dispute with the Indians at the pueblo over the use of the Rio Lucero for irrigation. For a century the squabble had continued. Each group still kept tearing down the other's little earthen dams, occasionally flashing a knife in the bright sunlight, then relapsing into months of apathy.

The Indians apparently were a slow-pulsed people, not easily aroused. Their roots sank too deep. The land had been there long before the Spanish and Anglo people came, and it would be there long after both of them had gone. But the water. That was something else. The Lucero came from high in the mountains, near a sacred lake to which they were said to make secret pilgrimages. With the Rio Pueblo, which drained from the sacred lake itself, it not only watered their pastures and their tiny fields, but their pagan beliefs.

Manby regarded this as nonsense. He intended to put a stop to it by utilizing the Lucero to irrigate the grant. He rode on resolutely to do his day's work.

There were a couple of other small clumps of adobes called villages. Arroyo Seco Abajo downstream, separated from Arroyo Seco Arriba upstream, and Desmontes, strung along the high rim of the Arroyo Hondo. Their villagers were similar to those of Arroyo Seco. Hardly much more advanced than the Indians, he thought, these aloof, swarthy men dressed in hand-sewn leather vests, carrying the look of far remoteness in their black eyes. Poor and uneducated, they still eked out a primitive existence by farming a few acres and grazing a few sheep. These were the descendants of Antonio Martinez who claimed to be the rightful heirs of his vast grant.

Manby's work was simple.[1] He would ride up to a squalid

adobe on whose earthen floor several naked children were playing
with a lamb or long-legged goat. The lady of the house might be
Filomena, Candelaria, or Maria Ascension. No matter. She
always looked the same. A scrawny, aged child, with quick fear
leaping into her black eyes as Manby's shadow darkened the
doorway.

Manby swept off his high-crowned Stetson. "Your husband,
Señora, is not here?"

"*Pues.* He has gone to the mountains this very day. Before
the sun was up."

"It cannot be true, Señora! With all this fine land to work?"

"But it is not fine land, Señor. *Seco, seco, seco.* You yourself
can see how dry it is. There is hardly enough water in the stream
to wet the tongue."

"And this land. It is all yours?" Manby settled himself on a
small bench. "How many acres may I ask, with your permission?"

"No, Señor. This land is very old. It comes from him who
fathered us all, the good Martinez whose name my mother bore.
It is not measured in acres. It is not cut into squares as is the
custom nowadays. That would not be right. It runs in the old
way, in strips from the mountain top to the river. Thus each
man has a bit of meadow to plow for corn, a bit of pasture for
his cows, a bit of forest for wood. The *vara* is the measure,
Señor."

"The *vara* is thirty-three inches, Señora. That I know."

"*Aye de mi!* That is the trouble. A man cuts his land into
strips for each of his sons, and they cut theirs into strips for
their sons. Soon there is little left. Twenty *varas* wide our land
is. No more. And dry besides. That is why my man cannot work
it. That is why he must take his sheep and goats into the mountains where the grass is free. Mother of God! How poor we are.
I cannot offer my guest a cup of coffee. He must sit there in the
sun because we have no curtains for the window. That storekeeper will not take the money I offered him. Look!"

She got up, raised the lid of an old carved chest and laid a
coin in Manby's hand. It was square, covered with grime, and
very heavy. "Under the floor it was, Señor. We looked for more.
But there were no more. Of what use would they be? That
storekeeper would not take it. He wanted a shiny new dollar."
Brushing back her hair, she spat with disgust.

Manby quietly pocketed the old gold coin and gave her a silver dollar.

"Take it. It is yours. Now, about that strip of land. It is too narrow. It is dry, besides. But I will buy it just the same."

"It is good land. We have lived on it, we have worked it, we have loved it. My father, and his father's father. What would my husband say?"

Manby stood up. "You will tell him, no? Then tell him I would not buy your home or these old apple trees in back where the children play. Only that land beyond the fence. A good price. A bag of new dollars. No?"

Putting on his hat, he walked slowly out to his horse. The woman followed. "All dollars, you say? Not on paper? *Ai, Ai, Ai.* My husband will come to see you, Señor! He will sell it, no doubt. I shall have my house and those curtains for the window. Bright yellow curtains with red strawberries on them to warm our hearts when the snow is high! And coffee, besides! Mother of God! What a lucky day this is, Señor!"

It was not always that easy. He would hunt up a taciturn, somber man in rags, herding his small flock of sheep and goats in a distant stretch of sagebrush. His name might be Jesus y Maria, or Juan Jose, or Librado. Whatever it was, he refused to sell his piece of land. He spat on the ground and refused to look at Manby's fat bay gelding.

"Well, that is too bad," said Manby curtly. He took out from his pocket a grimy bill from a supply store for groceries and supplies, unpaid all year. "That store in town was tired of waiting for its money. Your goats and sheep are thin and scrawny. They will not be worth anything. The storekeeper has refused you any more credit and was about to put you in jail. So I paid him for you. Now to me you owe $86. Here is the bill."

He waved it discreetly in front of the sheepherder, taking care lest he grab it. In a harsher voice he continued, "I had thought to be a friend to you as I have been to many of your *primos.* By taking that worthless piece of old land of yours in payment for this bill. But you do not want to sell your land. Good!"

He swung his horse around by the bridle, jumped into the saddle. "I do not pay $86 for nothing! I will let the sheriff come up and get it from you. Perhaps he will take all your sheep and goats instead. No?"

Setting spurs to his gelding, Manby was called back by the sheepherder. He had a frightened look on his simple face, and he was extremely polite. "Perhaps I was hasty, *compadre*. You see, my wife is sick in the chest. She cannot breathe. Perhaps she will not live many days now, God forgive me for saying so! So her *primos* have taken her and my children to live with them. Now I have no family. I have no home. I have only my sheep and my goats here to give me comfort. Do you understand!"

"I cannot listen to your troubles," said Manby. "Do you want to talk about selling your land?"

The sheepherder lowered his head and with a gesture of defeat opened his horny hands. "It will give her a funeral in church, as is proper. With candles, not many but some. The little incense pot will sweeten salt tears. Perhaps, if there is money enough, the padre will ring the bells." He suddenly began to beat his bowed head with his great fists. "*Ojala!* God have mercy and forgive my sins!"

So one by one Manby cajoled and harassed the residents into selling their inherited shares of the grant. The process was too slow. Moreover it was not endearing him to the people. Why not let a couple of lawyers do it for him?

Manby was shrewd enough to pick them carefully. They had to be smart enough to follow his instructions, but not too smart or they might double-cross him. As a further goad to their efforts and a check on their loyalty, he always underpaid them and was usually behind in his payments.

For the disagreeable job of harassing the residents to sell their parts of the grant, he obtained Antonio Gallegos—the same Gallegos who had attended the Court of Private Land Claims hearing as an heir of Antonio Martinez and a claimant to the grant. Assisting him were two other local Spanish attorneys capable and poor enough to drive a hard bargain. The land they obtained was turned over to another lawyer who bought it for Manby. For this he selected an Anglo attorney in Sante Fe, Judge Laughlin.

Napoleon Bonaparte Laughlin bore slight resemblance to the smaller, former illustrious gentleman for whom he had been named at birth in Grand Tower, Illinois. As a fiery youth of twenty, however, he had joined a mounted regiment of the Confederate Army at the outbreak of the Civil War. The experience had convinced him he was not cut out for another Little Corporal. Taking up law, he emigrated to New Mexico and engaged in politics. His rise was rapid. He became successively a member of the territorial House of Representatives, attorney general, and had just finished a term as associate justice of the Supreme Court and judge of the First Judicial District. Upon becoming a judge, he grew a little sensitive to his given name. He signed papers as "Napoleon B.," which he gradually reduced to "N.B.," and finally preferred to be known by the more august "Judge Laughlin." Under any name he knew his way around.

The combination of Gallegos and the Judge worked out as well as Manby had foreseen. He was no longer seen and the land was being sold ostensibly to someone in Santa Fe. Within a short time Gallegos was bringing in to Laughlin groups of a dozen or more resident grantees at a time to sign over their parts of the grant.[2]

The process was still too slow for Manby. A hundred square miles of land was too big a chunk to buy up in small pieces at a time. Cheap as he was getting it, he was running out of money. There was still another hitch. A small group of grantees was obdurately refusing to sell. It included Daniel Martinez and Francisco Martinez y Martinez who years before had first claimed ownership of the grant and who had attended the hearing in Santa Fe to which Manby had gone, and four stubborn Marias, all Martinez also: Maria Encarnacia, Maria Andrea, Maria Juliana, and Maria Filomena.

Manby probably restrained an impulse to arm a gang of roughnecks to run them off the grant, as the Maxwell Land Grant Company had planned with Jim Masterson. That would be the quick and easy way to do it. But the Maxwell Grant had taught him a lesson. Craft and intrigue were better, though slower. Also, he did not yet have title to the land. Some other solution would have to be found by which he could dispossess the remaining residents who still gave trouble.

Why not acquire title to the whole grant by inducing local county officials to reduce the value of the land so he could pick it up for payment of taxes?

On May 23, 1900 he wrote Judge Laughlin of his plan to perfect title, advising him of the need for extreme caution: "But the successful consummation of this, as you know, in a great measure depends on the skill and secrecy with which our moves are made, so that we shall not be held up by more plotters in unlooked-for quarters. And if we manage matters carefully and skillfully we shall have the Grant title perfected before others realize what we are after."[3]

If the plan seemed to be on the shady side of the legal avenue, the former attorney general, associate justice of the Supreme Court, and august judge, now fifty-six years old, offered no objections.

Leaving Laughlin and Gallegos to keep working on the people, Manby went east to raise more money, and then down to Mexico to see about his mines, all the while working out his projected scheme.

Upon his return he wrote Laughlin on October 7, 1901, "I have recently returned from Old Mexico where I have been for nearly a year,"[4] and resumed his discussion of the grant, concluding that the easiest and safest way to perfect title would be to have the grant sold for taxes after they had got the taxes reduced to as little as possible. He informed Laughlin that his friends in the east, representing large capital, were eager to go ahead. Then, in several pages filled with his bold handwriting, he submitted his detailed, year-by-year computation of taxes on the Antonio Martinez or Lucero de Godoi Grant from 1891 to 1901.

He believed that if delinquent taxes were due from February 14, 1901, taxes for only six years needed to be paid. Moreover, the 60,000 acres could be valued at only twenty cents an acre, making a total valuation of only $12,000 for the entire grant, which could be bought for a tax payment of $2,160.

Four months later he and the judge began their insidious campaign. On January 28, 1902 they filed a bill for partition in the district court, Manby as the plaintiff versus Daniel Martinez and his small, stubborn group as the defendants. Manby alleged that he was the owner in fee simple of more than three-fourths of the grant, the remaining one-fourth being claimed by innumerable Spanish settlers living in the tiny village of Arroyo Seco and in the straggly settlement of Desmontes on the high ridge along the deep Arroyo Hondo. Manby was cautious enough to plead that he did not want to disturb these settlers in the possession of their homes and fields. But he demanded that all the land in the grant be surveyed, partitioned to individual owners, properly taxed and paid. The bill was notarized by Laughlin and duly published four times in the weekly *Taos Cresset*.

One of the Eastern promoters Manby had secured was D. F. Morgan, general counsel for the Michigan Telephone Company in Minneapolis, acting for a group of interested investors. On April 5, 1902 he wrote Judge Laughlin in Santa Fe, questioning whether the Leroux or Lucero Grant had been made in 1742, twenty-six years after the Antonio Martinez Grant, or whether there existed a question of priority.

His question reflected the general ignorance about all these old grants. Judge Laughlin by this time seemed confused himself by the growing ramifications. Manby was not. He had become a practical historian of acknowledged ability. The Antoine Leroux Grant, he pointed out, had been made indeed on August 12, 1742 by Governor Gaspar Domingo de Mendoza upon the petition of Pedro Vigil de Santillana, Juan Beautista Vigil, and Cristobal Vigil. But it was not to be confused with the Lucero de Godoi or Antonio Martinez Grant, an entirely separate tract.

Ruthless and persuasive, he continued harassing the poor, uninformed county officials. They were easily manipulated. Almost all of them were ill-educated Spanish *politicos* named to office by their party's *jéfe* in return for the votes they controlled, and ready to bend the laws to Manby's interest.

On May 27, 1903 Manby reported to Laughlin that a nice tract of 9,200 acres in the grant had been sold at last to Taos County for $36.11 delinquent taxes. Manby had given this amount to the deputy treasurer, Henry Gonzales, who had mildly protested that this was too much land to obtain for such a small amount of money. Manby, however, had forcefully reminded him that he could not ask for more than the judgment. Two weeks later Manby delightedly informed the judge that after paying a few more dollars for court costs he had successfully redeemed the whole 9,200 acres for a total cost of only $52.99.

Another large tract of 6,200 acres was then put up for sale by the county for $126.25 delinquent taxes. This time Manby remained in the background, inducing Antonio C. Pacheco of Arroyo Seco to redeem it for him.

Manby was jubilant. Whatever ridiculous prices he had paid for previous small holdings, he had obtained these 15,400 acres

Arthur R. Manby, 1904.

A. R. Manby in the living room of his Taos home. L to R: Bert Phillips, Harriet Randall (Edith Kearney's mother), A. R. Manby, Mrs. Bert Phillips.

A. R. Manby at home, ca. 1904.

A. R. Manby and dog. *Courtesy Kit Carson Memorial Foundation.*

—a fourth of the whole grant—for a total cost of only $179.24.

The small and stubborn group of heirs and claimants headed by Daniel Martinez could read the writing on the wall. Finally capitulating, he and Andrea Martinez sold out their shares to Manby.

Manby was now in position to assert ownership to the entire grant of 61,605 acres. On October 6, 1905 he filed at last his suit to quiet title for the whole grant, pleading that any conveyance of interests in it be made subject to his own declared rights.[5]

9

The comparative ease with which Manby obtained possession of the Martinez Grant did not blind him to the possibilities of other lucrative ventures. During this time he met the Santistevan family.

Juan de los Reyes Santistevan was a prominent Taos resident descended from a proud old Spanish family that gave him the right to prefix to his name the familiar "Don," designating *De Origen Noble*. He had begun his remarkable career as a member of the Santistevan, St. Vrain, and Hurst mercantile company. As banks were few and unreliable, such influential merchants controlled the economy by issuing supplies on credit to sheepmen and farmers, and collecting when their flocks and grain were sold. The natural corollary to this prosperous enterprise was his establishment of the first and only bank in the county. Municipal and state offices followed. Don Juan served as postmaster, chairman of the school board, county commissioner, probate judge, twice as a member of the state legislature, and one term in the senate.[1]

Don Juan and his wife Doña Perfecta also had been blessed with six daughters. Three of them, Rafaelita, Margarita, and Jacunita, had successfully married into the reliable Pacheco, Cordova, and Romero families. The three younger daughters still lived in the family home, a large two-story house with a pitched roof on the north side of the plaza. Victoriana's and Perfectita's loyalties were bestowed, it was understood, and their formal betrothals were imminent. Only Circilia remained unattached. She was a young, slim girl spirited enough to be regarded as headstrong; and it was not too surprising that she was often seen with Manby.

Townspeople had wondered why he did not get married—this rich and rather handsome man in the prime of life, with a fine big house and so much land. They were certain he did not lack feminine companionship. He seemed to have a fondness for young girls, and one after another were seen at his home. But not for long. One would leave, weeping. Or another would flee the house in fear. Circilia was a different matter. Tongues began to wag.

"*Pues*. Young lamb is more tender than old mutton!" one would say with a shrug.

"But a Santistevan? It is a thing not to be believed! Of course he will marry with her."

"*Cómo no?* Business is business," another would answer.

It was indeed quite possible that mundane business affairs were uppermost in the minds of both Santistevan and Manby. For the elderly Don Juan was in financial trouble and, as a man of importance, feeling his community obligations deeply. For a time he staved off a crisis by borrowing money from the reliable old standby, the First National Bank of Trinidad, Colorado. Then debts began to overwhelm him.

"I must ask our good friend, Mr. Manby, to help me. He is a clever man," he confided to his wife.

Doña Perfecta was annoyed and alarmed. "And who is he, this stranger who has compromised our good name? Has he asked for Circilia's hand? No! That is a matter to be straightened out first!"

"But surely his intentions are those of an honorable gentleman. He has a big house and much land. He is not a foolish young man."

"He is three times her age! That I have warned her—to no avail. Now I warn you! Have no business dealings with this man."

"*Aye de mi*, Perfecta," sighed Don Juan. "You are well named."

'*Caras vemos, corazones no sabemos.*" Dona Perfecta snapped at him the old proverb—"Faces we see, hearts we do not know" —and flounced out of the room.

A few weeks later Don Juan, frantic with worry, appealed to Manby for help. Manby was glad to oblige. He advised Santistevan to go into bankruptcy and to turn over all his holdings to him to liquidate.

Santistevan took his advice. He assigned everything he owned to Manby: 21 pieces of real estate worth $20,000, several of which were owned and lived on by his married daughters although title was still in his name; book accounts and notes amounting to $15,000; merchandise in his store worth $30,000; 20,000 head of sheep including the Spring's lambs, worth almost $40,000; 75,000 pounds of wool with an estimated value of $9,750; and other assets worth $5,000. He then closed his bank and waited confidently for his shrewd and capable future son-in-law to salvage for him something out of the wreck.

Manby graciously persuaded several nominal friends of his to appraise all of Santistevan's holdings at the lowest possible value. They claimed that the store merchandise was old, worn, and damaged; the sheep were scrawny and worth little; and the twenty-one pieces of real estate worth only $9,000.

Having reduced these holdings to almost negligible values, Manby put the real estate properties up for sale—buying them himself through dummy purchasers, and evicting Santistevan's married daughters. It happened that several pieces were close to or adjoined his own town property. These he kept, enlarging his own estate. Others he sold at good profit, including a large house next to his own which he sold to young Doc Martin.

He then instituted suits against all of Santistevan's creditors. One of them was against Santistevan's daughter, Maria Rafaelita and her husband Manuel Pacheco, for $6,758.96 worth of family groceries and clothing bought from her father's store on an open book account over a period of several years. Santistevan protested, claiming that his son-in-law had paid for the goods in work. It was no use. Manby obtained a judgment of $5,134.96, taking four pieces of property in payment.

The rest of the creditors paid off at from 25¢ to 65¢ on the dollar. Manby collected $5,000 commission and $1,000 travel expenses, which included the rentals of a team and buggy at $3 per day, and the cost of meals at $1 apiece. He was then released by the court from all further obligations. There was nothing left for Juan Santistevan.[2]

Circilia, whom he dropped, wept in her mother's bedroom. Don Juan, completely ruined, began to fail rapidly. Doña Perfecta said only one thing to each of them. "*Lo que volando viene, volanda se va.* Easy come, easy go. You will see!"

Such shenanigans and shady dealings did not endear Manby to town. Nor did his frequent displays of violent temper. Early that November Jose Montaner, editor of the weekly paper, published a small squib about him during the political campaign. A few days later Manby, passing by the Columbian Hotel, noticed him sitting in the dining room with state senator Ramon Sanchez. Manby, his face purpling with rage, banged open the door and rushed inside.

"You blasted liar!" he shouted. "What do you mean attacking me in your paper? I'll teach you a lesson!"

Grabbing up a knife from the table, he flung himself upon Montaner, slashing him on the wrist and raising the knife to stab him in the chest. Sanchez was too quick for him. Jumping up, he grabbed his chair and cracked Manby over the head with it, averting a possible murder. Manby struggled up from the floor and stalked home in a daze.[3]

During his successful acquisition of the grant and the joyful building of his house, he had completely forgotten the shadow-creature imprisoned but so long dormant within him. Now suddenly and unexpectedly it had come to life again. Luckily nothing had come of its little outbreak. He could afford to ignore it. There were too many other things on his mind.

The Fergusons up at Elizabethtown, or E-town as it was usually called, were always a diversion. The raw-boned Scotch miner would be up at the Mystic with his daughter Francisca. She would sit watching him pounding away at chunks of ore, or panning sand in the stream and adding quicksilver to catch the flakes of gold. They were constant companions, these two.

The other little girl, Teracita, preferred to stay with her mother. When Manby rode up to the cabin, she would run out to hold his horse, the bridle was so pretty. Then she would take him inside to talk with her mother. Mrs. Ferguson sat beside the stove, spinning wool. Instead of using a wheel, English style, she followed the old Spanish custom of feeding the wool to a

long smooth stick which she twirled in a saucer. When the wool
was spun into yarn, she knitted it into socks which she sold to
miners for twenty-five cents a pair.

There was something about this black-haired, black-eyed
woman of Spain with her Moorish heritage that he liked, but
which he could not fathom. Living on a hard granite rock ten
thousand feet high had made her resourceful; and being married
to a dirt-poor, if not ore-poor, Scotch miner was making her self-
reliant. The girl Teracita was just like her. Manby kept watching
her too. She sat across the room without speaking. Quiet and
demure, but with a streak of granite in her too.

From Moreno Valley he went east again, making the rounds
of his financial associates. Money, money, money! He needed
more and more and more. The big booms at Amizette and Twining up Hondo Canyon had become big busts. There was no longer
a parade of stages and wagons full of hopefuls passing by, those
settlers whom Manby had expected to populate his grant. His
potential investors back east knew this very well. It made them
cautious about digging into their pockets. Still he raised capital
in Minneapolis, Chicago, Kansas City, and Lansing. More was
coming from investors found in Great Britain by his brother
Eardley. One of them, a particularly steady and heavy investor,
was a young Irish girl named Margaret Higgins living in Rosganna, County of Antrim.

Still it was not enough. Manby was not a man like Maxwell
to take pleasure walking through his grant in his bare feet. His
love for it was not that of a Spanish peon or an Indian. His whole
life hinged on developing it into a populous and thriving kingdom
of which he would be the undisputed, royal sovereign. So every
night at home, sitting under a lamp in his big adobe hacienda,
he wrote unceasing letters with a free, bold hand in blue ink on
blue stationery engraved "A. R. Manby, Taos, New Mexico,"
and worked out the details of his chartered kingdom.

For it had been chartered! On April 24, 1905, five months
before he had filed suit to quiet title to the grant, he had
organized the Taos Valley Land Company in which to invest
his title to the land. According to its articles of incorporation,
the authorized capital stock of the company was $1,000,000,
with an authorized issuance of 1,000,000 shares at a par value of
one dollar. "The amount of cash actually paid in on the capital

stock is nothing," the document asserted, but the cash value
of the property was $1,000,000.

Five men were named as the Board of Directors: Manby
himself; Napoleon B. Laughlin, his attorney in Santa Fe; and
three of Manby's investors, Schuyler S. Olds of Lansing, Michigan, Jesse B. Levy of Kansas City, Missouri, and E. G. Potter
of Minneapolis, Minnesota. Manby was named as the resident
agent in Taos.[4]

The Company! The power of a company! And now he had one.
That evening, in a late April snowstorm, he mounted its sign
on top of his adobe wall.

The articles of incorporation fully outlined for the first time
the extent of Manby's grandiose dream of empire with all its
wealth and power and glory. The stated purpose of the company
was to purchase, settle, and cultivate lands of every description,
including mineral lands; to mine minerals, coals, and salts;
to raise agricultural products and to breed livestock; to acquire
water rights; and to act as a brokerage house and to make loans
of money. It was empowered to promote immigration into the
property of the company and to colonize it; to lay out towns
and cities; to construct dams and reservoirs, canals, and ditches;
to build streets and roads, power plants and gas plants; and to
provide lighting and telephone lines, and yes, a trolley line
system for transportation!

It was all there—a magnificent paragraph that in the Book of
Genesis might have detailed in modern terms God's own
injunction to populate the barren earth, make the wilderness
blossom as a rose, and provide all the necessities and comforts
of civilization to colonists arriving on a new, unknown earth
from other distant shores.

Manby, however, was taking no chances, even on divine
providence. For on the same day of incorporation there was
issued to the directors of the company a certificate of non-
liability of stockholders.

Within six months from incorporation of the company, and
just a month after filing suit to quiet title, Manby set forth to
sell its million shares. In Chicago he found two enthusiastic
buyers, Charles H. Hill and his wife Martha S. Hill; and in
Rockville, Maryland three more, Mary R. Prescott, Alexander F.
Prescott and his wife, Edith H. Prescott. Already rich and

influential, they signed an agreement on November 12, 1906 which Manby assured them would swell their fortunes. The five persons jointly agreed to buy 200,000 shares in The Taos Valley Land Company, and to protect their investment Manby gave them a lien or mortgage on 2,000 acres in the Martinez Grant.

At home that winter Manby received a letter from his brother in England. Eardley had met in a small borough on the outskirts of London a man to whom he had taken a great fancy. William E. Hinde, or Bill as Eardley called him, had served on the police force and then had become an excellent mechanic. A stout-hearted man of adventurous disposition, he now wanted to go someplace where there might be a little excitement. Eardley was therefore sending him to Taos.

Manby's response was enthusiastic. A colonist for his grant! The first of the thousands who would soon populate his empire! Early that spring Hinde arrived with his wife and small daughter. He was a well-built man with blue eyes and yellow hair, adventuresome enough to cross the sea to an unknown land, but immensely practical. How was he to make a living? The grant, Manby explained, was not quite ready for colonists. Until it was, Hinde moved into a small house down the road and opened a blacksmith shop around the corner from Long John Dunn's livery stable.

Manby was friendly to him, but not companionable. He was preoccupied with planning how to spend the money obtained from the Hills and Prescotts. To begin with, he would build dams and ditches to divert water from the Rio Lucero, Rio Hondo, and Rio Seco to irrigate vast fields of corn, wheat, and alfalfa. Water rights were always a problem in New Mexico; it was necessary to avoid legal difficulties. Such a fragile egg would be insecure in Judge Laughlin's basket. He took it to the law office of Catron and Gortner in Santa Fe.

It was a young firm but a promising one. Charles C. Catron was only twenty-seven years old and had been admitted to the bar only three years before. But his father, T. B. Catron, had been the Maxwell Land Grant Company lawyer who had secured Manby's acquittal on a charge of murder.

Manby knew his selection of the firm was a wise one when on May 22, 1907 he received a long letter from Gortner. The lawyer had interviewed the territorial engineer, Sullivan, who had informed him the federal government would oppose any appropriation of water Manby might make that would diminish the flow in the Rio Grande. This opposition was unavoidable. If the federal government was to abide by its treaty of May 21, 1906 with Mexico, it must require all the flood waters, as well as the river's ordinary flow, to store behind Elephant Butte Dam in the southern part of the state. Gortner added, however, that it was possible for them to make "a scientific showing" to the effect that any water they might divert on the Martinez Grant for irrigation would eventually run off and find its way into the Rio Grande. In conclusion he advised Manby to get in his application immediately, and to induce Prescott to use his influence in Washington, D.C. to get it accepted.[5]

The advice caught Manby in a corner. A long winter had passed; he had done nothing to develop the grant; and both the Hills and the Prescotts were beginning to worry about their investment. Manby promptly wired them all to come to Taos as his guests to discuss their mutual affairs.

Late in May the large party arrived. He met them early that evening at the Columbian Hotel when their stage drove in: Charles and Martha Hill, Mary Prescott, Alexander Prescott and his wife Edith, and a young girl whom Prescott introduced as his daughter, Edith S., to differentiate her from her mother, Edith H.

In his warm welcome Manby explained that the hotel was comfortable enough, but the food was not of the best. Hence he was taking the liberty of putting them up. At his imperious beckon, a carriage drove up. Manby's home was only a stone's throw from the plaza; his guests were impressed by his providing a carriage for them. They were even more impressed when they alighted in front of his adobe hacienda. The warm May evening still held an effulgent glow that was thickening into a lilac twilight. Yet from the front gate to the door there glowed on each side of the flagstone walk a row of soft, mellow lights to mark the way.

They were *luminarios*, said Manby, simply a candle stuck in a paper bag partly filled with sand. According to the old Spanish custom they were usually reserved for the Christmas season, but they were so charming he had not been able to restrain himself from setting them out for his guests.

Taking young Edith by the arm, he led them out to see the garden before it grew too dark. Edith Stanley Prescott was sixteen, as fresh and beautiful in her pink and gold way as Circilia had been dark and handsome. She too was impressionable, slipping her hand in Manby's with a sly look at his broad pleasant face and noble forehead. He had removed his riding breeches and boots for once, and was wearing a dark blue English worsted suit. To offset its somewhat formal aspect, he still wore around his throat his flowing silken kerchief. A handsome couple, this distinguished looking man of forty-eight and pink-and-gold girl of sixteen.

Another long row of *luminarios* lined the walk through the garden. It was beautifully laid out. The close-cut grass looked smooth as velvet. The two hundred lilac bushes were in full bloom, filling the air with fragrance. Still farther in back the guests could see the trees Manby had set out, transforming his back pasture into a great park.

Returning to the house, Manby showed them through its innumerable rooms. Rough plank flooring, huge spruce roof-beams, walls washed with the native white clay called *tierra blanca*. But furnished with fine walnut and mahogany pieces from England and carven old Spanish chests, and hung with excellent paintings everywhere.

"Charming, Mr. Manby!" admitted Mrs. Hill grudgingly, wondering how much of her money had gone into it. "Where did you find this delicate watercolor?"

"Our family home in England. My mother painted it," said Manby. "Now I shall leave you to settle in your rooms until dinner. Eight o'clock, is that suitable?"

The dinner was excellent. Roast beef, of course, rare and cut thin by his dexterous hand. It was a pleasant evening too, sitting before an open fire, although Manby and Edith sat together holding hands on a sofa and doing most of the talking.

"You have become acquainted so soon and intimately with my daughter, Mr. Manby," observed Edith H. sharply, "you might as well call her Pinky like the rest of us."

"Pinky! Well, well! And may I call you Pinky?" he asked, turning to her.

Pinky giggled.

Still the evening was so pleasant that none of his guests had

the indelicacy to mention the object of their trip. That came
next morning when they gathered in the same room. This time,
in daylight, it wore a bleak and somber appearance to match the
looks on the faces of Manby's investors. The two Hills and three
Prescotts had put up a great deal of money some time ago, and
had nothing to show for it.

But they had, Manby answered pleasantly but firmly. Two
thousand acres!

It was a distinctly uncomfortable meeting, terminating in
Manby's agreement to transfer 50,000 acres of his Martinez
Grant to The Taos Valley Land Company, 200,000 shares of
which were owned by the two Hills and three Prescotts. The
Hills couple, still unsatisfied, left Taos the following day.

The three Prescotts, just as unsatisfied, were induced to
remain at the insistence of the fourth—Pinky.

Manby added his inducements, confessing that the charming
young Edith had captivated him completely. He had promised to
teach her to ride a horse so he could show her the grant of which
her parents were part owners.

The older woman, Mary Prescott, sniffing trouble, left on the
next day's stage. Pinky's parents capitulated. Something was
going on that they were powerless to fathom or combat.

Less than a month later, on June 22, 1907, Manby and Pinky
were married.[6] In applying for a marriage license that morning
before the probate clerk, Samuel Esquibel, Pinky in an attempt
to act grownup and dignified gave her age as seventeen, although
her birthday on September 20 was still three months away.
Manby also fudged on his age, stating that he was forty-two
instead of forty-eight. Even so, Pinky exclaimed forthrightly,
"Forty-two! Why, Mr. Manby, I didn't know you were *that* old!"

It was quite possible that Manby took an instant dislike of
her from that moment—this silly, pink-and-gold, sixteen-year-
old girl who on her wedding day was still calling him "Mr.
Manby."

Still, that afternoon at two o'clock they were married by N. R.
Nye, rector of the Episcopal Church of the Holy Father of Santa
Fe. As one of the three witnesses, Manby had brought along
William Elios Hinde, the blacksmith and the first colonist of his
Martinez Grant. The deputy probate clerk, however, was Jose
Montaner, editor of the local paper whom he had tried to stab

with a knife three years before. Manby, restraining his temper, trudged back home with his bride. There was one good thing about it: the Prescotts, by giving him a hostage, would make no trouble about their investment in the Martinez Grant.

10

The marriage, after a tempestuous courtship of hardly more than three weeks, embarked on a reality the Prescotts were unable to navigate. They returned to Maryland distinctly uneasy about both their daughter and their investment. Their qualms were justified. Pinky did not qualify for the role of a mature and resolute Mrs. Manby. Doc Martin next door characterized her as a pink-nosed little rabbit mesmerized by a boa constrictor, and volubly damned the whole affair.[1]

Manby himself probably was not overjoyed by the presence of an already pregnant, sixteen-year-old girl alternately weeping and screaming "Mr. Manby!" in the house. He shut himself up in his study, having more important things on his mind. Morgan's question regarding the Antoine Leroux or Los Luceros Grant had come up again and the federal government was preparing to make a survey of it; and Manby was apprehensive that its boundaries might conflict with the Antonio Martinez Grant. Indignantly he settled down to pen on sheet after sheet of his blue stationery a comprehensive letter to the United States Department of the Interior.

It was finally dated December 27, a brilliantly composed, fourteen-page historical resume of the Antonio Martinez Grant and a heated protest against the survey of the Antoine Leroux or Los Luceros Grant.[2] The latter had been awarded in 1742, twenty-six years after the Martinez Grant, he wrote. Moreover its papers had been tampered with; some of them were forgeries; and any belated claim for its title was unjustified. The title of the Martinez Grant, on the contrary, had originated long before the existence of either the United States or Mexico, and the international treaties took precedence over all subsequent acts of Congress. In short, it was a legally perfect grant whose title reverted back to 1716, and his Taos Valley Land Company was its sole owner by right of purchase.

The following day when he went to post the thick envelope, he was brought up short by a disturbing claim just filed in the district court. The plaintiff was Humphrey Purnell Blackmore of London, the brother and heir of William Blackmore, who claimed that he was the owner in fee simple of the Los Luceros Land Grant, east of the Antonio Martinez or Lucero de Godoi, and the Pueblo de Taos grants, and who was now asking that his title be established against all other claims.[3]

William Blackmore, Manby recalled, was the London barrister and promoter who had been a member of the English syndicate which had bought a large part of the immense Sangre de Cristo Grant. He had then become associated with General Palmer and Dr. Bell in promoting the Maxwell Land Grant and the town of Colorado Springs. From their manipulations Bell had become rich and fashionable. Palmer had grown fabulously wealthy and powerful, but during the process he had defaulted on the Maxwell Grant bonds that Blackmore had sold for him in England. Blackmore, left holding the sack, had become an alcoholic and committed suicide, leaving to his brother all that he owned.

For the first time Manby realized he was playing a fast and dangerous game. The stakes were high and now there was a new rival in the field. Manby set his mind against discouragement. He was not a man to be caught like Blackmore, or poor Twining either, who had been imprisoned for embezzling his bank's funds.

Everything was pending: the court decision on his quiet title suit to the Antonio Martinez Grant and on the Blackmore claim to the Los Luceros Grant, the new government survey of the latter, and his girl-wife's pregnancy.

It was a long, hard winter, but the thaw began on March 2, 1908 when Pinky gave birth to a baby daughter, Alice Rockfort (*sic*) Manby. Doc Martin next door was not called; and if he had been, he probably would have been glad to offer the excuse that he was delivering at that time a baby for a respectable Spanish laborer and his wife.[4] Manby obtained a doctor named I. N. Woodman instead, who helped to make out the birth certificate. Manby had aged considerably since he had given his age as forty-two on the marriage license nine months before; he now registered his age as forty-seven. Pinky, lately turned seventeen, gave her age as eighteen.

The baby was either stillborn or died soon after birth; no death certificate was issued. How deeply her parents felt was not known, for Manby seemed more concerned with the arrival of a sharp businessman from Chicago named Charles A. Watson. Watson was impressed with the possibilities of the Martinez Grant and promptly made an offer. He would buy a large chunk of the land for $128,000, the money to be paid in installments over a twenty-year period. During this time he would break and cultivate 200 acres a year at his own expense, planting 100 acres a year in fruit trees, mostly apple and pear, until there were at least 400 acres in orchards.

Manby felt a strange premonition but signed the agreement on April 1. He was hard up for cash and needed to show some development to quiet the Hills and the Prescotts. Perhaps he would not have to give away such a large chunk of his hard-earned grant, for he anticipated that Watson would default on his payments, leaving a part of the grant cultivated and in orchards. The agreement, however, was something of an April Fool's joke to them both. The deal fell through.

The Hills and the Prescotts, damn their hides, continued yelling about their money. To placate them this time, Manby went to Chicago carrying warranty deeds from the Taos Valley Land Company to the four investors: one to Martha Hill for 400 acres; one each to Alexander Prescott, Mary Prescott, and Charles Hill for 200 acres; and not to be left out, one made to himself for 200 acres. As an added inducement, Manby proposed that Prescott act as secretary of the Taos Valley Land Company. Perhaps this was small compensation for the loss of his infant granddaughter, but business was business. Prescott agreed.

That summer, on August 21, the ruined Don Juan Santistevan died and was given a great funeral befitting a man of his importance. It was dusk before all the mourners left the Campo de Santo. There then creaked into the cemetery a springless old wagon. From it descended a Spanish man in overalls carrying a small wooden box, and a young Spanish girl carrying a shovel. In the northwest corner of the weedy graveyard, the same corner in which the infant body of Alice Rockfort (*sic*) Manby had been laid to rest, the man dug a shallow grave and deposited the wooden box. Over it the young woman planted a wooden slab on which had been crudely lettered the name of the thirty-day-old male infant, parents unidentified: "Margaret Mamby" (*sic*).

Whatever it meant, if it meant anything at all, it marked the end of the marriage between Manby and Pinky. Doc Martin no longer heard her weeping in the garden and screaming "Mr. Manby!" According to gossip, she was often seen with a handsome young man in town. Then suddenly she left town.

Manby may have felt relieved. The grant! The dream! This was what concerned him most.

It was also of primary concern to the Hills and Prescotts, for late that fall they went on the rampage again. In another attempt to satisfy them, Manby drew up an agreement on November 13, 1908 between them and the Taos Valley Land Company.[5] Its purpose, in brief, was to execute the company's deed of trust to secure an issue of bonds in exchange for monies to be realized from the sale of these bonds, the monies to be deposited in the Central Savings Bank and Trust Company of Denver.

It was acknowledged that the Hills and Prescotts were owners of 1,000 acres in the Martinez Grant, held a lien or mortgage on 2,000 acres more reserved to them under their previous agreement of November 12, 1906, and the rights given them that spring. Furthermore they owned 200,000 shares in the Taos Valley Land Company. In addition to these rights, Martha S. Hill held a promissory note from Manby for $20,000, having as collateral 240,000 shares in the company.

Manby, expressing himself as anxious to clear these obligations, therefore assigned to them rights and interest amounting to seventy-five percent of the first $100,000 to come from the sale of the bonds, and fifty percent of the second $100,000. The money was to be credited to Charles H. Hill in the First National Bank of Santa Fe. The Hills and Prescotts were to place their

shares, deeds, and note in escrow in the same bank which would
return them if the payments had not been made at the end of
two years. Manby, however, was permitted during the two years
to sell the 2,000 acres for not less than $50 per acre.

It was further agreed that Manby should give a deed for the
2,000 acres, upon payment of the second sum of $50,000, to
Charles and Martha Hill and Alexander and Mary Prescott. By
another provision in the agreement Alexander Prescott and his
wife Edith were to give Manby title to the Hot Springs property
on the bank of the Rio Grande when the second sum of $50,000
was realized.

In any case the Hills and Prescotts were forced to be content
with the vague hope that the Taos Valley Land Company would
be able to sell $200,000 worth of bonds. Manby was hopeful too;
he wanted the Hot Springs property.

A sandy wagon road now climbed up the mesa and for mile
after mile crawled snakily across the high sagebrush plateau.
Here it suddenly ended on the 1,000-foot-high rim of the steep-
walled, basaltic gorge of the Rio Grande. Looking closely, one
could detect a rocky trail twisting down the sheer cliff to the
wild churning river below. Here among the narrow sandpits
gushed up the hot springs Manby had discovered.

It was a remote, wild, and desolate spot. Yet every spring one
could see solitary sheepherders climbing down the tortuous
trail, throwing off their ragged, lice-infested clothes and soaking
their winter-chilled bones in one of the shallow, steaming pools.
Occasionally too came women to wash their clothes in the hot
water and spread them out to dry on the great volcanic boulders
while the children made *pic-nic*.

Manby had cleaned out the largest and deepest spring, built
around it a crude plank shanty, and went there so often to bathe
that the place had come to be known as Manby Hot Springs. He
loved the place, projecting it as a health resort of great importance to the thousands of settlers who would soon come to
buy lots and estates on his Martinez Land Grant. Sometimes
reminded of the resort of Morecambe back in England, he
thought of constructing a twelve-mile-long promenade along
the rim of the spectacular gorge. More often he recalled the
many iron and soda springs at the English-style spa of Manitou
Springs near Colorado Springs which Dr. Bell and General

Palmer were promoting. In any case, the property had a potentially high sales value that he was quick to point out to prospective buyers. There were few of these. To clear a road through the sagebrush, construct an elevator on the steep wall of the gorge, and erect a well-equipped bathhouse below, safely protected from the river's spring floods, would be an expensive undertaking.

Manby's main worry now, after his agreement with the Hills and Prescotts, was to protect his immense grant against any further assaults by forming a bulwark of several interlocking corporations. He accordingly got busy to complete without interruption the organization of the new company which he had mentioned in his letter to the Department of the Interior, and drew up plans for the formation of still another. If the ramifications of this multi-company organization were deviously complicated, their general pattern paralleled General Palmer's scheme for developing Little London.

Palmer's initial problem was getting land. To help him get it, he engaged another influential promoter, Alexander Cameron Hunt, former governor of Colorado. Hunt managed to secure some 9,300 acres of public land that could be bought with Agricultural College script. This federal script was issued primarily to aid various states in acquiring large tracts of land to be used for establishing agricultural colleges, but it also could be used for locating unoccupied government land. Each script was worth $1.25 and would buy an acre of land. Palmer began to shop around. He found that the value of the script had depreciated, enabling him to buy the 9,300 acres for eighty cents an acre with money Dr. Bell raised in England.

To handle the purchase and sale of the land he formed the Mountain Base Investment Fund, with himself as president. This company sold the land for fifteen dollars an acre to the Colorado Springs Company, a second company that Palmer organized with himself as president, which in turn promoted the sale of townsite lots for $270 acre. The townsite was limited to 2,000 acres which he immediately sold for a profit of some $538,000. The remaining 7,300 acres Palmer reserved for himself and a few helpful friends, without cost, enabling them to sell the land without restriction at still more enormous profit. It was a scheme even more profitable than the one Palmer had promoted as president of the Maxwell Land Grant and Railway Company.[6]

Manby detected this pattern behind its confusing facade and built his own upon it. If Palmer had acquired 9,300 acres for eighty cents an acre, Manby had obtained 9,200 acres for only $59.99—and he had over 50,000 acres more. He was also forming two companies to handle their purchase and sale: the Taos Valley Land Company already chartered, and the Taos Land Company which he was now setting up.

But unlike Palmer, Manby did not have a townsite to promote to settlers arriving over a new railroad which he owned. The Antonio Martinez Grant lay in a sparsely inhabited valley that had never and would never hear the whistle of a train. It was still a sagebrush wilderness, and to develop it—clearing the land, planting it to wheat and corn, irrigating it, bringing in utilities, and breaking it down into lots for sale—would require an enormous amount of capital. So Manby was going Palmer one better. He was organizing a third company, the Colonial Bond and Security Company.

The Taos Land Company had not been incorporated yet for good reason, but on February 19, 1909 he incorporated the Colonial Bond and Security Company. Of its capital stock of 50,000 shares at a par value of one dollar, Manby owned 49,990 shares, his brother Jocelyn five shares, and a Golden Barret of Denver five shares, these three men constituting its board of directors.[7]

Two years before, Manby, in need of a little ready cash, had sold to Jocelyn his shares in their patented mining claims in Moreno Valley: his one-third interests in the Golden Era, Fairfax, and Twin, and his one-half interest in the War Eagle. Now he demanded that Jocelyn in payment for the honor of being included as a director of the Colonial Bond and Security Company and his participation in the great future of the grant, transfer his full ownership of the four mining claims to the company. Jocelyn objected.

"Never mind," said Manby. "When the shares of the Taos Valley Land Company are issued, I'll have a thousand shares made out in the name of "Laura.""[8]

Jocelyn, unenthusiastic if not surly, grudgingly made over quit claim deeds to the company for the four mining claims that Manby later evaluated at $10,000.

Manby felt vastly relieved upon receiving the Colonial Bond and Security Company's certificate of incorporation. Now he could transfer mining claims, land, shares, stocks, bonds, mortgages and notes between his companies too fast for any lawyer to follow. His first major transfer was practically all the shares of the Taos Valley Land Company that had not been bought by the Hills and Prescotts—the company of which Prescott himself, that poor dupe, was the nominal secretary.

That poor dupe, however, undoubtedly realized he had little chance of recovering his investment and that his daughter's marriage had been a forlorn folly. Manby just as certainly saw that he could get nothing more out of the Prescotts; Edith Prescott had served her purpose.

Pinky evidently realized it too. She had gone to the little town of Kiowa, Colorado, on the edge of the Black Forest. Here on June 1, 1909, she and Manby were divorced. Judge George H. Fahrion of Elbert County granted the decree to Mrs. Edith S. Prescott Manby on the grounds of "extreme and repeated acts of cruelty," awarding her an alimony of $1,700. Manby had no money to pay it.[9]

It was then, during the summer and fall of 1909, that wisps of mystery began to gather about him. They were insubstantial as all auras, of course, comprised only of rumor and gossip. Indians no longer saw him, sturdily built as his gelding, riding past the pueblo on the way to his grant. Nor was he seen often in the plaza.

No, he seldom went anywhere save to ride alone across the empty sagebrush plateau to bathe in Manby Hot Springs. A secretive recluse, he remained shut up in his adobe hacienda. Here all day and late into the night he sat alone in lamplight, his quick mind ticking ever faster and faster to work out a devious scheme of inter-company organization beyond the reach of a dozen nosey lawyers.

By December 1 it was completed at last—a bulky, adroitly written, new third agreement he presented to the Hills and Prescotts. The agreement, in brief, was a contract to convey the Antonio Martinez Land Grant from the Taos Valley Land Company to a new company, the Taos Land Company.

The previous agreement of November 13, 1908 provided that

the Taos Valley Land Company was to purchase from Charles and Martha Hill, and Alexander and Mary Prescott, land and stock out of money to be derived from a bond issue to be made by the company. The bond issue had never been made, so not a cent had come in from sales, and the four investors were furious.

They still owned 200,000 shares. How much these shares were now worth was probably less than the paper they might have been printed on. For of the 1,000,000 shares issued, Manby had just transferred 570,053 shares to the Colonial Bond and Security Company, 175,000 shares to his own name, 1,000 shares to Laura Manby, and five shares to his brother Jocelyn. Hence Manby owned practically all the stock except the shares owned by the Hills and Prescotts.

These four investors were now demanding a return on their nebulous holdings. Manby had no means of paying them—yet. Wherefore in the agreement he now proposed to incorporate a new company, the Taos Land Company, to which the Taos Valley Land Company would convey the grant. The new company would be set up with a capital stock of $300,000 in 3,000 shares with a par value of $100.

When these shares were sold, the Hills and Prescotts would be paid $100,000 for which they would surrender their 200,000 shares of Taos Valley Land Company stock and release Manby from all further obligations. With the remainder of the money, the new company would construct a dam on the Rio Hondo and a network of canals to irrigate 12,000 acres.

Complicated and obscure as was this long and involved agreement, its intent seemed simple enough. If the Hills and Prescotts had invested perhaps $120,000, they would receive back at best only $100,000, incurring a loss of $20,000. But this return was even more nebulous than had been their expected return from the stock sale of the Taos Valley Land Company, for it depended upon the sale of the new company's capital stock and they stood to lose their whole investment.

The Prescotts realized they had been made the victims of a colossal swindle and dropped out, but Charles Hill stubbornly hung on with the hope of salvaging something out of ruin. Manby encouraged him in the same way he had Prescott, by naming him one of the directors of the new company.

It was incorporated on December 23, 1909, having after all this ambitious planning only $2,100 actual capital on which to start business. There were five incorporators, each being issued five shares of stock: Manby; his brother Jocelyn; Charles H. Hill; Charles A. Watson of Chicago—who was still trying to buy into the grant; and Andricus A. Jones of Las Vegas, New Mexico.[10]

On the following day Manby sprung another surprise. He incorporated his fourth company, the Taos Irrigation Company, with a capital stock of $1,000,000 representing 50,000 shares at a par value of $20. Yet it too had only $2,100 actual capital on which to start business. Its directors were the same: Hill, Watson, Jones, Manby, and his brother. Each was issued twenty-five shares except Jones who was given only five.[11]

Manby had been shrewd enough to include in the articles of incorporation of each of his four companies the same grandiose purposes of all Creation. Each one of them now was authorized to do everything under the sun except create synthetically the lives of the vast population which would soon inhabit his Martinez Grant. And between all four companies he could transfer rights and titles and debts more adroitly than even Palmer.

Manby wasted no time. On the afternoon of the same day, December 24, he filed a deed transferring the 61,605 acres of the Martinez Grant from the Taos Valley Land Company to the Taos Land Company, and another selling for ten dollars all its water rights to the Taos Irrigation Company. He then filed two more deeds for sales he had made to give him money for development. One was for the sale of 5,120 acres to the Mesa Irrigation Lands Company for $150,000, and the other for the sale of two-and-a-half sections of land to the Taos Valley Fruit Company for $30,000.[12] It seemed apparent that he had held these sales amounting to $180,000 until after he had incorporated the two companies with a combined capital stock of only $4,200.

Satisfied with the day's work, Manby went home to a solitary Christmas dinner. It had been not only a busy day, but a successful year.

11

On New Year's morning Manby rose early, stalked into the plaza and filed public notice that the Taos Land Company claimed all the surface and flood waters of the Hondo, Lucero, and Pueblo rivers and the right to conduct them through ditches to irrigate the Antonio Martinez Grant.[1] By this amazing display of arrogance he claimed virtually the complete run-off of waters from all the surrounding mountains through the major streams—the very lifeblood of the Indian pueblo, the Spanish villages of Arroyo Seco, Arroyo Hondo, Valdez, and Desmontes, and most of Taos itself. If successfully put into effect, the theft would place the population of the entire valley at Manby's mercy.

Only one man seemed to realize it, the now disillusioned Golden Barrett of Denver who the year before had been given five one-dollar shares of the 50,000 shares of capital stock in the Colonial Bond and Development Company for serving as a director with Manby and his brother Jocelyn. On January 4th he filed suit on behalf of himself and a few other persons against the Taos Valley Land Company and the Taos Land Company, each "a pretended corporation," to restrain them from doing business.[2] Nothing would come of it Manby was sure. All the ancient valley seemed to maintain its traditional attitude of sleepy indifference.

Late in March, Manby rode up to the mouth of the Lucero, intending to pick a site for a dam by which he could control the water for his use on the grant. It also occurred to him to ride on up the narrow high-walled canyon which flanked the mysterious sacred peak; he might find traces of gold. The day was clear and bright, but as he rode past the pueblo a curious feeling of apprehension, like an invisible shadow, fell upon him. Unable to shake it off, he rode on around the shoulder of the mountain into a great open meadow flanked by huge cottonwoods. It was one of his favorite spots. The snow had melted, but it was too early for the vivid color that would carpet it later—the dark purple larkspur, pale lilac bluebells, sparkling white daisies, brilliant orange-red Indian paint-brush, and scarlet St. Joseph's bells. Yet the wild iris were out in full bloom, showing pale blue against the blue-green spruce slopes rising ahead. A wild and beautiful glorieta. Still he could not enjoy it, gardener that he was, for the ominous feeling that seemed to poison the very air.

Was it that damned mountain exuding its negative spell again? Or was someone following him? Manby wheeled his horse about. The meadow was empty and the sagebrush flat beyond it. Even the pueblo behind him looked like a weathered rock barren of life. A single thread of pale smoke rose from the highest housetop, was suddenly cut off, and then a moment later replaced by another. What it meant Manby did not know. He rode on toward the mouth of the canyon.

The trail was getting narrower now, leading through a thick growth of piñon and scrub oak that seemed to rise on each side like waves ready to break upon him. All at once that intangible miasma of danger and evil coagulating around him was loosed like a torrent across his path—a barrier that seemed dense as water and violent as wind, but invisible. His horse sensed it too. The gelding broke into a sudden nervous sweat. His ears thrust forward; his nostrils widened. Then, unaccountably, he spooked, lurching sideways so abruptly that Manby was almost unseated. Jerking up the reins and regaining his balance, he flung a fearful look around. A brown, brittle oak leaf had been whipped under his horse's feet by a sudden gust of wind. Manby was not a man to be frightened by a leaf. He yanked up his mount's head in a burst of anger that expressed his great relief and dug in his spurs.

"Damn you! What's wrong with you today!" Just the same, he felt his own knees quivering.

All at once the mouth of the canyon yawned open to engulf him. Great pines and spruce thrust upward around him, revealing in their dark shadows the thin white shafts of leafless aspen. On each side, the high rock walls drew down to a narrow opening through which the Lucero poured, foaming white over the rocks. Here at the narrowest point was the site for his dam; the abutting walls would stand the thrust of any water pressure.

Manby, however, was in no mood now to make even a casual survey, let alone any preliminary calculations. He felt trapped in this dark glade, as if in the fanged mouth of some invisible presence ready to close upon him. It had been a long, hard ride. He should rest his horse, eat the lunch he had brought in his saddlebag. Yet he found himself unable to dismount for the unaccountable spell cast upon him. Beneath his own quivering knees, he could feel the muscles of his gelding twitch. Beads of sweat broke out on his forehead.

At that moment Manby saw him standing immovable at the far end of the glade. A single Indian, a pale cotton blanket swathing his whole figure and drawn up to his eyes, obscuring his face. What there was about this ghostlike figure to freeze him with a deathly fear, Manby did not know. The Indian did not speak. He made no move within his blanket to raise a hidden gun or knife. He simply stood there, materializing all the apprehension, premonition, and foreboding sense of evil that had followed Manby all morning.

Something intangible, something that existed in a dimension unknown to him, had come to a climax. Too petrified with fear to reach for the gun in its scabbard, Manby flung a despairing look backward. What he expected to see, he did not know. What he did see was a clear trail. Without thought, he jerked his horse around, brought his quirt down on his rump. The gelding cleared a trickle of water in one leap and bolted. Manby leaned forward over his neck and raced to safety, feeling his heart pound like the hooves beneath him.

What the strange incident meant Manby did not know, but it worried him for days. It was as if a secret and unknown self within him had apperceptively encountered an invisible something existing in a realm beyond the rationally known, and it had thrown up an intangible barrier before him. Whatever this irrationally fantastic realm of pure feeling was, it now threw

back at him also a number of remembrances of trivial things he
had not been aware of noticing at the time. The way Griffin's
jaw had suddenly dropped when the bullet struck him in the
head, leaving him to fall face forward with a ludicrously gaping
mouth. The peculiar nasal timbre of Pinky's voice shrieking
or crying, "Mr. Manby!" Don Juan's courtly gesture of assent
as he nodded his graying head with the slight wave of his open
right hand. Yes, and the dark perfume of Circilia's warm body on
a summer night. A strange fragrance which always seemed
familiar, but which he could never identify. Now, unaccountably,
he knew what it reminded him of. Chokecherry blossoms, their
tubular shapes pale in June moonlight, swollen with life, and
emitting the perfume of his desire. It was fantastic that these
insignificant sounds, smells, and gestures should now leap out
at him so long after he had dismissed their instigators and the
incidents connected with them from his mind! As if time and
memory alike, with all their mere sensuous and transiently
emotional details, were a part of that realm of feeling which as a
sensible man he had resolutely ignored. The devil take that
damned Indian up at the mouth of the Lucero who had stirred
up such unreasonable thoughts![3]

Upset, he left for Mineral Springs, Claremore, Oklahoma to
take the hot baths. Here he persuaded Dr. John H. Sloan to
to send a sworn statement back to Taos that Manby, whom he
was attending as a physician, was too ill with rheumatism to
attend the May term of court when Barrett's suit was scheduled. Damn Barrett! Nothing would come of his suit anyway.[4]

More disturbing was the news that the government survey of
the Antoine Leroux or Los Luceros Grant that he had protested so bitterly had been completed. John Walker, the surveyor, set the boundaries: the Arroyo Hondo on the north,
the summit of the Sangre de Cristo range on the east, the bed
of the Del Norte or Rio Grande on the west, and on the south,
a line two leagues south of the Arroyo Hondo. This conflicted
with the boundaries of the Antonio Martinez Grant.

Judgement on his suit to quiet title was still pending. A few
Spanish people were straggling into the courthouse claiming
a share by right of inheritance. Who they were, and how many
actual heirs there were, no one knew. Hence Judge John R.
McFie had appointed Charles F. Easley, who was a member

of the bar and had been in charge of the Antonio Martinez
Grant survey, as a special referee to take oaths and proofs,
build up a genealogy, and submit his findings.

Stopping in E-town on his way back home, Manby found
the old mining camp greatly perplexed. The great Aztec mine
had been forced to close down again because of losses from high-
grading. The owners, a Dutch corporation with offices in New
York, had done everything possible to prevent thefts, tracing
one shipment to Chicago where it had been sold for $15,000.
Yet they had not been able to discover the highgraders nor
their method of operation.

The Mystic and the Ajax just below it, on the contrary, were
poking along. Wilkerson lived alone in a cabin on Mt. Baldy
and worked the mines. Ferguson ground the ore in a crude
arrastra for shipment to Colorado. The returns were small, but
the two men often showed considerable sums of money.

Such was the gossip being bantered around the stove in
McIntyre's store on the day Manby dropped in.

"Where's it all come from?" an old-timer asked forthrightly.

"Ask Manby here," replied Brankfort, an old prospector.

"If I were you boys, I wouldn't be too nosey," said McIntyre.
"You ain't forgot what happened to Gutierrez and Gallegos
and Brunner, have you?"

"What did happen? They just plain disappeared, ain't it so?"

"Or that Mexican cowhand named Varos who used to work
for Manby," McIntyre said again.

Manby snorted. "His horse kicked his head off! Everybody
knows that!"

McIntyre shrugged. "Well, I ain't goin' to have my head
kicked off for blabbin' about somethin' I don't know nothin'
about."

The next day Manby told Ferguson tersely, "There's too
much talk. From now on ship your ore to El Paso. I'll see it's
taken care of there."

At the Ferguson cabin he found Teracita no longer a black-
eyed splinter of hard granite. She had developed a curious fey
streak which enabled her to read cards or palms. When they were
alone, Manby asked her about it.

"A band of gypsies stole me for awhile," Teracita replied
gravely. "When I asked the old woman I was staying with to

teach me, she threw a crust of bread on the ground. 'You don't get anything to eat until you stoop and pick it up. You've got to humble yourself'."[5]

Manby laughed. Perhaps she had made up the whole story, but she had imagination! Moreover she was rounding out into a young woman, like Circilia and Pinky, to whom he felt peculiarly attracted.

Returning to Taos, he noted a number of changes and new people in the old mud town. A German immigrant peddler named Gerson Gusdorf had set up in the plaza "The Largest Store in the World Away From a Railroad," replacing Juan Santistevan's former proud establishment. He even had the temerity to bring in by stage a tin bathtub to display in the window. There had come Walter Witt who supported his large family by rounding up wild horses and shipping them to St. Louis for seven dollars a head. Across the road from Manby's house a young Indian trader, Ralph Meyers, was opening shop in an old gambling house once run by the notorious Doña Tules—nine rooms and two patios which he rented for four dollars a month. Long John Dunn, the gambler, had built a new livery stable on the corner of the plaza and was driving the only stage into town from the Chile Line railroad stop. Across from his livery stable Pete Nolan had opened a general store that was gaining a reputation for foreclosing on pieces of land given as mortgages for grocery bills. This frank but not too successful rivalry outraged Manby who refused to speak to him. Two more newcomers, Harry Tarleton and King Hopkins, had the effrontery to open a movie-house showing two-reelers to the clatter of a mechanical piano. A few horse-thiefs and even a couple of artists... People like this, with whom no English gentleman would care to associate. New people with Anglo names straggling in to add variety to the traditional Martinez, Santistevan, Sanchez, Gallegos, and other old Spanish names. American immigrants coming in to colonize Spanish New Mexico.

They were, in fact, the very settlers Manby needed to populate the Martinez Grant if he could find a way to accommodate them. Blacksmiths like Hinde. Farmers. Surveyors. Carpenters, masons, craftsmen, artisans. Doctors and dentists. Workers of all kinds to lay out the streets and trolley lines, to build up the towns and cities he envisioned. And scrubby trades-people too,

Taos Plaza, southwest corner ca. 1900. *Courtesy Kit Carson Memorial Foundation.*

Taos Plaza. L to R: Liebert's Livery Stable, the Columbian Hotel, home of Juan Santistevan.

who might supply its human needs for food, shelter, and amuse-
ment.

Despite his distaste for making friends, he would need their
support. The way to get it was clear. These people loved politics
with its slogans and symbols, and a new party was gaining favor:
Roosevelt's Progressives challenging Taft's Republicans and
Wilson's Democrats. So Manby promptly allied himself with the
Bull Moose, heatedly denouncing the Elephant and the Burrito
in the corridors of the courthouse and on the plaza lawn. By
acclamation he was elected chairman of the Taos delegation to
the Progressive Party meeting in Albuquerque during the thirty-
second state fair. It was a great occasion. Stiffly holding the
banner of his delegation, he posed for his photograph in the
front row: his Stetson hat set straight as his black bow tie, his
mustache bristling, his light jacket neatly buttoned.[6]

Arriving back home, he ripped off his jacket and tie, and
slumped down in the big chair at his desk. What a farce! It had
exhausted his patience. Why should he associate himself with
a bull moose, elephant, or jackass! He needed to raise money
from every possible source. In response to his feverish entreaties
a little came in from New York and Chicago. Then Margaret
Higgins in Ireland resumed sending regular amounts enclosing
with one draft a photograph of herself: dark-haired, demure,
and trusting.

The months dragged by, Manby becoming more and more
impatient. What could be holding it up?

Finally it came—the day he had been waiting for so long
and anxiously. Easley, the special referee, had turned in his
report and Judge Thomas D. Leib was to render the final decree
of the court.

Manby rose early, carefully tied his black bow tie, buttoned
his jacket, and put on his Stetson. Then he encircled with a
red pencil the date on his calendar—May 20, 1913—stalked in
his riding boots to the courthouse, and settled down on a hard
bench to wait for Easley's report to the court to be read.

12

The doors were closed on the big room. The rap of a gavel sounded silence. Court came to order and the long hearing began.[1]

From the start Manby knew that Easley's statement of facts and findings of fact could not have been more thorough. Beginning with the granting of the original petition of Antonio Martinez for a tract of land in 1716, he had reviewed the grant's entire history to date. Antonio Martinez had left him surviving an only child, Maria Rosario Martinez, who married one Mariano Sanchez. From this, Easley had patiently interviewed and taken depositions from a hundred or more persons who claimed to be rightful descendants and heirs, and had drawn up a complete geneaology.

To each of the proven heirs he had then apportioned various shares ranging from 1/24 to 1/140 of the total grant of 61,605.48 acres. He recognized that Manby had obtained title to about three-fourths of the land by conveyances from all the heirs with a few exceptions. He accordingly reported to the court that 59 persons, each entitled to 5/1800 of the grant, had now conveyed their interests to Manby. There were only 16 persons who had not, and they as a group were entitled to 80/1800 or 2/45 of the grant. Manby then was clearly entitled to 43/45 of the entire grant, amounting to 58,867 acres, except for a few tracts at Ranchitos, Arroyo Seco Abajo, and Desmontes.

Manby felt a shiver of apprehension run up his spine.

Easley then took up the matter of the Antoine Leroux or Los Luceros Grant. This had been claimed in 1907 by the brother and heir of William Blackmore, he recalled, but the claim on it had been renewed on September 19, 1910 by Walter Wynne and George Herbert Newman, trustees for the Land Company of New Mexico, an alleged corporation under the laws of Great Britain and Ireland. Easley found, as Manby had previously discovered, that the alleged grant had been made on August 9, 1742, twenty-six years after the Antonio Martinez Grant, and that the Walker survey had been made fifteen years after the Martinez Grant survey. As no proofs had been offered to establish a genealogy or any right to the grant, Easley recommended dismissal of the English firm's claim.

Manby gripped his knees, waiting for a counsel to offer objections. No voice spoke. The reading of the report continued.

There remained the claim of the Pueblo de Taos to two tracts. One was the Garcia de la Mora tract derived from Captain Sebastion Martin in 1785. The other was the Tenorio Tract based on a deed drawn in 1818 by Miguel Tenorio, an attorney for the son of Sebastion Martin, Antonio Martin, whom the Indians evidently had confused with Antonio Martinez. In conclusion, Easley found that the Pueblo was not entitled to either tract.

Hence with the exception of 16 persons entitled to 2/45 of the grant, Easley recommended that Manby's title to 43/45 of the entire grant be duly approved. For his lengthy and exhausting research and investigation, he now submitted a bill of $1,030.

A recess was in order. The big court room emptied save for Manby who sat staring blankly at the wall. Then it filled again with a shuffling of boots and a spitting in the sand boxes. The rap of the gavel brought silence.

The court did not mince matters. Judge Leib accepted Easley's report and in his final decree ruled that all claims against the Antoine Leroux or Los Luceros Grant be extinguished; that the Indian Pueblo claims to the Tenorio and Garcia de la Mora Tracts were void; and that Manby's Taos Land Company was the owner in fee simple of 43/45 of the entire grant. It was also recognized by the court that the Hadley

Tract of 1,500 acres within the Los Luceros Grant had been
sold for delinquent taxes to William Frayne who had conveyed
it to Manby.

Manby, crouching on his hard bench, was stunned by the
overwhelming completeness and finality of the court's decree.
In 1892, when he first had heard of the Antonio Martinez Grant,
he had known this moment would come. For twenty-one years
he had planned, intrigued and lied, cheated, cajoled, begged,
bribed and stolen to bring it to pass. And now that it had come,
he had no word, no thought, to express his curious amazement
that it had come so quickly and easily! He could only see, as if
it were an etiolated projection of his obsessive desire, the vast
wasteland of the grant itself, which with additional fringe areas
he claimed without title, comprised, he now reckoned, an empire
of some 100,000 acres. His! Wholly, incontestably, all his!

Suddenly aware that he was sitting alone in an empty courtroom, he got up and walked slowly out through the crowded
corridor to the front door. Silent and surly clumps of Spanish
villagers dressed in their work-worn dungarees and ragged shirts
stood lighting cigarettes and expectorating into stained brass
spittoons. None of them rushed up to him with a loud *"Mi
patrón!"* to congratulate him and fawn upon his favor. An Anglo
hurried by without speaking, not knowing who he was—or not
caring if he knew. Manby did not notice them at all.

He pushed open the door and stood blinking a moment in the
bright May sunlight. An Indian was leaning against a portal
post, his blanket as usual drawn up almost to his eyes. Those
reptilian, black Indian eyes! Yet even as Manby looked into
them, he could see the invisible shutters close over them.

It was court day; the plaza was crowded with horses and
wagons, a shiny tin lizzie; the long, open portál was thronged
with people giving each other the *embrazo*, whacking backs, and
offering to buy a beer for a visiting *primo*. Manby pushed
through the crowd without greeting and walked up the dusty
road to his house.

It was May again, with its electric green and cloudless blue,
with all the springtime of youth bursting through leaf and
blade. Manby did not notice it either. Reaching home, he sat
down as usual at his desk.

The grant was his, his, his, irretrievably at last! He was only

fifty-four years old, and the hour of his great victory was pealing
in his ears. He could hear church bells ringing, the clang of
trams, the clatter of carriages and motorcars, the multitudinous
roar of life rising from the towns and cities on his immense
grant. Listening more closely, his big head with its faintly graying hair, noble brow, and thin merciless lips bent toward the
open window, it seemed to him he could make out the shouts
from a distant plaza acclaiming him the sole ruler of an immense domain.

If no one had congratulated him on his great triumph, Manby
had no one to share it with either. Thought of his brothers
never entered his mind. Nor for the moment even that of a
young, black-eyed and black-haired Spanish girl in a high mountain valley. If he thought of anybody at all, it was of those dam-
nably stubborn sixteen villagers who had defied the immutable
laws of Providence by not subscribing to his own injunction.
One of them, he knew, owned a rare old Spanish chest worth
a dozen acres. Such a random thought was not out of keeping
even now. After all, he was not an idle dreamer but a practical
man!

Motherless, wifeless, childless, and friendless as he was at his
great moment of triumph, Manby was not alone. With him sat
that invisible mistress to which he long ago had given full
allegiance. She may have robbed him of the best years of his
life, sucked him dry of all human warmth and compassion, dis-
torted his every thought; but she also had alleviated his loneliness and fed his greedy dream of empire—that great folly by
which he was to attain the only immortality he was ever to
achieve. And now Manby was hers, all hers, as completely as
the grant, the dream, the lost kingdom were all his. So she
clasped him to her breast, tight against her flat and milkless
paps, and held him fast as with claws of steel.

Darkness came over the high adobe wall with its barred gate,
and across the close-cropped English lawn. Manby got up and
went to bed. He had forgotten his supper of cold cornmeal
pudding.

The Folly

1

From the very start the crown weighed heavily on the ruler's head. Manby was hard up for money again, and wrote his brother to step up the amount of investments in the grant. This was impossible, wrote Eardley; things were slow in England too. Manby then hit up Eardley for a large loan. The major was reluctant. He already held a promissory note from Manby for $1,000 and a mortgage deed for property, both dated in 1898. Still, as Manby assured him, the court had just passed favorably on his long-delayed suit to quiet title. These things took time and patience!

The result of their protracted correspondence was that Eardley on July 14, 1913 loaned Manby another sum of $11,500 with interest at eight percent, but demanded a mortgage deed to Manby's entire hacienda—land, house, outbuildings, and even the furniture and paintings.[1] The major seemed as sharp as his brother.

A little discomfited, Manby went up to E-town. Mt. Baldy's bare head was still capped with white although wildflowers were brightening the open meadows. Manby enjoyed getting back to this high valley, particularly upon seeing Teracita. Something had happened since he had seen her last, one of those mysteries no one could explain. She had suddenly become a woman.

Manby knew it the moment he saw her; and knowing it, he fell in love with her at once—and for the first time in his life,

121

at the age of fifty-four. His little princess!

Her older sister, Francisca, had married a man by the name of Abad Varos and moved to Taos. Teracita wanted to go too. Manby agreed that this dwindling and isolated mining camp was no place for a beautiful young woman.

"What would I do down there?" she asked.

"The old town's starting to grow," Manby assured her. "New people coming in all the time. You might get a tourist camp to run. Come to think of it, there's one up for sale. What do you think of that?"

Teracita thought well of it, indeed. "I'll have to bring my father with me, of course." Her big black eyes were guileless, her soft voice carried the tone of loneliness. Yet in her, as in her mother, ran that streak of hard granite.

"Why not?" he answered casually. "I'll find out how much they want for that old tourist camp."

As a matter of fact, Ferguson and Wilkerson were not getting rich from the Mystic by any means. Their shipments of ore to the smelter at El Paso were returning less all the time.

"Give it up, Ferguson. Let Wilkerson manage it," he said abruptly to the old Scotch miner one morning. "You're getting too old for this hard work."

"What's easier than a pick handle I can swing?" Ferguson asked cannily.

"A tourist camp down in Taos. Teracita wants to buy one."

Their glances met and broke. Ferguson shrugged assent.

Early that fall the deal for the tourist camp was settled. It lay up Taos Canyon Road, a short horseback ride from Manby's house. On October 6, Ferguson shipped his last carload of ore and with the $1,950 it brought moved down to Taos with Teracita.[2]

Manby then hired a rig and drove down to Santa Fe to resume a promising friendship with a woman he had met the year before at Mineral Wells, Texas. She had been sitting alone on the rim of the pool when he first saw her. Rather tall, with dead white legs and arms in contrast to her loose, walnut brown hair which she was drying, she looked attractive. Manby paddled over and hoisted himself up beside her.

They introduced themselves, and from their friendly chat he learned a great deal about her. Miss Margaret A. E. Waddell was a cultured Scotswoman obviously of a good family who seemed to be endowed with quite adequate finances. She lived in Los Angeles, California, but recently she had gone to Santa Fe, New Mexico on a brief visit. Its unspoiled charm and the beautiful countryside had delighted her. She was now thinking of moving there. Perhaps to buy a few acres and build a modest house in which she could live comfortably in agreeable surroundings.

Manby's approval was enthusiastic. He lived just upriver from there, in Taos, he told her; and immediately launched into a vivid description of his hacienda, hot springs, and immense grant.

Miss Waddell listened intently. It was an imposing background, and he himself was a good looking, mature Englishman evidently of some importance and with a promising future.

So they had dined and wined together the few days she was there, and when she left she promised to let him know of her arrival in Santa Fe.

Her note had come the week before, saying she had moved into a small house up Canyon Road. Manby was enchanted with the place when he drove up in his rig and was welcomed into the house. It was an old adobe, of course, and furnished with a few pieces of excellent Spanish-Colonial make. What good taste she had!

They saw each other often. During Manby's frequent calls upon her, he described an ambitious project for which he was drawing up plans. It was a resort hotel to be placed on his own estate, close to the town plaza. Not as large as General Palmer's Antlers Hotel in Little London perhaps, nor the other English-style hotel Dr. Bell was operating at the spa of Manitou Springs. But Spanish-style, well-built, and beautifully furnished; one that would attract people coming to settle on his grant.

Miss Waddell expressed great interest in it, suggesting he bring down his plans for her to see. Manby demurred. How could she visualize a building without seeing its background? One had to fit the other to blend into a whole, he insisted. There was only one thing to do; take her back with him to see the site.

Driving her to Taos, Manby showed her the back part of his estate where he planned to set the hotel. Then he conducted her through his own immense hacienda, an excellent example of his architectural skill. After inspecting its nineteen rooms she remarked casually that it was a man's house, but that a woman could live in it quite comfortably.

Manby did not blink an eye. Miss Waddell was as honest and straightforward as her large, loose handwriting.

The result of their association seemed inevitable despite Manby's predeliction for young girls and his new love for Teracita. They became engaged, and Miss Waddell had no hesitancy in turning over to her future husband some ten thousand dollars of her savings.[3]

During one of Manby's visits to Santa Fe a few weeks later, she proudly showed him a portion of the large trousseau she was having made. Happy and excited, she then brought out her most extravagant purchase.

Manby could not restrain his surprise at seeing the fine linens stacked on the table and chairs. He was even more surprised to find that each piece had been beautifully initialled "A.R.M."

"Why, that's the old English custom, using the bridegroom's initials!" he exclaimed.

"Of course! I wanted them just right!"

Manby became a fervent lover, writing her often when he was away:

"Dearest! One watches and loves while the other sleeps and dreams of love. Now it is my watch while my sweet Bess sleeps, and as I kneel to brush my lips near hers, her eyes open and she awakens, knowing that I am near her but cannot see me, and a dear sweet smile comes over her lips, her eyes, and she is asleep once more."[4]

Miss Waddell, whom he now called "Bess," returned his endearments by calling him "Rochie." Still nothing was being done about the hotel she was helping to finance. Nor was Manby pressing the marriage. She suggested, quite sensibly, that they get married, move into his hacienda, and start building the hotel together.

Manby frowned. A vast grant like his required a large amount of capital to develop it properly, he explained, and his capitalists and investment brokers were telling him money was tight. They would have to wait.

Once again Miss Waddell raised money to give him in return for stock in the venture he promised her. As he was still short of cash for living expenses, however, he soon decided with regret to part with one of his great art treasures—the beautiful "St. Agnes" hanging in his drawing room.

The masterpiece, he told her, had been painted by Hubert Van Eyck about 1396. It had been brought to the United States sixty years ago by a French nobleman who had mortgaged it to the chief justice of Minnesota. He had been unable to redeem it as he was killed by Indians soon after. The picture then had come into the hands of Judge Emmett in Santa Fe who bequeathed it to his daughter, the wife of Governor Otero, who in turn had sold it to Manby.[5]

The painting, he went on, was worth $100,000, but as they needed money so badly it could easily be sold for $10,000. Hence he offered her one-half interest in it for $500, this payment being equivalent to a $5,000 equity.

Miss Waddell was somewhat perplexed, but gave him the $500 in cash and accepted his conveyance of one-half interest in the painting. At Manby's insistence, she then took the painting East, at her own expense, trying to sell it in New Orleans, New York, and Washington. When it did not sell, she wrote him warmly and generously from Washington:

"Whatever are you going to do for money to live on? I am just miserable at the thought of the bad time you are having and the lack of care and all the worry. Rochie, everything you do proves that you are a thoroughbred, and that bad luck can't be helped. Ever loving, your Bess."[6]

While she was away, Manby rode daily up the road to see Teracita. She and Ferguson were living in one of the cabins of the tourist court until they could move into a small, separate house nearby. Teracita, with a larger and more interesting world to live in, was more vital and beautiful than ever. And more inquisitive.

"And who is that woman in Santa Fe I hear so much about?" she asked. "You're in love with her, no?"

"An older woman, much older than you. In fact, the skin on her thighs is wrinkled."

"And how do you know?"

"I saw that when we were taking the hot baths. Her legs probably had been swollen and the hot water, taking down the swelling, had left the flesh wrinkled. It disgusted me!"[7]

Teracita frowned. "*Pues.* You don't see her any more?"

Manby scowled. "She's a business associate! And not attending to business! She's not selling my painting!"

Teracita stared dreamily up the canyon. She suddenly had
become a fey woman immersed in another world. "No good!
That woman no good! She will bring you trouble!" She jumped
to her feet and took him by the hand. "Come. I will run the
cards for you. They will tell you!"

Miss Waddell apparently felt a change in the wind, for she
soon wrote: "The only thing that would make me desire you
to have your freedom would be that you could marry someone
with money, for money is a necessity to your success."[8]

Her letter irked Manby. He wrote her a cool reply, accusing
her of being incompetent to sell such a fine painting. Miss
Waddell in turn forthrightly requested that he make an effort
to return the money she had given him.

Her change in attitude upset Manby so much that he fled to
Hot Springs, Arkansas. From here, late that October, Dr.
Estill D. Holland wrote a notarized letter to Judge T. D. Lieb
in Raton saying, "Mr. A. R. Manby is my patient. He is suffering from neuritis and arthritis, unable to walk, and utterly
unable to attend to any business for several months. . . . It
might prove fatal if he went to any cold country or high altitude
in his present condition."[9]

Manby evidently made a rapid recovery. By December he
was back in the high altitude and freezing cold of New Mexico.
He had thought of a way to dispose of the St. Agnes painting
which Miss Waddell had indignantly released to him, and also
that other old masterpiece he had bought in London twenty
years before. Clearing this latter painting into the country
through the U.S. Customs Service, Port of Denver, Manby wrote
a friend there, Reverend H. Martyn Hart, that the masterpiece
was entitled *Marriage Feast of St. Catherine* and believed to
have been painted by either Titian or Anton Van Dyck about
1626. He also gave the history of the St. Agnes painting.

To back up his assertions, he sent his friend a copy of the
book *Masters of Art*, with a reference to the lost painting by
Van Eyck on Page 317, and another book on Titian. Reverend
Hart discussed these unusual finds with Frank M. Taylor, director of the Colorado Museum of Natural History, who expressed great delight in the opportunity to exhibit them.

Manby accordingly shipped the two paintings to the museum on January 1, 1914 and settled back to await offers to buy them. None came. At the end of their showing he shipped the two paintings to another friend in Philadelphia.[10]

Miss Waddell had grown bitter. On January 19 she wrote Manby from Los Angeles:

"You should be ashamed of yourself, living on my money, when I have to move into cheap rooms. I am having a struggle to live. So much for an Englishman and one whom I have helped when he was down and out. I call it stealing."

By February 12 she had made up her mind to do something about it. She wrote coldly:

"Before taking steps which will have more far reaching consequences than you at present realize, I want to put before you certain thoughts that your self satisfaction precludes you from seeing yourself.

"When I came out here bringing a certain sum of money to invest, I brought that for my own use, not for the benefit directly or indirectly of any other party.

"You, by your making me change my plans in order to marry me tacitly agreed, definitely agreed, to my spending money to that end—and by your exaggerated talk about your extensive possessions, fine home, grand friends, causing me to make more extensive preparations than I otherwise would have done—took that money from me just as directly as if you had put your hand in my pocket and stolen it.

"As Mr. Stoddard Jess says—the deadbeat Englishman is the curse of England and America, and the pity of it is that they can fool women with the plea of old family. Both he and Miss Graham say that judging from your letters, you, from the first, had no objective but to use me as a business tool, and you know how much lower than that you stooped.

"To think that I had to pawn my jewelry and my mother's jewelry in order to live. That I had to do in Dallas, Texas."[11]

A few months later she took steps to file suit against him.[12]

2

The first clouds were already beginning to gather at the edges of Manby's resplendent dream. After twenty-one years of impassioned effort, he finally had quieted title to his Martinez Grant. He owned the land; he claimed all the water rights; and he had set up four interlocked corporations to juggle titles and rights, and to issue stocks and bonds for the huge capital necessary to develop the grant.

But of the money he had raised, Manby had not spent one cent to make a single improvement. He had bought more land with some of it, and spent the rest on his large estate in town and on his own foibles. This had helped to make investors back east and abroad leery of his nebulous project. There was no railroad into the region bringing trainloads of new settlers eager to buy and settle the land. Moreover, Manby had alienated the local people whom he might have used as a nucleus for a colony. He found himself, in short, with a kingdom on his hands but no subjects and no way to get them.

What had gone wrong, he wondered. Perhaps he should have concentrated more on raising capital to finance the whole venture from the start: actually issuing the stocks and bonds authorized by his companies; making gradual improvements on the grant; and inducing at least a few families to form a colony which would draw others. That he would do now with all his strength and talents. The promise of fulfillment he could read in the land before him spreading out from mountain to river, unbroken and untouched save by the shadows of clouds in the sunshine!

What Manby did not realize, was that it was now too late. Time and tide and fate at last had turned against him. It was 1914 and a spark had ignited the vast conflagration of World War I. People in Europe could not be interested in an undeveloped piece of real estate in America; they were marshaling all resources to defend their own homes. Even in America, investors were jittery and money scarce.

Manby soon discovered that things were worse than this. For years he had been cadging, borrowing, and begging money with no regard for when he might repay it; ownership of the grant would take care of that. Now he began to find that it didn't. On the contrary, his vast grant was beginning to draw vultures to its fat and overripe carcass. Everybody to whom he owed money began to clamor for payment.

On March 1, 1910 he had borrowed $4,000 in the name of the Taos Valley Land Company from the First National Bank of Trinidad. Now on July 18, 1914 it filed suit for payment of the note with interest.[1]

Somehow he managed to pay it, and on January 1, 1915 obtained from the bank in the name of the Taos Valley Land Company, the Taos Land Company, and the Taos Valley Fruit Company two more notes: one for $6,000 and one for $5,000.[2]

Six months later he was desperate for cash again. He had not yet paid his attorneys their legal fees for services in quieting title to his grant; both Laughlin and Catron were demanding money. Other creditors were pressing him; a mercantile house in town was getting nasty over a minor bill.

From whom could he borrow now?

In desperation he saddle-soaped his riding boots, put on his best jacket and high-crowned Stetson, and late that evening strolled through the plaza to the ivy-covered adobe on the edge of town known as the Vine House. From the dark, dusty road outside, he could hear the rattle of a piano, the whine of a guitar. Saddled horses, teams and wagons, and cars and trucks in front reminded him it was Saturday night. Repressing his distaste for such a place, he pushed open the door and stepped inside.

Manby had never been in the Vine House before, and his first sight confirmed all that he had heard about it. Through the whorls of smoke he made out a long bar extending down the left side of the room. It was flanked with the cowpokes, ranchers, and Anglo newcomers who were beginning to give Taos the color of a Western frontier town. The bartenders he recognized under their preposterous nicknames: Luis Guara, "The Kangaroo Keed"; Morro, "The Buffalo"; Joe Buckland, "Kokomo Jo." The blast of music from the right side of the room stopped; and as the dance floor cleared, he could see Nat Flores, "Mister Flowers," and his musicians beckoning for refreshments. More bartenders—"Shotgun," "Chepa," and "Knee High"—staggered through the crowd with loaded trays. The blare of voices, English and Spanish, a woman's high-pitched yell, were worse than the music. How tawdry it all was![3]

"Manby! For God's sake! What are you doing here?"

Manby was spun around by a hairy paw to look into the bearded face of a giant in overalls he vaguely recognized. Jenkins was his name, something like that. A fellow who rounded up wild horses to break and ship east, and from whom he had bought a fine animal only to find it branded.

"Just don't stand there, man. Have a drink!"

Jenkins bellowed at The Buffalo, put a glass in Manby's hand with a wink. "Funny how a wild broomtail picks up a brand, ain't it?"

Before Manby could reply, he was gone. Manby seldom drank, but he gingerly took a sip from the clear liquor. It was as if he had been struck by a bolt of lightning. He could feel it sear his tongue and lips, race down through his interior, and explode in a burst of fire at the pit of his stomach. Taos Lightning! He remembered now that the Vine House distilled its own potent firewater from dried peaches, prunes, corn, wheat, rye, old boots and anything else handy. A foul concoction!

The music began again. When the bar began to clear, he set down his glass and made his way through the dancers to the gambling tables in the back room. Under the overhanging lights the place was jammed. At every table men were wheeling and dealing, pinchin' 'em tight in draw, stud, One-Eyed Jacks, Merry Widow, Down the River, and Fiery Cross. He recognized Curly running the roulette wheel, Pete Perez dealing blackjack, and "The Lord" at the crap table. And at every table, planking down stacks of new Denver-minted silver dollars and leafing through rolls of green paper money, Manby saw men whom he had ignored in town but whom he had now come to see.

There was Bing Abbott, "Keed Bar Fly, the Geezer," who had watched the deputies try to run the squatters off the Maxwell Land Grant, raced horses in Colorado, worked as a cowpuncher with the Diamond outfit, and was now standing high as a pine in town. There was Abe Bowring who had baked thousands of bricks hauled by old man Ferguson to the mining camps of Twining and Amizette, and had become a successful builder in town. Walter Witt, his partner, from E-town who had rounded up wild horses, driven a stage to Twining, worked in Chihuahua, and now had a prosperous ranch. A dozen others —gamblers, confidence men, ranchers, all staunchly individual and stubborn men who gambled, traded in land and were not above stealing horses and cattle, and in general lived by their wits. Entrepreneurs who were cracking open the gates of settlement and bringing the refinements of American civilization to the crude and backward Spanish province of New Mexico that had lately been admitted into the Union as a proper state. They too knew what it was to run into a streak of bad luck, to be down on their heels. And for a friend in need, not one of them would hesitate an instant to peel off a roll of bills. No questions asked. No receipt necessary.

Manby, alone and friendless, had never taken up with these newcomers. Still the English gentleman, he had eschewed them as he had the old Spanish families and the Anglo tradespeople. He regarded this sporting clique, using the correct term of "chicken-shit gamblers," as far beneath his notice. Their vulgar pleasures did not appeal to him. But now necessity impelled him to strike up an acquaintance with one of them. Certainly they knew who he was and admired his audacity; undoubtedly they would loan him any amount he asked. But which one should he approach?

As his gaze searched anxiously one face after another, a man got up from a poker table and offered him his seat.

"Change in! Change in!" the dealer said curtly.

Manby hesitated, his hand freezing on the few dollars in his pocket. There was not the slightest doubt that he would be

mercilessly robbed unless he were shrewd enough to rob others.
Something within him refuted them all. As they had their own
code, he had his. He was not out to filch a grubby dollar by
a dexterous flip of a card. By his own sleight-of-hand he already
had gained more land than all these men could see across!

He drew himself up stiffly. "I don't gamble!" Drawing down
his hat, he stalked home in a rage.

The only Paul from whom he might borrow to pay Peter,
whichever one was pressing him hardest, was his next-door
neighbor, Dr. T. Paul Martin. After all, Martin owed him an
overdue favor for having been allowed years ago to buy the
house which Manby had stolen from the wreck of Don Juan
Santistevan's estate. So about nine o'clock next morning Manby
imperiously strutted to the large adobe adjoining his own.

Doc Martin's cramped and dirty office was on the ground floor
and his small, bare waiting room was already crowded with
patients. Most of them were poor Spanish folk: a man with a
broken arm, women bloated with pregnancy, half-naked children
covered with sores—a miserable bunch. The two wooden benches
were full and the rest of the patients squatted forlornly on the
floor. Manby stood waiting in the corner, distinctly aloof.

After awhile the door to Martin's office opened and Doc Martin
appeared, short and nervous, profane as always. "Manby! What
the hell's wrong with you on a day like this? Come in!"

Manby slouched into the office and sat down on the only available chair. The room was a mess. A battered desk in front of
the open window. A crude pine table on which he presumably
operated on groaning patients. Around the walls dirty shelves
and cabinets cluttered with medicine bottles, forceps, syringes,
knives, tablets, pills, rolls of gauze, wads of cotton, all the
paraphernalia which constituted the tools of his trade and stacks
of books and medical journals. Everything covered with dust,
stained with spilled liquids and powders. And in the corner a
brass spittoon overflowing with cigarette butts. Manby shud-
dered. It was a wonder that every patient didn't go out infected
by a worse disease than he had brought in.

Martin plunked down in his chair behind the cluttered desk.
"All right, now. What is it?"

"I need a thousand dollars," Manby answered curtly.

Martin gave him a sharp look, settled back in his chair, and let out a profane laugh. Then reaching behind him, he yanked down a quart bottle and poured a hearty libation in a filthy glass tumbler which he offered to his patient. "Here! Relax! It's 'Old Grandad,' the best elixer I've got in stock!"

"You know I don't drink bourbon!"

"My God, man, don't you have a single vice?" With a quick gulp, Martin downed it himself.

Manby scowled. Martin always got on his nerves, and never more than this morning. Twenty-five years ago, young Martin of Shippensburg, Pennsylvania and fresh out of medical college in Baltimore, Maryland, had come here to begin practice as a country doctor. In those intervening years, curt, profane, and vulgar though he was, he had become one of the most trusted and loved men in the valley. At any hour of the night he would arise on call, hitch up horse and wagon or lately crank up his battered tin lizzie, and drive through snow and cold to a mountain cabin, an isolated adobe, or to the remote village of Arroyo Seco, to set a bone, break a fever, or deliver a baby. For what? The people seldom paid. But all summer they would bring him fresh fruit and vegetables, and in the fall a leg of lamb, a venison roast, or a few scrawny chickens. How he managed to keep alive, Manby could never understand. Nor could he understand why most of the people in the valley proudly called themselves Martin's Babies.

"What about it?" asked Manby. "Can you loan me a thousand dollars?"

"With all that land you've got, why don't you sell a chunk? You'll never miss it."

"Sell my land?" The question was its own answer.

"I was up to see Doña Encarnacion the other day," Martin said quietly. "You finally got that old carved Spanish chest of hers."

"Yes," said Manby casually. "I picked it up cheap. It fitted very well in a spare corner in my study. An excellent piece!"

"Congratulations!" Martin said. "Doña Encarnacion paid me three dollars out of the seven you gave her for it. So you see we both profited."

His irony was lost on Manby.

Martin scowled. He might have made Manby squirm and sweat for his loan, but he didn't. "All right. You can have a thousand. But I want a nice piece of land for it."

"I don't sell my land. I'll give you a note backed by a piece to secure the loan."

Martin shrugged. Accordingly that June afternoon two promissory notes for $500 each, with two lots and their water rights to secure them, were signed in the name of the Colonial Bond and Security Company and Manby hurried out with his money.[4]

For a year it kept up. This constant borrowing, paying a little here and there, borrowing again. Staving off the ever-increasing creditors. Following the news of the disastrous war in Europe. Hearing rumors that the United States might be drawn in, too. What had happened that the inexorable flow of time had carried him to this? Where had the years gone—those many long years since he first had heard of the Antonio Martinez Land Grant? It was as if it had happened only yesterday, that day in the courthouse at Santa Fe which had determined the course and temper of his life. Brooding alone, Manby felt that he was suffering a horrible dream.

Late in the evening he would rouse himself from his chair in the study, go out and saddle a horse, and ride up Canyon Road to see his Princess Teracita. Never before in his life had he experienced what he now felt for her. What it was, Manby did not know nor care. It was like awakening from one dream to plunge into another. Black-eyed, black-haired Teracita, princess of his crumbling kingdom and of his uneasy dreams.

3

At precisely 11:07 on the morning of June 6, 1916 a thunderbolt tore down through the cloudless turquoise sky and exploded in the Taos County courthouse with a clap whose thunderous echoes shook the very Sangre de Cristo range on its bedrock foundations.

Manby, badly singed and shaken, escaped dazedly out of the courtroom, wandering across the plaza and up the dusty road to his home. June had come with all its usual gaudy trappings of blossom, leaf, and bud. Even the Indians had changed their winter blankets for white cotton sheets. Stalking by him, ghostly white shadows in blinding white sunlight, their anonymous shapes reflected the monstrous sense of unreality that possessed him.

Why, it had been only two weeks ago on May 20—or was it three years ago?—that the court had decreed him sole and incontestable owner of the Antonio Martinez Grant. Now the same district court had ordered the Antonio Martinez Grant to be sold at public auction to the highest bidder.

It was preposterous, of course! Not for an instant could Manby believe it. The whole thing was a fallacy instigated by a host of quarreling creditors, greedy *políticos*, and shyster lawyers. To imagine that such men could steal from him that immense grant for which he had slaved devotedly now for almost a quarter of a century—and only three years since he had gained clear title to it!

Still he was badly shaken. The legal action was at least an omen of what could possibly happen if he could not circumvent the scoundrels who sought to ruin him. He too had lawyers, tricks up his sleeve, four incorporated companies, and pieces of land he could part with if absolutely necessary.

It was easy to persuade officials to drag their heels all summer in obeying the court's order. Meanwhile, careful lest he lose his own home and estate to Eardley who held a mortgage on it, he wrote his brother. After some correspondence, the Honorable Major sent him in October the power of attorney to bargain, sell, and join in all conveyances with the Colonial Bond and Security Company. Manby made sure the certificate was notarized in Great Yarmouth, Norfolk, England, and certified by the consulate general.[1]

Receiving this, Manby began to dicker for money to pay off his brother. In November the Colonial Bond and Security Company executed through Manby a deed to Eardley Blois Manby paying off the $1,000 promissory note of May 2, 1898 at five per cent interest; the mortgage on land given on August 17, 1898; and the mortgage for $11,500 at eight per cent interest taken by Eardley on Manby's house, outbuildings, furniture, and pictures on July 14, 1913. Major Eardley, struggling in wartime England, was damn well pleased to finally get out of the whole unfortunate venture. No one else had been so extremely lucky.[2]

Two weeks later, Manby, acting on his brother's power of attorney, sold a piece of Eardley's land held by the Colonial Bond and Security Company to Emma W. Gusdorf, wife of the now prosperous German storeowner. She was a good business woman and got it for $700.[3]

Meanwhile other vultures were moving in. The First National Bank of Trinidad, in order to protect its loan of the year before, had persuaded the court to segregate 734 acres of the Antonio Martinez Grant from public sale. Now the court indomitably ordered that the land be put up for public sale to satisfy the bank's notes for $6,046 and $5,546 at eight per cent interest. How galling it was to Manby when Charles A. Watson bought it for $7,053. Watson, whom he had made an incorporator of both the Taos Land Company and of the Taos Irrigation

Company, was after the grant too![4]

Six weeks later even his next door neighbor, crusty Doc Martin, took over two lots with a three-room house and full water rights on Manby's failure to redeem his two promissory notes for $500 each.[5]

Fighting against the incredible tide dragging him down, he made one last effort. In February he obtained a court order to postpone the sale of the grant. Just long enough for him to concoct out of thin air something, someone, to save it!

The tragic day dawned bright and clear, as do most tragic days. It was June 5, 1917. Exactly a month before, the court had ordered the Antonio Martinez Grant to be sold at public auction on this day, and Judge Lieb had appointed William J. Barker as Special Master to conduct the sale. Public notice of it had been duly printed in four successive weekly issues of the *Taos Valley News* in English, and in *La Revista de Taos* in Spanish.

The sale was scheduled to be held at ten o'clock in front of the south door of the courthouse. By nine o'clock the whole plaza was crowded with interested spectators: Anglo businessmen, Spanish villagers, and white-sheeted Indians gathered to see Manby lose the land he had stolen.

A few minutes before ten, Barker came out. He was a resolute young man of thirty-three from Washington, D. C. who had begun the practice of law in Santa Fe only the year before; an ambitious new attorney who was later to become the U. S. district attorney for New Mexico. He was followed by an imposing group of lawyers, clerks, county officials, and a wary sheriff conspicuously wearing his gun on his right hip. Manby strolled up in his dusty riding breeches and boots, wearing a red silk kerchief around his throat in the manner of a matador ready to flaunt it in the face of a charging bull, but standing inconspicuously in the crowd.

Exactly on the hour Special Master Barker rapped his gavel on a wooden table brought out to support his papers, and bellowed out for bids on some 48,000 acres representing the 43/45 of the Manby-owned 61,605 acres of the Antonio Martinez Land Grant.

Immediately a man named W. G. Haydon bid $40,000, stepping up to lay in front of Barker a certified check for the full amount drawn on the First National Bank of Trinidad.

Barker then called for other bids. There now stepped forth an unidentified man who bid $50,000. When questioned by the Special Master, he identified himself with proper papers as the authorized representative of Miss Nellie Gray of Chicago, Illinois, and tendered a New York draft for the full amount, duly endorsed.

There being no further bids, the grant was sold to Nellie Gray. Barker took her representative aside to make out a Special Master's Deed and a map of her new, great tract. It showed the grant bounded on the west by the Rio Grande; on the south by the Rio Don Fernando de Taos and the north boundary line of the Pueblo de Taos League and Rio Lucero; on the east by the top of the mountains which were the source of the Rio Lucero; and on the north by the line established by the official survey. There was no doubt about it. Nellie Gray now owned the grant that Manby had devoted a quarter of a century to obtain.[6]

As the crowd began to drift away, a few pitying looks were directed at his indomitable figure. Curiously, he showed no sign of ill-effects from the ruin that had engulfed him. He stood there, the breeze flaunting the red kerchief around his throat, his face set in an impassive mask. Then he walked home.

There was no such person as Nellie Gray. Somebody had concocted her out of thin air. But who had put up the $50,000 purchase price?

Months before the sale, on January 27, Manby had released a public notice stating that on May 17, 1913 the Taos Valley Land Company had conveyed the grant to the Taos Land Company under a contract among minority stockholders, dated December 1, 1909, for payment of $300,000. This had not been paid. The stockholders of the Colonial Bond and Security Company, which owned 745,000 shares of the TVLC, did not authorize transfer of the shares from TVLC to TLC. Hence notice to the world was given that any sale of land in the Antonio Martinez Grant owned by the TVLC, and now claimed by the TLC, was subject to the trusts mentioned, together with the rights of the 745,000 shares of TVLC owned by the Colonial Bond and Security Company.

This superbly impudent "notice to the world" said in effect that Manby of the CBSC did not approve of the transfer of the grant by Manby of the TVLC to Manby of the TLC; and that no matter what Manby No. 2 and No. 3 had done, Manby No. 1 still owned the grant![7]

By now all the persons involved were thoroughly confused, and the best legal firms in New Mexico were also baffled by the transactions. It seemed, however, that multi-headed Manby had squeezed out of his fix. The Colonial Bond and Security Company which Manby No. 1 owned still claimed ownership of the grant even if it had been sold to Nellie Gray.

Despite all this, Manby's creditors wanted their money. This was simple enough. The court appointed receivers for the Taos Valley Land Company and the Taos Land Company, and the infuriated creditors massed to present their claims. One of them was the Taos Mercantile Company to which Manby owed a trifling $295.97; but in its claim against the Taos Land Company in October there were listed sixteen other claims of unusual interest.[8]

Four of them seemed reasonable enough to recommend payment: $10,000 each to C. C. Catron and Horace W. Cook for legal services rendered while Manby was quieting title to the Martinez Grant; $8,475.90 for legal services given by Judge Laughlin who still had not been paid; and $17,282.92 to the First National Bank in Trinidad for its loan and interest.

There then cropped up two claims, one for $37,561.67 and the other for $33,416.68, from Martha S. Hill whom Manby had fleeced with the Prescotts. A man named E. G. Potter claimed $166,446.19 and a Frederick H. Jephson claimed $9,638.31. Then followed $7,000 in claims from four members of the Martinez family, and several minor claims for a few hundred dollars each.

Among these claimants was a familiar name: Edith S. Prescott Manby Allnutt—Pinky, who had remarried and now sought $1,500 with eight per cent interest of the alimony which Manby had never paid. Nor was it recommended to be paid to her, for it represented a personal liability of Manby, not that of the Taos Land Company nor the Taos Valley Land Company. The final result of the claim, after much dickering, was a full settlement of judgment of $900 for her tragic two-year marriage.[9]

Pinky's attorney was A. B. Renehan, also the administrator of the estate of Matilda Cox Stevenson who had held $20,000

worth of stock in the Taos Valley Land Company. In presenting
Pinky's claim, he asked the court to set aside Judge N. B.
Laughlin's claim of $8,475.90 and Horace Wright Cook's claim
of $10,000, for the legal services rendered by these attorneys
were antagonistic to the interests of the owners of the remaining
3/45 of the grant. Furthermore Cook seemed to be acting for
undisclosed clients. Renehan also asserted that Nellie Gray was
not the real purchaser of the Martinez Grant, being but a dummy
acting for the estate of Martha S. Hill whose attorneys were
these same men, Manby's lawyers, Laughlin and Cook. Martha
S. Hill had been a heavy stockholder and creditor of the Taos
Valley Land Company, "and later the Taos Land Company
was formed and became or pretended to become interested as
a successor in some manner unknown ... in said grant of the
Taos Valley Land Company."

Just how much this company was in debt, he did not know.
But he believed and asserted the only real result of all the
manipulations was a loss of $150,000 "to certain persons called
settlers."

All these claims, however, totaled approximately $320,000.
The last big item was the sum of $300,000 claimed by both the
Taos Valley Land Company and the Colonial Bond and Security
Company. This again threw into focus the complicated relationship between Manby's three companies. I. W. Dwire, receiver
of the Taos Valley Land Company, addressing himself to
William J. Barker, receiver for the Taos Land Company,
presented four objections which revealed the deviousness of
Manby's organizational methods. He objected to the claim of the
First National Bank in Trinidad on the TVLC because it was
outside the power of the TLC to pass upon; to the Taos Mercantile Company's claim against the TLC because it was but
an alleged claim against TVLC; to the Colonial Bond and
Security Company's claim for $2,000 salary for Manby as the
manager of the TVLC; and to the Colonial Bond and Security
Company's claim for the $300,000 purchase price of the Antonio
Martinez Grant sold by the TVLC to TLC, because it was the
claim of the TVLC and not that of the Colonial Bond and
Security Company.

With all these claims against him, one thing was certain.
Manby was busted.[10]

On July 12, 1919, Barker, receiver of the Taos Land Company, was authorized by the court to sell all the assets of the company at public sale. Nellie Gray again offered the highest bid of $2,500 for all the remaining assets—chiefly the water rights held in the name of the Taos Irrigation Company, particularly the diversion and surplus waters from the Rio Hondo and Arroyo Hondo to the Antonio Martinez Grant. This marked the dissolution of Manby's third corporation.[11]

The end came not quite two months later when Nellie Gray, for the stipulated sum of ten dollars, released a quit claim deed to the entire 61,605.48 acres of the Antonio Martinez Grant, with all its water rights—to Charles A. Watson![12]

Watson, who had done what neither Prescott nor Hill had been able to do!

Manby could believe it now, trudging home on that September 1st from the courthouse in which for twenty-seven years he had cheated, cajoled and threatened, bribed and betrayed to obtain the grant, and in which he now at last had been betrayed and cheated out of it himself. During all these agonizing months it had seemed too preposterous a fantasy to believe the grant could ever be taken from him. Those sweeping miles of mountain, forest, and sagebrush, all that vast domain stretching out unbroken in sunlight and shadow was rooted in an ownership no man could question; a royal title to which, after two centuries of neglect, he had fallen heir as the rightful sovereign.

He could have endured with some equanimity its loss by catastrophic change, fire, flood or earthquake, a war or a social revolution; such great and unavoidable calamities bring natural ends to the sovereignty of royal empires. Manby, as an imperialist, deserved the compliment of high tragedy. But to be cheated out of his kingdom in the same corrupt and greedy manner as he had obtained it—and by a mere conniving promoter like himself whom he had blindly nurtured like a snake at his breast—violated every vestige of false pride, every corrupt instinct, every shred of greed within him. To be dispossessed by Watson! This admission was what now finally drove the cold blade of inescapable failure into his brain. He had completely, irretrievably lost the Martinez Grant.

Manby's Folly!

The thought kept pounding at his mind like the blood in

his graying temples as he trudged home. There was no denying
it. A dispossessed sovereign, he saw his scepter raised by another
hand. He was condemned for the rest of his life to the slow
torture of watching his grant blossom as the desert rose, the
proud towns and cities growing upon it, and the money come
rolling in to a treasury not his.

Manby's Folly!

Whatever role he played, Manby was still a man of flesh and
blood, and for all his sturdy body and brilliant mind he had the
delicate inner mechanism so often to be found in natures like
his. It was not surprising that it could not be unaffected by such
a blow, and indeed something did happen on his short walk
home. Perhaps that fragile and complicated apparatus slipped
a gear or a microscopic pin crystallized and snapped under the
pressure, necessitating his whole mechanism to change its
rhythm. Manby did not notice it himself. He simply continued
home to the miserable twenty-three acres left of his large estate
and to his nineteen-room adobe hacienda. Here he slumped
down on a stiff chair in his study, staring out at the peak looming
beyond his garden.

It was a view of which he had always been justly proud, that
softly rounded spruce-blue peak so exquisitely framed by two
hundred lilac bushes and the great narrow-leaf cottonwood
trees in his park, and which at sunset glowed red as the blood
of Christ, the Sangre de Cristo. Yet beneath his surface
admiration there had lurked an uneasy feeling about it which
reflected his growing apperception through the years of a
subtle quality of resistance beneath its soft, amenable shape.
It was a mountain of many mysteries. In a large cave on its
opposite side, near the mouth of the Lucero, human sacrifices
allegedly had been made by ancient Indians. Behind it lay the
pueblo's sacred lake to which the present Indians still made
secret pilgrimages to conduct rites never witnessed by a white
man. The mountain too was said to contain rich lodes of gold
that no man had been allowed to prospect. Manby could discount
most of the tales about it, but he could not ignore the fact that
it was an Indian mountain standing on Indian land, blanketed
like their own soft shapes, and hard and inimical inside as they
themselves. If the benevolent aspect it often showed mirrored
his own love of the beauty of the land it overlooked, the shadowy

Taos Sacred Mountain seen from the road in front of Manby's house.
Photo by Mildred Tolbert.

and sinister quality it showed just as often reflected all the silent negation of the Indians against him. Such changeableness of character in an inanimate heap of rock irked him; a mystery he could never fathom.

Perceiving the peak now through his awry sensory apparatus, it seemed to him that it suddenly had become alive and was almost imperceptively pulsating. He could hear, as if with ears which were not his own, its slow rhythmic beat. The momentary delusion of this apperception of its hidden reality, if that was what it was, seemed strangely comforting. The beat, for the first time, drew an unacknowledged hidden self within him in tune with the mountain and the spirit which informed it. The rapport did not last. Within an instant the Manby he had always known himself to be saw the peak was wracked by unrest, as if the benevolent blue spirit had metamorphosed into a baleful creature frantically trying to break out of its dark confinement. A great sentinel spokesman for this vast hinterland of America that he had never really known, of all that land which had perversely rejected him, it was churning under the pitiful cries and antics of that creature imprisoned within, ready to erupt upon him the intolerable folly of his own long incomprehension. Regularly, in an unendurable rhythm and with painful pressure, it pounded at his temples, kept pounding in his mind.

Unable to stand it, he flung out of his chair to close the window against the sound. Then suddenly he realized what it was. Indian drums! A group of those blasted Indians were holding another meeting across the fence from his park, and beating their cursed water-drums. With all his strength he hurled the window shut, shattering the glass in the dusk and cutting his wrist. With a shriek of rage, both bloody hands clapped over his ears, he ran out of the room.

Doc Martin, passing by, heard the shatter of the glass and Manby's scream. Luckily the house had not been locked up yet, enabling him to rush inside. Manby was lying on the floor of a far room, kicking and shrieking, with blood spurting from his cut wrist. Martin lit a candle and stood looking down at him.

"What a bloody mess you are, you old fool! Shut up!"

Manby's eyes cleared. He stopped kicking and sat up with a look of incomprehension on his tortured face. Martin worked swiftly, stopping the bleeding and giving him a sleeping powder. Then guiding the old man to another room, he stripped off his bloody clothes, and pushed him into the dirty bed.

'That'll teach you to take out your temper on a window pane! For God's sake! At your age, too!"

He turned on his heel and stalked out.

4

During this troublesome time Manby became aware that the still remote village of Taos, rendezvous of Kit Carson and the mountain men of the century before, was receiving another small but unusual influx of residents to add to its already cosmopolitan population of barely two thousand souls. They were, of all things, artists!

Years before, three accomplished painters who had studied art in Paris—Joseph H. Sharp, Ernest L. Blumenschein, and Bert Phillips—had discovered the valley as a place to paint. The wild beauty of the mountains, the serene little adobe villages, the colorful Indians—this was an America still fresh and untouched, not yet put on canvas.

Establishing homes and studios, these three artists were joined by two more academic painters, Oscar Berninghaus and Irving Couse, and a former cowpoke who had become a popular magazine illustrator, Buck Dunton. The six men in 1914 had formed the Taos Society of Artists, adding two more members that same year, Walter Ufer and Victor Higgins. It was not surprising to Manby that their paintings caught the fancy of the public. Indians and aspens! Exhibitions of the work of these *Los Ochos Pintores*, as they were called, were booked in all large cities throughout the east and sent abroad.

Manby, as a cultured Englishman, might have found in these newcomers the companionship and congeniality so long lacking in his life, but his relationship got off to a bad start. Bert Phillips had been the first artist to establish a permanent home and studio, and the site he picked was across the street from Manby. For a time they were good friends, enjoying together the company of a young woman in town. How deep Manby's interest in her became no one knew, but rather abruptly she stopped seeing him and married Phillips.[1]

A short time later, Phillips, who always had admired the great cottonwoods Manby had planted along the road, set out a row in front of his own house. When they began to leaf and seed, Manby rushed over to his studio in a rage.

"Look at that cotton fuzz blowing off your trees into my fine garden!" he shouted. "What do you mean planting female cottonwoods just to spite me?"

"How did I know they were female trees, Mr. Manby?" asked Phillips in his gentle voice.

"You damned artists don't know anything!"

Manby stormed back across the road. From then on he seldom spoke to Phillips and his wife. He foreswore all artists, although this did not prevent him from picking up some of their work when he could get it cheap. He and Doc Martin by now hated the looks of each other. There was no one with whom he was friends. And with his empire crashing into ruins about him, he shut himself up in his house, becoming a lonely recluse.

Then, on a cold December morning, there sounded an imperative knock on his door. The callers were the artist and sculptor, Maurice Sterne and his wife, Mabel Dodge Sterne, already famous for her gatherings in Paris, at her villa in Florence, Italy, and in her salon at 23 Fifth Avenue, New York. A short, energetic, and intuitive woman with ample means, she had popped into Taos for a quick one-day look. It was enough. She was tired of worn-out Europe, of the overcrowded cities of America beginning to be stifled by an ever-increasing materialism. This was the place to make her home at last! Mabel, as she was familiarly known everywhere, was like that. When she knew what she wanted, she wasted no time nor words.

When Mabel opened the door she saw, as she was to write later in her memoirs,[2] a man dressed in filthy riding trousers, flannel shirt, and frayed waistcoat; a man with bloodshot eyes, "completely negative" and "breathing out a dark and bloody anger to the world."

"What do you want?" he growled in a surprisingly cultured voice.

Mabel answered immediately, "I want to rent your house, Mr. Manby! It's the largest and most attractive house in town and my husband must have a comfortable place in which to work."

Manby, taken aback, showed them through the house. The huge rooms, she observed, were well furnished with walnut and mahogany pieces, some of which had been brought from England, and many fine carved chests and tables. The walls were hung with oils, and several delicate watercolors which Manby said had been painted by his mother. Everywhere was a litter of ore specimens from his mines, fossils, old rifles, Indian jewelry and artifacts. Yet, like himself, the whole house gave off a feeling of defeat and decay. The black iron-barred windows were covered with grime; dust lay thick upon floor and furnishings; cobwebs stretched across the ceilings.

"I'll take it!" said Mabel. "I've got to have it!"

Manby's bloodshot eyes gleamed with a resurgence of hope. He agreed to rent the huge house to her for the exorbitant sum of seventy-five dollars a month, reserving to himself a small apartment that lay in a wing protruding toward the road and adjoining Doc Martin's house—isolated of course by a two-foot-thick adobe wall.

There now began for him—and for Mabel—a fabulous year. She moved in with maids and workers, cleaned up the old house. Soon divorcing Maurice Sterne, she married an Indian at the pueblo, big Tony Lujan. They then began to build their own big house at the edge of the reservation, a house later surrounded by five smaller guest homes for the steady stream of visitors that began to pour in.

Ever since his strange experience at the mouth of the Lucero, Manby had been frightened of Indians. The presence of one in his own house now was distinctly ominous. There was nothing he could do about it, though he confided his danger to Mabel.

"They want to kill me, so I must be very careful," he explained. "That is why I must insist that the gates and doors be locked every night before we retire. And if I were you"—he lowered his beautiful voice to a confident whisper—"I'd be very careful of letting in too many of Mr. Lujan's friends. They are not like we are, you know."

"Oh now, Mr. Manby! You know Tony isn't a dangerous man! He wouldn't let any of his friends harm you. There's no reason for them to hate you."

Manby's voice changed. "Those damn heathen Indians!," he shrieked. "Their blasted sacred mountain is full of gold and they won't let me get it. They don't want me to have any water for my land. They think all is theirs—land, water, gold, and everything else."

Nevertheless there grew up between these two a peculiar friendship. Mabel saw him as a queer, dissolute old man, but a cultured one. Cleaned up, the house revealed his architectural skill, and the garden in back his taste and green thumb. There were acres of lawn bordered with roses, poppies, hollyhocks and lilacs, locust, linden, elm and cottonwood trees—a typical English park. But like Manby, it was a devious park; there were no straight lines. All the walks and passageways wound through the shrubbery in curves except a lane of great trees which Manby called his "Avenue."

"This Avenue," he explained, "will extend eastward and join the Boulevard which will encircle the whole valley." He pointed out to her the course he had laid out: along the curving range of mountains to the Rio Grande, down the river, and back across the wide plateau to the tree-lined Pueblo road he already had prepared.

"We have here in Taos Valley," he went on, "one of the great gardens of the world whose scenic splendor may be equalled only by the Valley of Mexico and the Vale of Kashmir. I intend to develop it for future generations before its natural beauty is destroyed."

"Yes! You're right, Mr. Manby!" Then recalled to his filthy riding trousers, old puttees, and greasy shirt, Mabel asked, "But when?"

"Not long. I'm being delayed right now by a few difficulties being encountered by my land companies. But let me show you the sketches I've drawn for a great hotel to be built here on my estate—on this very spot."

Mabel was impressed by his drawings and a painting he had made of the exterior. She insisted years later she saw a smaller replica of it in the Biltmore Hotel at Santa Barbara, California.[3]

One morning he drove her out to Manby Hot Springs, deep in the somber gorge of the Rio Grande. The old wooden shack he had replaced with a small stone bathhouse built around the main spring.

"Boiling hot and impregnated with radium," he boasted. "The finest water in the world for invalids! This spot lies on the Boulevard I've told you about. On the rim of the gorge here I'm going to build another hotel, and at the bottom a bathhouse with all modern facilities to house the pools of varying temperature filled from the spring itself. Yes, it'll make a renowned spa. No doubt of it!"

Back home, Mabel wrote Robinson Jeffers, the poet in Carmel, California, of the peculiar fascination of the hot springs:

"The water itself, Jeffers, is the most wonderful water in the world. Hotter than blood-heat, and so buoyant that it is difficult to keep oneself below the surface . . . Perhaps most strangest of all, Jeffers, outside the stone house there were two great rocks with faint but indelible incisions on them. One was a fragment of the Greek key pattern . . . on the other, close beside the entrance to the water, was the symbol of that oldest of human wishes—the dot within the circle, the sign of eternal life.

"Our local legend from the Indians is that the people who lived near the river long, long before the Spaniards came, took care of this spring until the white men appeared and heard tales of it; then the Indians tried to hide it from them lest they too bathe there and live forever. The Indians wanted to live forever, but they did not want the white men to! So they covered the bubbling water with sand as best they could, and to mark it for their own kind, they cut the sign into the rock—as if to say: 'Close by this stone is hidden the way to eternal life.' "[4]

Later she brought out her guests often to soak in the remote, strange spring. One of them was that other tortured Englishman of genius, the writer D. H. Lawrence.

A couple of weeks later Manby saddled horses and took her around the mysterious mountain to look at the immense landscape spread out before them.

"Look!" said Manby. "Sixty-one thousand acres of virgin land waiting to be planted to wheat, corn, and barley. To be divided into estates and building lots for the thousands of people who will flock in. Room for at least two towns! There's

plenty of water. Lucero there"—he pointed with his whip—
"and Rio Hondo to the north. That's a river for you! Look at
the gorge, cut from the mountains to the Rio Grande. One of
these days I've got to dam it to preserve the water for use. That
will mean a lake for fishing, swimming, boating. A recreational
resort."

"But Tony tells me his people own the Lucero, Mr. Manby.
It comes from the high mountains surrounding their sacred
lake."

"Those damned Indians!" Manby spat with disgust. "What
don't they claim, those lazy, ignorant heathens!"

Mabel ignored his outburst. "It will take a great deal of money,
all these developments."

"We will talk about that later," answered Manby, quieting
down. "I first want to show you the great extent of planning
I have done with my financiers."

"No!" said Mabel at once. "All that is a man's business. I have
no feeling for such things—money, planning for the future, great
undertakings. I've come here just to *live*, today, now, every day,
for the first time in my life!" Just the same, she felt a great
respect for this old man's visionary plans, his taste, and
judgment.

Manby's temper flared up. He lashed his horse. In a few
minutes she caught up with him and they rode slowly home.
There Tony had been waiting for them. He was a big man
wrapped in his blanket, more than six feet tall and solidly built.
There was a scowl on his broad, dark face.

When he and Mabel were alone in the house, he said quietly,
"No good. Goin' ridin' with that old man. I don't like him.
Nobody like him. He bad."

"He's just a little queer, Tony. Why don't you like him?"

"Him trying to steal all our land, all our water. Indian land.
Our mother who borns us all."

That strange feeling of Indians for their land! It was rooted in
their very bones! She was just beginning to understand it.

Then Tony told her of an incident a friend of his, another
Indian, had witnessed. Some years ago this Indian had seen
Manby riding up the canyon, a rifle slung on his saddle. Knowing
Manby's reputation, the Indian carefully followed him up the
canyon to a solitary miner's hut. Hiding behind a boulder on

the hillside, he watched Manby dismount, unsling his rifle, and
walk up to the shanty. He knocked loudly, then stepped back
with his rifle raised. The door was opened by the miner. Without
a word, Manby shot him. Then he carried the body to a ravine
and buried it. The Indian, without saying a word, returned to
the pueblo.[5]

As Tony finished the story, Mabel felt for the first time an
intuitive suspicion that there were two Manbys embodied in that
cultured but dirty frame. She began to feel a little frightened.

Impulsively she wired two more artist friends in New York to
come to the wonderful place she had found—and to bring a cook.
A week later they arrived, with the cook, and also took up
quarters in Manby's huge house. One of them was Robert
Edmond Jones, a noted stage designer on Broadway. The other
was Andrew Dasburg, an American painter born in France, who
had become one of the first and foremost exponents of modern
art in the United States.

How strange it seemed to Manby to have so many people in
the house for the first time. He got acquainted with Jones and
took him around the valley, pointing out with an architect's
appreciation the irregular lines and planes of the adobe houses,
and the fantastic, crooked crosses on the roofs and in the
graveyards. Jones was impressed by Manby's acute observations:
as a stage designer, he found these values stimulating. Soon
after returning to New York, he designed settings for *Macbeth*
and for the Metropolitan Opera's production of *Til Eulenspiegel*
which reflected this semi-abstract style with its fantastic leaning
and crooked houses.

Dasburg also found Manby cultured, intelligent, and extremely well informed about the native arts. He became
interested in collecting *Santos*—those old Spanish paintings of
Christian Saints done on wood slabs known as *retablos*, Manby
told him, or as *bultos* when carved out of wood. For hours he
would sit in the kitchen with a treasure in his lap, wiping off
with kerosene the bedbug eggs, dust, and grime. Beside him
sat Manby.

"You will observe," Manby would say, picking at the corner
of a *Santo* with his grimy fingernail, "that the paint used in
those times was composed of pigments of colored clay mixed
with the white of an egg. *Yeso*. It accounts for the durability

of the color and its cohesion to the wood for so many years.
Also the mellow tones of the colors."[6]

He seemed to be something of an authority on old embroidered
Spanish *colchas* and *serapes* too, teaching Dasburg how to darn
them when torn. To him also Manby showed the painting and
the drawings he had made for the big hotel he intended to
build in back of the house. But Dasburg observed, like Mabel,
that there were two Manbys, one of them destitute, devious, and
unreliable. Periodically he would sneak out of the house an old
firearm or an Indian piece, placing it for sale with the Indian
trader, Ralph Meyers.

One evening when Mabel and Tony, Jones, and Dasburg
were gathered under the big brass coal-oil lamp in the kitchen,
there sounded overhead a peculiar noise. "Drat those mice!"
said Mabel. "I told Filomena to get them all out of the house!"

Tony held up his long brown forefinger for silence. "Them
ain't mice. That Manby up on the roof. He listenin' down the
chimney."

It made them all feel uncomfortable.

"Has he hit you for a big investment to put in his crazy
venture?" Jones asked Mabel later. "He hasn't asked me yet,
but he's working up to it."

Mabel, getting acquainted around town, learned a great deal
more about Manby. Phillips told her to be careful. Ralph Meyers,
taciturn as an Indian himself, only shrugged when she asked
about him; but the shrug was eloquent. Doc Martin condemned
him vociferously.

"He's crazy as a hoot-owl, and he's no good! Doesn't he lock
you all in the house every night? And them dogs he keeps
chained in the patio. Ask Tony. He knows that the Indians might
get him. Or the Spanish people around here. Or even me! And
all that digging in the garden he does every night! What's that
for? Is he burying all the money he's stole, or digging it up just
to see if it's all there? That damned old coot! You be careful
of him!"

There was more talk, more rumors. Then Mabel learned
Manby already had lost all that land he claimed was his.

Bobbie Jones returned to New York. Andrew Dasburg stayed
to paint with an abstract technique the landscapes for which he
became famous. Mabel's own Big House was finished, and she

was glad to move away from that cultured but grimy old Englishman who "breathed out a dark and bloody anger to the world."

She saw him seldom after that, and felt somehow relieved.

5

Once again Manby resumed his solitary life in the big adobe. Did he miss the rich, selfish woman who had married a blanket Indian and built a big house of her own instead of financing development of his grant? At least he missed the sound of footsteps, the pleasurable excitement of creeping down the hall or climbing up to a rooftop chimney to listen to their voices.

Closing up most of the house to gather grime and dust and cobwebs again, he lived in one room. Dust lay thick on the piles of documents and papers, the bronze ink-well and many pens lying unused on the table. The bed was unmade, without sheets, the filthy gray blankets tossed back from the uncovered pillow on which his tortured head rolled back and forth at night. No matter. Every few nights he moved to another room to sleep after bolting all gates and locking all doors against the baleful influence of the mysterious mountain, and seeing that his watchdogs were chained in the patio to keep out Indians.

In the morning he got up, made tea and a porridge out of cornmeal brought from Anderson's mill. He always made enough so that he could eat what was left over for lunch as a cold pudding with milk and sugar and a bit of currant jam. During the day he puttered around, letting bushes and trees grow in his garden to shut out sight of that baleful peak, and wondering how he was to sell his two paintings for enough money to regain his grant.

His friend in Philadelphia, George Thomas Lambert, had asked Professor Pasquale Farina, an art expert, to authenticate them. Farina said nothing about the St. Agnes but believed the St. Catherine had been painted by Van Dyck instead of Titian. He wrote:

"Late in 1631 Sir Balthazar Gerbier, British Minister at Bruxelles, sent Van Dyke's *Virgin and St. Catherine* to the King and Queen as a New Year's gift. After the execution of Charles I, the Puritan government, or the victorious Roundheads, compelled painters to flee England; and in 1645 Parliament voted that all pictures at York House and other galleries be burned.

"If this picture is the one bought by Gerbier, it must have been smuggled out of England and sent to the Continent. There were three Van Dyck *Marriage of St. Catherine* pictures.

"My conclusion is that your picture is original, and painted by Van Dyck. The flesh colors in this picture cannot be found in other master works, but in Van Dyck's only. There is remarkable purity of form, silvery clearness of tone, mastery of pigments . . . which is entirely his own . . . No traces of hesitancy . . . which could lead one to think it the work of a copyist."[1]

Lambert then referred Manby to Dr. V. C. Thorne in New York, an extremely wealthy man. Manby, excited by such a good prospect, wrote Thorne at once. Professor Pasquale Farina, he explained, had been the last word in painting to the late John G. Johnson of Philadelphia, a lawyer of international fame who had bought one of the finest art collections in the world, valued at $6,000,000. Farina had stated this painting was one of the finest Van Dycks in the world. "The beauty is in its gorgeous colors and magnificent free painting," went on Manby. "This is supposed to be the painting purchased by the British Minister in Brussells, December 1631, and for which Lord Treasurer Weston paid 2,500 guineas. This is thirty decades past, and if money doubles every ten years it would make this picture today worth $393,750."[2]

In another letter Manby added that Professor Farina valued the painting at $125,000 at least. "If I could make a quick turn I would sell it for $75,000, and possibly $50,000 might tempt me as I need the money in our business. I would gladly pay you, say, 10% or 15% if you would allow me to."

Thorne wrote that the next time he was in Philadelphia, he would go to the Trust Company vaults and look at the painting. He was interested! He was friendly! Manby's imagination began to work and there was indeed a large field for it.

Dr. Victor Corse Thorne, as he found out, came from an old Quaker family which had made an immense fortune out of buffalo hides and leather on the Great Plains. The family had then moved from its old home on Second Street, New York to a huge new brownstone mansion on 84th Street and 5th Avenue, near the Metropolitan Museum. Young Thorne himself had been born in Florence, Italy in 1871 and had secured his degree in medicine at Yale University. When his father died, leaving him and his brother a fortune of some $11,000,000, he had taken a degree in law at Columbia University in order to fit himself for the management of the estate. His brother Brink had married, his wife bringing in still another fortune for him to look after.[3]

Dr. Thorne now lived in Greenwich, Connecticut, maintained offices at 120 Broadway, New York, and devoted himself to administering his fabulous estate. If there was any man fitted for Manby's pressing needs, it was Dr. Thorne. He could not only buy or obtain a buyer for the Van Dyck, but could finance any reasonable venture presented to him. Manby had no trouble proposing one whose immense profits would restore to him his lost kingdom.

So now, day after day for months, he brushed the dust off his desk with his frayed elbows and scribbled away. He could no longer afford engraved blue stationary and wrote in black ink on thin white paper. His handwriting was as bold as ever, perhaps bolder, for he wrote hastily, with the enthusiasm of a born promoter. "My dear Dr. Thorne"—page upon page, letter after letter.

He had temporarily lost the Antonio Martinez Grant, but still claimed 18,000 acres of the disputed Antoine Leroux or Los Luceros Grant. He had title to at least 1,649 acres of it, known as the Hadley tract, which had been picked up by William Frayne for payment of taxes and then transferred to himself. Manby in turn had transferred the title to the Colonial Bond and Security Company.

What he now had in mind for this Los Luceros property, as he called it, was simple. They would raise sheep on it, beginning with a flock of ten thousand. He carefully reviewed the methods of grazing, the cost of wages for sheepherders and of supplies for them, transportation, fleecing, the rate of animal multiplication, the state of the market, and the likely profit to be derived. La Bajada Sheep Company! That would be its name!

Not satisfied with this, he went into a lengthy discussion of a vast copper deposit on Copper Mountain that could be profitably mined, conservatively estimating that about $7,000,000 worth of copper ore was awaiting them.

Nor did he forget the land embracing his hot springs which could be developed into a resort, a renowned spa.

Finally on September 5, 1919 he combined all his data in a conclusive La Bajada Sheep Company Prospectus which he mailed to Thorne. There were three objectives: to buy and graze 10,000 sheep, to mine $7,000,000 worth of copper ore on Copper Mountain, and to cut 10 million feet of timber.

The financing assets were equally simple. There were 18,000 acres in the Los Luceros property at $10 per acre, representing $180,000. About 1,500 acres in the La Bajada Tract or Hot Springs at $50 per acre, $75,000. And some 530,000 shares of the Taos Valley Land Company, representing the controlling interest in the Antonio Martinez Land Grant, $265,000. All that was needed was a surplus fund of the corporation for purchase of the sheep, $180,000. All totalling $700,000.

Two weeks later Manby rushed off another letter embroidering the above facts, and also mentioning the prospect of oil on the Navajo Reservation. He reminded Thorne again of the Van Dyck masterpiece lying unseen and unsold in the safety vault of the Philadelphia Trust Company. "If you can sell the Van Dyck I will gladly pay a commission of 25%," he added.

All this took a great deal of time and thought each day. Almost before he knew it, it was sunset and his Princess Teracita had come to fix his supper.

When she did not come, he saddled his black horse, "Nigger," with trembling hands, called his watchdogs, and rode up Canyon Road. Ferguson was getting old. Wilkerson up at E-town had closed the Mystic and mysteriously vanished.

"Any news?" Manby always inquired upon arriving.

The old Scotchman shook his head.

Betrayed again! A shadowy something deep inside Manby

came alive again at the thought; from it rose a slow, intense, burning anger that suffused his whole body. Just as quickly it disappeared when he saw his Princess come in the door. She alone would never fail him.

Teracita was now a mature woman of strength and determination, showing more clearly every day that hard streak of granite Manby had detected in her years before. He depended upon her completely. Whether she loved Manby with equal fervor her friends did not know, although they could not question her loyalty and devotion to him. She always insisted that Manby was like a grandfather, an uncle to her; not a lover.[4] There was indeed thirty years difference in their ages. Yet they suspected some of her long evenings must have ended in embraces with someone, for by now she had two children and was about to have another.

To baptise them, she always obtained Milton Arthur Spotts: Captain, Reverend, and Mister. Named after the small town of Milton, Pennsylvania where he had been born, he had graduated from Susquehanna University and was ordained a minister of the Lutheran Church. After obtaining his Ph. D. at Princeton, he served as pastor at the St. Mark's churches in Saxon and Pittsburgh, and in Trenton, New Jersey. Upon the outbreak of World War I, he was commissioned a lieutenant in the Navy, serving as chaplain, and then as a captain in the New Mexico National Guard. He had now come to work with the Board of Missions in New Mexico, was a county commissioner, and was taking over an abstract company.

A big, heavy-set, and jolly man, he enjoyed the baptisms at Teracita's house. The paper for each child he made out in the name of Ferguson. Afterwards Teracita served a chicken dinner to celebrate the event. On one of these occasions he met Manby, and called on him next day.

Showing him inside, Manby opened the door of a large ceiling-high safe and began taking out cigar boxes filled with gold nuggets and specimens of rich ore. They contrasted so oddly with his poor and disreputable appearance that Spotts could not forebear asking, "You're a rich man, Mr. Manby! Why don't you sell some of this gold?"

Manby gave him a quizzical look. "Whenever I need a little money, I just take a nugget or two across the street to Bill

Hinde and he loans me all I need. This is just like a safety
deposit vault. But I always put them back!"

There was something queer about this. Spotts could not
imagine the blacksmith Hinde having much money on hand
from merely shoeing horses.

Manby put back the boxes and locked the door of the safe.
"There's more where this came from, and only I know where.
You see now why I keep my dogs to guard it, and lock up the
house every night. Those rascals! They think they'll get me
yet!"[5]

Another person he permitted to call was a Spanish widow
named Mrs. Demetrio Rodriguez who lived with her two small
boys in a nearby adobe on Bent Street. She had been born in
E-town where her husband had been fatally injured in a mine
accident, and like Manby she knew all the people in the high
valley.

"Why in the hell do they call me '<i>La Pocha</i>' up there?" he
asked.

Mrs. Rodriguez giggled. "That word. I do not know what it
means. But that is what the people called the girls—how do I
say it?—those girls who lived in what you call Red Houses.
For these girls, you understand, cut their hair short to be pretty."

"<i>Las putas. Las cucharachas.</i> Whores!" exclaimed Manby.
"Blast them!"

"You see, Mr. Manby, your hair is cut very short too."

"You mean I'm beginning to get bald!"

Mrs. Rodriguez giggled. "Perhaps that is so."

Manby liked to hear her talk, and let her wander through the
big house to admire its furnishings. She was greatly impressed
by the fact that he slept in a different bed every night. What
a rich man!

"A different bed every night. Sometimes three!' insisted
Manby. "On moonlight nights I change to another bed at mid-
night, and then to another one just before dawn." Lowering his
voice, he added, "You see, we all have enemies. Mine want to
kill me."

"But I have no enemies, Mr. Manby."

"Yes, you do! But they hide themselves, pretend they're your
friends. You must be smarter than they are!"

She was a simple woman. She loved flowers, and in the whole

world there were no flowers like those in Mr. Manby's garden!

"That's right!" agreed Manby, immensely pleased. "Pick all you want. You can come into this garden anytime. But only you. Nobody else. Don't ever bring anyone with you. Understand? They might be my enemies, pretending to be your friends."[6]

On sleepless nights Manby dug in his garden, his back bent in a frenzy over pick and shovel. A hole here, another there. Always neatly raked over by morning. Doc Martin could glimpse him in the moonlight or hear him on dark nights. That goddamned, everlastin' diggin'! The crazy old coot! Was he buryin' it or takin' it out?

On winter nights after making cryptic entries in his diary, Manby read a little. Not the complete sets of Dickens and Thackeray on his shelves, but from his favorite book: *The War in the Air*, a 1908 novel by H. G. Wells, which prophesied the collapse of modern civilization after a world-wide war of new flying machines. Once again Manby would read:

> No one troubled over the real dangers of mankind. They saw their armies and navies grow larger and more portentous; some of their ironclads at the last cost as much as the whole annual expenditure upon advanced education; they accumulated explosives and the machinery of destruction; they allowed their national traditions and jealousies to accumulate; they contemplated a steady enhancement of race hostility as the races drew closer without concern or understanding; and they permitted the growth in their midst of an evil-spirited press, mercenary and unscrupulous, incapable of good and powerful for evil . . . One is incredulous now to believe they could not see.

Then suddenly the air-fleets swept in over the seas—the beginning of the end. . . .

The shadowy prisoner within Manby responded instantly to this grim tale of horror, as it in turn reflected his own dark, bloody anger against the world. He read it over and over, fuming with hate, his mind storing away scenes, lines, paragraphs.

There came unexpected good news. One of Thorne's many

companies was the Radium Company of Colorado with main
offices in the Radium Building, Denver, and branch offices in
New York and other large cities throughout the country. Now
Thorne was on his way to Denver and would come down to Taos
for a brief visit to see him! Manby snapped out of his lethargy,
cleaned up the house a bit, and attired himself in his best
manners. Dr. Thorne was not another Hill or Prescott—not
with all his millions! No doubt he was coming to put the La
Bajada Sheep Company on its feet!

Thorne and his wife arrived in September, in ripe Indian
summer when everything was at its best. He was a short, alert,
quick-moving man, very friendly, and Manby did his best to
please him and his wife. They stayed overnight at the hotel,
but Manby proudly took them out for a look at his hot springs.
"The water is radioactive," he told Thorne. "Your Radium
Company will be interested in that."

"Very interesting. We'll look into it," replied Thorne.

Friendly as he was, he seemed extremely cautious. Evidently
he was not interested in raising sheep, mining copper, or cutting
timber. Nor had he found a buyer for the Van Dyck. Manby
did not show his disappointment. He had found the peg now
on which to hang his best efforts—the hot springs—and restrained himself from overselling its virtues too soon.

Several Navajo families had come to town for the San Geronimo fiesta, and the women were squatted along the road in
front of Manby's house with their blankets spread out for sale.
"I love this one!" Mrs. Thorne said, stooping over a beautiful
one, white with red and blue designs.

"How much?" asked Thorne.

The Navajo woman, understanding English, replied, "Thirty
five dollars."

"Too much!" said Manby promptly. "Don't buy it!"

"But I want it!" said Mrs. Thorne.

"Still, if it's too much, maybe we shouldn't," said Thorne
cautiously.

"Thirty five dollars!" the Navajo woman insisted.

"Let's go!" interposed Manby, taking Mrs. Thorne by the
arm. "These damned Indians always ask too much!" Down the
street he added, "I know how to deal with the buggers. I'll
get it for you and ship it."

Mrs. Thorne showed her disappointment by a huffy manner that did not escape her husband. He bought her two other small, cheap throw-rugs down the road.

A week after the Thornes had left, Manby wrote the doctor: "Patience rewarded at last... I succeeded in buying you the lovely white robe for twenty-six dollars—one of the most delicate designs I've seen in many years. I have shipped it with the other two you bought to Connecticut." He added that the postage was $3.23.

A short note came back; Thorne had thought Manby was not going to succeed in his negotiations, but his manner of handling the matter had been correct. Mrs. Thorne was delighted.

Manby too was encouraged by the firm basis established for their friendship. It did not occur to him that a multi-millionaire financier so anxious to get nine dollars the best of a Navajo woman who had spent six months or more weaving her blanket, would not jump too quickly at any new proposition Manby could offer.

Fall set in with its cold rains, mud, discomforts, and more pressing debts. Then came the day, just a year and a half after Nellie Gray had given up the grant, when the last screw on Manby's torture rack was given its final twist. It was January 15, 1921. Watson had organized the Antonio Martinez Grant as the Watson Land Company, and its certificate of incorporation was issued that day. Manby read it carefully. The company was authorized a capital stock of $500,000, to be issued in 5,000 shares with a par value of $100, including 250 shares of preferred stock. There were three incorporators: Watson, with 980 shares, including all the preferred stock, William J. Barker with ten shares, and George M. Neel of Santa Fe with ten shares. The war was over; the country was entering the boom period of the twenties; and Watson evidently had encountered no difficulty in raising plenty of money. The capital stock paid up to start business amounted to $100,000.[7]

Manby let out one last howl of unendurable anguish which never escaped his lips, and fell headlong into the dark deep prison his tormentors had prepared for him.

In the days and nights that followed the world did not exist. There was only a raging turmoil of subterranean forces whose

walls, shapeless, silent, and pitiless, formed within him a pit
of bottomless despair. A hopeless and helpless and whimpering
creature, he made tea and porridge, tossed sleeplessly in his
grimy blankets. The prison itself ached to break, to set him
free. But it could not; he carried it or it carried him wherever
he went. Only at times a ray of light, a trickle of flowing time,
seeped in.

To escape the pain and misery they brought him, he took to
getting up while it was still dark and trudging to a greasy
loncheria on the plaza. It had five stools set before a stained
oilcloth counter, and one decrepit table in front of the window.
Here he would sit, while his tea steeped in a brown, cracked
pot, watching the dawn. The snowcaps on the mountains would
flush saffron, sassafras, or salmon-pink, the adobe walls would
lighten, a glass window wink. Then the dark well-like plaza
filled with light. He could make out the shapes and signs of
Gerson Gusdorf's "Largest Store in the World Away From a
Railroad," the courthouse, Don Juan Santistevan's two-story
house, Burch's general store, the Columbian Hotel, post office,
and Anastacio Santistevan's saloon, *"El Castillo del Moro."* No
one walked down the boardwalks. No horse nor wagon team
stood at the hitching racks. Deserted as the plaza was, it seemed
impossible that people could be stretched out like logs in their
narrow, hard beds inside the hotel. With the deep sense of unreality that possessed him, he saw the town now for exactly
what it was—a theater-set in which a cast of insubstantial characters played out their habitual, nonsensical roles in a life so
short and trivial that it had no meaning at all. He wondered
what had brought him here and why he had stayed so many
years in this crude and flimsy habitation on a wide and lonely
earth; and this momentary illusion of freedom somehow com-
forted him; it absolved him from the necessity of allowing
himself to be borne by the remorseless flow of time from one
effectual cause to another causal effect; and it left him content
to rest in a shallow eddy on its shore. Suddenly then he remembered the dream, the folly, his lost kingdom; the mountain-
ous walls of his prison rose about him, and within it he could
hear a hurt and frightened little creature begin to whimper.

Then he banged irascibly on his saucer with a tin spoon.
"What do you mean bringing me a cold cup?" he shouted as

the slatternly girl came running. "Hot tea in a cold cup! Almighty God! Blast your manners!"

The scrawny little rabbit of a waitress and the greasy cook with a cigarette stub always glued to his protruding lower lip learned to humor him, warming his cup with hot water before they brought it to him. Manby detested the big, coarse-pored, thick cup even when warm; he felt like a horse with a bit between his teeth whenever he took a sip of his tea. The brew itself was execrable, a cheap, strong leaf without fragrance. Still he kept returning every daybreak for this moment of mindless release between nightmarish night and tortuous day.

Driven from an empty, silent house by a frantic need for some semblance of life, he found himself strangely and paradoxically content to sip his tea alone at the window in a deserted town somewhere on the face of a barren earth, free of passing people, garrulous talk, the sound of strife and worry.

"What did you say, Señor?" the scrawny girl-waitress asked, coming up to his table.

"I said nothing at all!" Manby shouted. "Are you hearing things? Don't disturb me while I'm having my tea!"

He became aware one dawn that the air outside was filling with swirling tufts of cotton. That was strange; there were no cottonwood trees in the plaza. He noticed then that its straggly elm, its few shrub lilacs, were starkly bare of leaves and that the ground was whitening with snow.

But the wintry dawns, with dark blue shadows stealthily creeping back from greyish-green drifts, and the cold mist draped like gauze over the flat rooftops, took on a still more ineffable ghostliness and unreality. Soon the silence was broken by a team and wagon clattering into the icy plaza and drawing up in front of Burch's store. Two Indians sat on the plank seat, a woman and a man, both swathed in cheap red blankets. The hour was too early for the store to open and the distance too far for them to drive back to the pueblo, so they sat waiting behind their scarecrow team, freezing in the bitter cold. There was no need to complain, no need to shiver and blow on their bare, brown-blue hands and beat their bodies with their stiff arms. The cold, like a corrosive, would still eat through their thin cotton blankets. So they just sat there, as Indians sit, patient and enduring.

Two cowpokes rode in, dismounted in front of Anastacio's saloon and beat impatiently on the door with the butts of their revolvers. Tousle-headed and half-asleep, he let them in for an eye-opener. Gusdorf, short and plump, hurried by to open his store before anyone else.

Day had begun. People were coming out. It was time for Manby to return home and make his bowl of porridge.

His prison longed to break and set him free, but it could not. Yet little by little the creature within whimpered less loudly. Manby's delicate mechanism was adjusting itself to a new rhythm. Perhaps the slipped cog had righted itself a little, or the rough edge of the microscopic broken pin wore smooth.

He had lost his grant but not his obsession.

6

In September 1921 Wilkerson reappeared in E-town after his mysterious disappearance five years before. He did not say where he had been or what he had been doing, but he had a great deal of money on him—reportedly $78,000. Outfitting himself in the best clothes the mining camp could produce, including a gray hat, a suit, and a pair of high shoes, he set off in high spirits to Taos.

A number of old-timers, long suspicious of the Mystic, put their heads together and conjectured what had been happening. Wilkerson had bored a tunnel into the closed-up Aztec mine and kept stealing out small quantities of highgrade ore. Ferguson had shipped it, presumably from the non-profitable Mystic, through El Paso into Mexico. Here it was received by Manby who sold it as coming from his Chihuahua mines. Wilkerson apparently had gone down to take Manby's place in Chihuahua while Manby was tied up by business in Taos. Now he was back with the last profits.

Still, his future did not look too bright. Stone, one of the first partners in the Mystic, had been found mysteriously dead. Wilkerson had a bad reputation, Manby was known to be ruthless and unscrupulous, and old Ferguson was failing.

On the evening of September 28 Wilkerson arrived at Teracita's tourist court in Taos. Marguerita Tafoya was working in Teracita's house as a servant girl, helping to take care of old

167

Ferguson and Teracita's several children. She noticed that
Wilkerson was dressed in new clothes and sported a great deal
of money. Soon Manby arrived, followed by a young man named
Flavio Salazar. Marguerita helped to put the children to bed
and then served supper to the grownups: Ferguson, Wilkerson,
Teracita, Manby, and Salazar. Immediately afterward, Teracita
ordered her to go to her own room and not to disturb them.

Waking next morning with a strange uneasiness, Marguerita
noticed a bulky mattress heaped on the floor across the room.
She jumped out of bed, drew aside the mattress. Underneath it
lay the body of Wilkerson with a mass of blood on the left
breast coagulated around a wound stuffed with cotton. Marguerita let out a frightened cry, then burst into tears.

Manby and Teracita ran in. "Shut up and quit crying!"
Manby ordered, his bloodshot eyes blazing. "This is none of
your business!"

Shortly afterward Flavio Salazar came and carried the body
out to a pickup. Marguerita was not sure, but she believed
Manby and Ferguson drove away with him.

The house was never the same to Marguerita after that. She
was frightened and dared not talk. Old Ferguson got steadily
worse. He couldn't sleep, and when he did he woke everybody
up screaming something about Wilkerson's head. Before long
some men came and took him to the insane asylum at Las Vegas.
Here he was kept for several months. Then he returned to live
at Teracita's tourist camp, a white-headed mumbling old man.[1]

Hardly two weeks after Wilkerson's reported murder, Manby
scribbled a short note to Thorne: "For the last few days the
weather has been simply gorgeous, and the shades of silver,
green, and gold in the drives and walks, with the purple mountains peeping through, gives the impression of a wonderland."[2]

He noticed more than the weather. More artists were moving
into town, buying land, building homes and studios. One of
them, he found out, was John Young-Hunter of Glasgow, Scot-
land, the son of a noted marine painter, who had studied at the
British Royal Academy with Sargent and had become a portrait
painter of distinction. Coming to America, he established a
studio in New York and was now building a home here in which
to spend the summers. The site he had picked irked Manby.
It was off Canyon Road, just past Teracita's tourist camp, on

a wide expanse of sagebrush facing the mountains. Moreover it was right on the Boulevard Manby had projected to encircle the valley.

Grinding his teeth with rage, Manby rode out there often— only to discover something worse. Out in the sagebrush in back of the house Young-Hunter was building a great studio modelled after a Scottish baronial hall. Manby rode back to Teracita, storming. "Preposterous! A baronial hall! Right on my Boulevard! The upstart! The insult!"

"Never mind," said Teracita. "The time will come when you can get even."

Ward Lockwood and his wife Clyde came, remodelling into a home and studio an old Penitente *morada* on the Loma. "They've got a German shepherd," Manby reported to Teracita. "Just exactly like those I use for my watchdogs. What do you suppose that means? It makes me suspicious."

Then came Nicolai Fechin, a great portrait painter who had escaped from Bolshevik Russia. He and his wife Alexandra, or Tinka as she was more familiarly called, wanted a homesite too. The site they picked was just past Manby's house. Here Fechin built a huge, two-story, Russian-style house, carving all the woodwork himself. The incessant hammering and pounding, the lumbering of trucks passing by, almost drove Manby crazy.

Then one afternoon Tinka came to see him. She was a small and vital woman, very Russian, whose English was hard to understand. Still Manby could make out that she wanted to buy a small piece of his land.

"What for?" he demanded angrily.

Apparently Fechin wanted to build himself a separate studio behind the house. With room, she added, for an outdoor bath.

"A bath!" snorted Manby.

Tinka patiently explained. Her Russian husband was a strange man. He liked to get up early in the morning, run outside naked, and dive into cold water. *Russo*. No?

"A swimming pool!" shouted Manby. "No!"[3]

But he was desperate for cash and sold her a few acres. The sale hurt him. Why, not long ago he could look from the plaza to Placita, a mile away, across his own land in town. And now they were moving in on him, squeezing out acre after acre!

He hurriedly wrote Thorne to do something about his Van

Eyck and Van Dyke paintings. The reason he gave was that he did not want the paintings here, for they made the work of local artists suffer by comparison.

Becoming aware that his rheumatism was worse, he took to carrying a cane and began to wear an iron ring for which he had sent to Germany; it possessed medicinal properties that obviated the necessity of his going to that damned rascal, Doc Martin. Then his straggly, discolored teeth began to ache with a pain that seemed to split his skull. This drove him at last to Dr. Fred Muller.

The first appearance in town of Saca Muelas, the tooth-puller, did not augur his unqualified success. Twenty-four years old and fresh from a dental school in Kansas, he breezed into Taos wearing a double-breasted suit and a new chocolate-brown derby. A welcoming society promptly escorted him to a saloon, filling him with compliments and Taos Lightning until he was too genial to care. Then they ripped the buttons off his double-breasted coat, smashed in his derby and thrust it through a point of a deer's antlers mounted over the bar.[4]

Young Muller bowed to the tradition of a flannel shirt, sloppy trousers, and a medium-sized Stetson.

Pulling teeth was not at first a lucrative business. To make ends meet, he bought a hearse, rented a team to pull it on due occasions, and took up undertaking as a sideline. Not content with this, he joined editor Jose Montaner in running a movie and dancehall in Montaner Hall. Saca Muelas played the slide trombone or bass horn for every dance, and obliged during every fiesta.

Manby had no use for a man who indulged such frivolities, yet Saca Muelas began to prosper. As there was no electricity, he rigged up a portable Singer sewing machine operated by a foot pedal so he could drill teeth and shape inlays. With this in his buckboard, he made the rounds of the small Spanish villages.

His reputation was made when he mounted four gold teeth in one side of a sheepherder's jaw, two above and two directly below. The sheepherder came back a few months later. "Señor Saca Muelas," he said beaming, "these gold teeth are so good for castrating my lambs and cutting wire, I please have four more other side!"

Manby was not so convinced of Muller's skill when he grump-
ily slumped down in the canvas dentist chair and spit nervously
into the tall brass cuspidor beside it. Nor was he relieved when
Muller, after one look inside his mouth, said cheerfully, "Those
old snags! They ought to have come out long ago. Never mind.
I'll fix you some dentures that'll make a new man of you, Mr.
Manby!"

"I don't want false teeth!" growled Manby. "I want this
pain stopped!"

Muller ignored his protestations. "Here's how I do it." He
showed Manby a set of false teeth shipped from a dental supply
house—sixteen crude molars in sets of four each, and twelve
single front teeth. "Now all I have to do is whittle them down
to size and mount them in vulcanized rubber. Like this!" He
sat down at his Singer sewing machine, pumped the foot pedal,
and began to polish one of the single teeth.

"How much?" asked Manby.

Muller pushed Manby's head back, gave him a shot of cocaine,
then daintily sterilized his forceps by holding them in a wisp
of steam rising from a water kettle boiling on the woodstove.

"How much, damn you!" yelled Manby.

"Not one word, Mr. Manby! I've got to yank out those old
snags before the anesthetic wears off!"

The tedious process took three weeks. There were many
interruptions. One of the callers was Toribio, a rather backward
resident of town whom Saca Muelas had presented with a key-
winding watch. Promptly at two o'clock every day Toribio
would come to the office and proudly present the watch to Muller
who would gravely take down the key from its nail and wind
the watch. He would then give Toribio a glass of water with
a sugar pill. Toribio, himself and his watch wound up for the
day, would then leave in high humor.[5]

Saca Muelas would resume pumping his treadle, shaping and
polishing Manby's teeth, while Manby, grinding his toothless
gums at the dentist's constant talking and whistling, watched
him with a growing, secret admiration for his skill. He was
sharp, shrewd, and amazingly dexterous.

"You're a good hand with that drill, Muller," he admitted
grudgingly.

"None better, Mr. Manby! I can grind bone, shape the ivories, engrave pictures on steel if I have to!"

"You ought to be a counterfeiter, then," said the old man.

"Why not? If a rich and clever man like you has any good jobs, bring 'em around!"

Manby gave him a curious look, but did not reply. The finished dentures fit in his mouth as well as could be expected, but he noticed that the corner of one molar was slightly chipped.

"My foot must have slipped on the treadle," said Muller casually.

"It's an imperfect job!" accused Manby. "I want some money back!"

"I'll take off two dollars, Mr. Manby, but you owe me two more for the identification mark if you ever lose 'em!"

The argument ended in another of Manby's rages. He stalked out the door shouting, "Cheat! Mountebank! Damned robber!"

Just the same he often recalled a certain look on Saca Muelas' face he could not explain, but which seemed vaguely familiar.

Manby's teeth were not his only cause for trouble. Miss Margaret Waddell's suit for breach of promise and fraudulent securing of capital from her was still dogging his heels. Several years before, she had gone to A. B. Renehan, a lawyer in Santa Fe, who agreed that a suit against Manby should be filed. It would be expensive. Miss Waddell managed to scrape up the $2,300 he demanded, then waited week after week for him to do something. Finally she went to another lawyer, F. C. Wilson, who took $350 from her but did nothing. In despair she began searching for another. At last, in 1916, the case came up in court. She was awarded by the jury a judgment of $16,700. Federal Judge E. H. Pope reduced this to $7,000 and denied Manby a new trial.

Two years later she was still unable to collect. Manby had been too shrewd. As president of the still-existent Colonial Bond and Security Company, he had transferred the 49,990 shares he owned of its total 50,000 shares to Teracita whom he had named vice-president of the company. Princess Teracita! The only human being he had ever truly loved.

Miss Waddell went to court again on November 19, 1918. Federal Judge Colin Neblett ordered seizure of Manby's property to satisfy the judgment with accumulated interest. And again there was no way to collect; Manby had lost the Martinez

Grant. Miss Waddell returned to San Francisco where she became ill with a heart complaint brought on by poverty and worry. Still she had not given up hope, for now again she was back in court demanding jugdment.[6]

If the whole world kept pressing in on Manby, he was delighted by a turmoil among Indian, Spanish, and Anglo residents alike that raised the question of just who owned not only the Martinez Grant but the whole valley.

The Commissioner of Indian Affairs came from Washington to attend a Council meeting at the pueblo. Here he curtly informed the Indians that their native religion made them "half animals," and forbade them to withdraw their boys from school for tribal instruction in their sacred underground kivas. When the old men refused to comply, the commissioner ordered the whole Council thrown into the town jail for violating the religious crimes code.

Manby, walking back and forth in front of the jail, could have howled with glee. Those damned, secretive, and pagan Indians at last had got what was coming to them!

The old Council members, finally released by the federal district court under the press of public indignation, began to clamor for the return of their land. They demanded all their own Pueblo Grant, part of which had been infringed upon by Spanish settlers. They wanted back that piece of the Martinez Grant known as the Tenorio Tract, which the court had ruled belonged to Manby. They claimed, in fact, that the very ground upon which stood the town of Taos was rightfully theirs.

Mrs. Mabel Luhan gave filip to the hue and cry by filing suit against the "purported village of Taos," claiming that neither the incorporation of the village nor the election of its officers was legal.[7] Even a member of the national Congress agreed that there was not a single town or business lot in Taos where the legal title was vested in the white man.

Over this mammoth absurdity, over all this hue and cry, Manby chortled. But standing in his weedy garden and staring north and west towards evening, he heard those blasted Indian drums beating again in the big communal pasture beyond his fence. Slow, soft, and measured, the beat echoed the volcanic pulse of the mysterious mountain beyond. And suddenly, despite himself, something within him attuned itself to the pulsing voice of that dimensionless and immortal earth that had never and would never have a master. Let man scratch twelve inches of its surface with his plow, mine a few hundred feet with a jack-hammer. Upon it let rise the obelisks and pyramids, the tall towers and proud cities of countless civilizations. Let rains and rivers carve channels down its leathery hide, and the angry tides of the swelling seas beat and lash at its rocky shores. Always like bedrock it stood firmly resistant to inner quakes and outward blows that sought to cleave its unity. Oh, wide and naked and timeless earth, great mother of all that existed for their brief lives upon her succulent breast! Oh, little mote of dust that whirled for its own brief time through eternity! Whose was the illusion that a worm could claim an infinitesimal burrow as its own domain, that a man could plat and register fee simple title to an acre of the topsoil of its immeasurable depth? For the earth, that mighty and eternal earth which was but a speck of stardust revolving ceaselessly about a luminescent solar hub, was not a chunk of matter to be divided, subdivided, fenced, sold, and resold. It did not exist as matter. Surcharged as was its every single stone, it was a mass of creative energy, dormant and unawakened, waiting but to be freed of its fleshly form. Vibrantly pulsating, its waves beat at his temples, pounded into his bloodstream.

And then, as suddenly, they stopped. Manby came to himself. An intolerable rhythm, those blasted Indian drums! No matter! Time and events were conspiring to restore title to his lost kingdom to him. His gaze leaped past the blood-red shape of the mountain and the gray-green sage to span the high mesa stretching toward the sinking, reddening sun. The land was still there—still his! A little hazy himself now about his often transferred titles and many claims, he went back into the sprawling old house, lit a lamp, and scribbled in his diary that he now owned 245,000 acres—or was it 745,000 acres?

A little vague as he might be at times, Manby's sharp and brilliant mind, like a clock suddenly shaken, started ticking again on a new and last venture—a full development of his hot springs on the Rio Grande. This, after everything else that had failed, would restore to him the Martinez Grant.

7

Next to the Martinez Grant, Manby loved the hot springs named after him. Perhaps he loved the springs more; for if the grant was in reality only a nebulous domain, a projection of his imperialistic dream of empire, there was nothing nebulous about the hot springs. Submerged in their hot and healing waters, he felt his tired body losing its tenseness, his nerves relaxing, his tortured mind clearing. The wild and lonely canyon reflected his own nature. He could hear an eagle scream high overhead, watch a solitary hawk floating noiselessly and without movement across the dark chasm. For twenty years it had been his place of refuge, and now, sixty-three years old, he poured into his plans for its development the last of his strength and feelings.

Manby was a thorough worker, and his mind cleared and sharpened for the task. To begin with, he compiled a long history of the springs.

Known among the Indians as *Wa-pu-mee*, the Spring of Life, he wrote, they had been visited since antiquity by natives who made long journeys to drink and bathe in the waters. Many cures of nervous and intestinal troubles had been attributed to the waters. They were especially beneficial to those persons suffering from rheumatism, particularly in relation to ossification of the joints which the waters eliminated from the system; they dissolved lime from the arteries which brought about premature old age, and thus established their claim as the Spring of Life.

The legend of the Pueblos, Manby went on, related that Montezuma was born on the headwaters of the Rio Grande. Subsequently it was revealed to him that by the will of the Great Father that he, Montezuma, was to become ruler of the people; that he should follow the great eagle to the south and found the city of Mecitl, whence he should return again provided the Pueblos kept burning the sacred fires in their underground kivas. To this day the fires were still kept burning in anticipation of his return.

The legend of the Aztecs according to Spanish historians, continued Manby, was that Mecitl or Tenochtitlan, now Mexico City, was indeed founded in 1125 by a people who had journeyed far from the north. They had come from Aztlan, near which city were to be found the springs of perpetual youth. Many Spanish expeditions were made to discover these springs which were sought as far north as Santa Fe. The expeditions resulted in the occupation of New Mexico, bounded on the north by the sierra of Taos in full view of the springs.

Recent discoveries west of the Rio Lucero had been made of many *tumuli* or mounds, and of long rows of rocks resembling foundations of streets of houses which were thought to be ruins of the ancient city of the Aztecs. To the west of these ruins lay the *Wa-pu-mee* hot springs, flowing between large rocks on which were inscribed old Aztec carvings signifying perpetual life.

Two of these inscribed symbols, one to the north and one to the south of the spring, Manby sketched in his paper. He then recorded the temperature of the water as 98 degrees Fahrenheit, the flow of the spring as one-half cubic foot per second, and an analysis of its chemical components.

"Should it develop," he concluded, "that these springs are the long lost springs of the Aztecs, and the fact coupled with history seems to indicate such a belief is well founded, then these springs, located as they are amid magnificent scenery, and the bright sunshine of New Mexico, should ultimately develop into one of the world's greatest resorts."

Hardly had he sent this off to Dr. Thorne than another promoter, Dr. Rankin S. Reiff, showed up and offered Manby $80,000 for his house and estate in town and the hot springs with 500 adjoining acres, provided he could interest a group of oil and cotton men in Texas. Manby rushed a letter to

Thorne saying that if Reiff could pay $80,000 and spend $100,000 in development, the owner had the advantage. Manby preferred to sell; he needed the money. "Now if you could only find a purchaser for my Van Dyck masterpiece!" he wailed suggestively.

An answer came right back: "Don't lease the hot springs to Dr. Reiff who only offered $1,000 a year rental with option to purchase. I am not particularly flush at present, but will see to it you have $1,000."

Thorne was interested! He was on the hook! Pleased and excited, Manby now settled down to develop plans and drawings for a levee wall along the river, conversion of his present bathhouse into a reservoir, construction of a swimming pool and dressing rooms. There would be a small country inn above, with stables and tennis courts. He also revised his plans for the large hotel in Taos, to which water from the hot springs could be piped to supply guests.

Late in February he sent Thorne his tentative plans. "They are simply evolved from their natural environments and local material. It is cheap to build here—8¢ per cubic foot." He suggested issuing preferred stock in blocks of 25,000 each. "The vendor must look to his profits in the common stock issued to him in lieu of cash for his property. This will keep down capitalization and avoid bonds and protect the vendor. Probably we will have to provide $25,000 of preferred stock for commissions to whoever placed the $100,000 of preferred stock. It works out as follows: to investor, $100,000 of preferred stock; to commissions, $25,000 preferred stock; to vendor, $25,000 plus all common stock; total $150,000. These days it is a case of sink or swim—anyway poor policy to sit still and see others doing things and making money."

A week later he suggested capitalizing for $250,000—2,500 shares at $100 per share. This would provide $100,000 cash for development, $25,000 to be expended on bathhouses, and $25,000 in the hotel above, with $50,000 placed in the treasury for running expenses. He also mentioned that although he was in pressing need of funds, he had written to Mr. Whittemore in Denver about testing the radium emissions from the water.

A few days later he sent in the testimony of four men who had been cured by the water of the hot springs: Mr. Armstrong

LA BAJADA HOT SPRINGS

Taos County, New Mexico.

Containing 2,000 acres, confirmed by United States Congress
March 3, 1869, and title finally decreed to owner by the District Court
June 18, 1915.

Known among the Indians as Wa-pu-mee, signifying the Spring of Life,
are located in the beautiful Canyon of the Rio Grande in Taos County,
and about eleven miles northwest of the picturesque old Plaza of
Don Fernando de Taos, in the heart of the Sangre de Cristo Mountains.
Very little is known to the general public about these springs, due
no doubt, to the fact that the title has only recently been perfected to
the owner, and also due to the fact that these springs are off the railroad,
and are chiefly patronized by the natives, who make long journeys
overland to bathe and drink the waters. Many marvelous cures are
attributed to the use of these waters in cases of nervousness and intestinal troubles, which cover about ninety per cent of the human ailments.
These springs have to their credit many wonderful cures of rheumatism,
particularly in relation to the ossification of the joints, which the
free use of these waters eliminate from the system. This has led to the
claim that these waters will renew youth by dissolving lime from the
arteries, which brings about premature old age; so, that after all, the
claims made by the ancient Aztecs to the early Spanish conquerors, of
the existance of wonderful life giving springs, many days journey to
the north of Tenochitlan (Mexico), may yet be found to be based on
something more than myth.

The Legend of the Pueblos

Is that Montezuma was born on the head-waters of the Rio Grande,
within the Tegua Pueblo, born of a Virgin, who was given a pinion to
eat, and by the will of the Great Spirit, conceived and bore a man
child, who suffered in poverty, and by the will of the Great Father
became the Ruler of the people, and subsequently married the Zuni
maiden, Malinche, and made her queen, and thereafter it was revealed
to him that he should follow the great eagle to the south and found
the city of Mecitil (now Mexico) whence he should return again, provided the Pueblos kept alive the sacred fires in their Estufas, and
which to this day are still kept burning in anticipation of his
promised return.

The Legend of the Aztecs

As related by the early Spanish Historians, is that they founded
Mecitil on Tenochitlan (now Mexico) about the year 1125, having
come from the great city of Aztlan, many days journey to the north,
and that near this city were to be found the springs of perpetual
youth. Spanish history tells us that many expeditions were out-
fitted by the early Spaniards to discover these springs, which were
sought as far north as Santa Fe, and resulted in the final occupation of
New Mexico, bounded on the north by Sierra of Taos, and Rancherias
in view thereof.

Recent Discoveries

Show that west of the Rio Lucero, in Taos County, are many
Tumuli, or mounds, also long rows of rocks, resembling foundations
of houses, streets, etc., which are thought to be the ruins of Aztlan
the ancient city of the Aztecs - while to the west of these old ruins
are to be found the Wa-pu-mee Hot Springs, flowing between large rocks,
on which are inscribed old Aztec carvings, signifying perpetual life.

These carvings are in semi-bass relief, are weather worn and indicate great antiquity.

Should it develop these springs are the long lost springs of the Aztecs, and the fact coupled with history seems to indicate that such a belief is well founded, then these springs, located as they are, amid magnificient scenery, and the bright sunshine of New Mexico, should ultimately develop into one of the world's greatest resorts.

ANALYSIS OF SPRING NO. 1

Parts in mil   Flow 1/2 cubic foot per second

Potassium Chloride	31.5
Sodium "	77.8
Sodium Sulphate	195.9
Calcium Bicarbonate	120.5
Silica	65.7
Magnesium Bicarbonate	40.3
Sodium Bicarbonate	139.5

Temperature Farh.   98 degrees
Very strong radium activity.
Flow 1/2 cu.ft. per second.

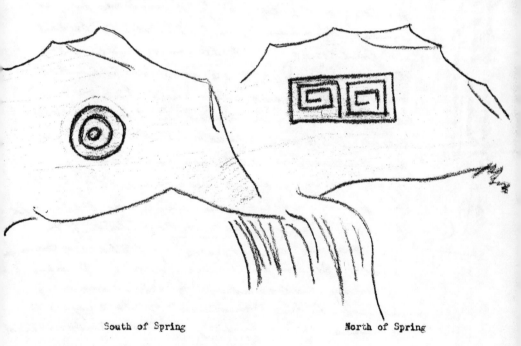

South of Spring   North of Spring

Above sketch shows two old Aztec inscriptions on each side of Spring, signifying perpetual life. W.

Two-page typescript of Manby's history of "La Bajada Hot Springs," and chemical analysis of the waters. It contains a pencil sketch of two ancient Indian markings which appear on the sides of the spring.

E 4 I

Rio Grande Hot Springs.

with 1½ miles of frontage to the Rio Grande and 1.500 acres of land. as decreed by US Court 6-18-15. with taxes paid in full upto Jan 1920 —.   procedure

Capitalize in 2500 shares @ $100⁰⁰ per share - non liability. fully paid & non assessable = $250.000 —

Issue $150.000 shares of first preferred stock @ 7% interest payable semi annually — to be distributed as follows — $100.000 cash for development. $25.000. the expended on Bath House etc. and $25.000 to be expended in Hotel in valley alone. $50.000 placed in the Treasury for running expenses. etc — $25.000 of said Treasury stock to be paid as commission or brokerage in obtaining above capital. x x

a Bonus of 1 Share of Common Stock $100⁰⁰ par value - will be given to every subscriber of the Treasury stock to the amount of every 50 shares of Treasury stock subscribed

Two-page handwritten letter from Manby to Dr. V. C. Thorne, dated March 7, 1922, which outlines Manby's plan for capitalizing the "Rio Grande Hot Springs."

at a par value of $100⁰⁰

vendor agrees to accept $25.000
of said Treasury stock – plus balance
of common stock in payment
of property – giving the privilage
of the holders of the preferred stock
to purchase same at par value
should same be at any time be for
sale —.
                    A.R.Manley.

Taos N.M.
3 – 7 – 22 –

                Referring to the attitude of
New York investors in Bonds and
Industrials – It would be advisable if they
would take into consideration first
as to Bonds – The inflation of currency
in Relation to papers which stands about
50 to one of gold – and which grafting
recklessly piling up – politicians without regard to
Redemption. Query what is the
breaking point. The U.S. Treasurers
announced Feb 11th 1922 – that the Public
debt now stands at 23. Billion dollars
with 6½ Billion due within 17 months – ///

                American Industrials
     The value of these securities carry
doubtful future values – due the vagaries
of Tariff. and politicians on one side
     with labour troubles on the other ///

Note the relationship proposition is unique
from these elements of fact – this license or
public right being deben interested with the
account of the value and annuel of the way
and only for this purpose and they so elect
X

of Liberal, Kansas was in dreadful condition, having been unable to eat and sleep but little for years. He filled two bottles
of one gallon each at the spring, one of which he broke, and
the other he drank. Within a week he was eating and sleeping
as well as anyone ... John Foote, a miner at Copper Hill, could
not eat, walk, or even stand up, and it was thought he could
live but a few days. Mr. Turner, the mine manager, sent him to
the springs. In about sixty days he was back at work again, well
and strong as ever ... James Sothers was just another such
case ... Bert Phillips, the Taos artist, was also in bad shape with
stomach trouble. He drank two gallons of this water and got well.

Thorne replied to this mass of information with a brief and
cautious note saying that he would show Manby's plans to
anyone he happened to run across who might be interested, adding: "I will finance Whittemore in Denver to go to Taos and
take samples of the water. It will cost me $150 but it is a good
gamble."

The report on the water samples showed that each of the
three springs contained from 57 to 168 grams of radium per
liter. What did this mean? Through his Radium Company,
Thorne arranged for the chemistry department of Yale University to run more tests. The report to him was brief: "Results of
the examination of specimens of water from Mr. Manby's springs
are interesting. The radioactivity of the waters is of about the
average order of magnitude for cold spring water; the waters
are not conspicuously radioactive ... As a general rule the
activity of hot springs is lower than the activity of cold springs
because of the fact that radium emanation is much less soluble
in hot water than in cold water."

Manby meanwhile was pressing hard. He was having difficulty
keeping up with taxes, owing $300 back taxes for two years on
his house and $200 for three years on his hot springs. "Do you
think it possible to get a loan of a few thousand on the Van
Dyck?" he asked. Thorne refused him, referring him to local
banks. Manby wrote back that he was unable to find in the
West any money for development.

Undeterred, he made an outright appeal. "I would like to
include you with me in developing the project. The property has
a perfect title, with a mile-and-a-half river frontage, and 1,500
acres—1,000 of this, fine farming land. Ultimately most of this

land will be occupied as a townsite with parks etc. Am enclosing
a sketch—showing a riverside drive. Would like quick action:
first, I am getting along in years; second, people should realize
there is such a big thing out here."

He followed this with a long letter containing a beautifully
drawn and crayon-colored sketch map of the hot springs tract
of 1,500 acres with its mile-and-a-half river frontage, showing
how it bounded the Martinez Grant on the southwest corner—
"the Martinez Grant which I formerly owned *and still claim*,"
he added significantly; also an ink profile of the spectacular one-
thousand-foot-deep gorge of the Rio Grande. On the map he
marked out five springs, including the one in the river which
he had discovered years before while standing on the rim of
the gorge.

It was quite possible that the small-boned, quick-witted Dr.
Thorne with $11,000,000 in trust had never, in his entire finan-
cial history, encountered a promoter with such prolific ideas for
making money. Five days later he received another proposition
from Manby:

"It has been my purpose all along to stake you in with me
to one-third of a big gold mine in the Navajo Reserve, papers
of which with the survey were turned over to me by my old
Mexican friend Jose Leon Mondvajon, now dead. Many years
ago when I was flush I helped him just as you have helped me,
and he entrusted me with everything a year or two before he
died.

"It would take too long to go into the full history of this:
the killing of the old man and capture of his daughter by
Apaches who sold her into slavery, and who sixty years after
took my friend to his place who managed to break off a piece
of the cropping before the Navajos descended on him and ran
him off, and which sample he had assayed and which showed
$17,000 per ton surface cropping ... Of course there may be
nothing to it, and for which reason I would like to investigate
at my own time and expense."

To afford this expense, if Dr. Thorne were interested, something would have to be done about—yes, the Van Dyck. "Farina
had my 'St. Catherine' for over a month and submitted it to
every test known, and pronounced it a genuine Van Dyck
masterpiece. This painting is inspired in colors and grouping

from Titian's 'Holy Family,' which Van Dyck studied in Italy and known as his Genoa inspiration ... In view of the money market we may not obtain more than $30,000. In the event of a possible sale, I would expect you to deduct at least $10,000 of this sum for yourself in order to pay in small part your many kindnesses. Should a loan be affected I would not care to come down on $7,000.

"If this could be arranged I would pay you back the $1,000 you so kindly loaned me recently, which after paying up everything would leave me with $4,000 clear ... It will be agreeable to me that you bring to New York both paintings in the vaults of the Phil. Trust Co. if you know of any place where you think they could be safely hung.

"In this event probably Prof. Farina would clean up the Van Dyck which should have a plate glass placed on it ..."

It was now the middle of the summer and Manby had been doing nothing for months except sitting at his cluttered desk and composing epistles to Dr. Thorne. Now he was getting writer's cramp. The financier, friendly as he was, had not evinced monetary enthusiasm, or any other kind, for raising sheep on the La Bajada tract, mining copper on Copper Mountain, cutting timber, exploring for oil and a secret gold lode on the Navajo Reserve, building a hotel in Taos, developing the hot springs into a famous world-wide resort, or even buying or selling the Van Dyck.

The Neiff deal too had fallen through. Victor Morowitz, former chairman of the board of directors of the Atchinson, Topeka and Santa Fe Railroad who had visited Manby some time ago, also had shown some interest in the hot springs but had done nothing about it.

"Mr. Morawitz (sic), like most German Jews," Manby wrote bitterly, "leans to operations in Bonds and Stocks in Wall Street. Some day they will have a rude awakening when the people demand that their ten thousand millions invested in these securities be made to pay taxes and share in the general burden of taxation ... You see I write straight off the reel, just as I think."

Manby's peaceful dawns, when he was briefly and miraculously lifted from the flowing stream of time to sit at ease in a quiet eddy on its shore, had ended. The current had caught him

Taos N. M
May 9ᵗʰ
1922

E
B

21

My dear Dr Thorne

Yrs of 4ᵗʰ with map Received
The long tail appendage along the
Rio Grande — & South of the Rio Grande
that Springs tract. is that portion of
los Luceros grant which did not
conflict with his martinez grant.
The martinez grant which I formerly
owned & still claim — was made
by the viceroy of Spain in 1716 —
The los Luceros grant in 1742 —
without prejudice to 3ᵈ parties —

Rio Hondo

N.W cor of a the grant
or
mounds on
plat —
point over I looked down in 1908.
from which I looked down
mesa

martinez grant

1716.

Rio Grande

2 Spanish leagues

W S

x

south line of the Leroux grant in
conflict with the martinez grant which I
knocked out

at A

A on West Bank of Rio Grande / is a small lake
warm Spring with slow flow as thick as a pencil
and is submerged most of the time by the Rio Grande
all the other Springs known are on the
East side of the Rio Grande on our land

B at point B is a very big Spring of cold
water - marked on Sketch map sent you

C Is a fine cold Spring. close to the
water's edge - visable only when River
is low - This water is rich & very
delicious —

D are the Rio Grande Hot Springs with
strong Radio activity.

E abt Two miles below Bath House etc —
at point marked E. are strong springs
to the River - said to be Hot - but are only
visable when the Rio Grande is low — These
I saw from the Top of the mesa in Aug. 1908
there are also on our land —

Three-page handwritten letter from Manby to Thorne, dated
May 9, 1922, describing the Hot Springs. It contains two drawings: one in colored crayon of the location, and one ink drawing
of the profile of the Rio Grande gorge.

Los Luceros or LeRoux grant as
his junior grant — I fought all
parts in conflict into his Martinez
grant — The part colored green
was decreed by the Court. in cause
820 — June 18ᵗʰ 1915. this was not
in conflict with with his Martinez grand.
the west & north boundary of which
is marked by Red Line —

The Survey of his Martinez grand
on which his patent was issued May 8
1896 did not include his cañon
of his Rio Grande. marked purple —

This tail like apendage. I hold
under old deeds & tax title
This gives me 6 Spanish miles or
about 5½ statute miles frontage to
his Rio Grande — from his middle
of the current — i.e. 1½ miles frontage
to River as decreed and 4 miles
caudal appendage confirmed by all.

There is only one way of
getting down to his River from
his mesa — namely by our private

of Congress — as his twicet boundary of Los Luceros grants
to which did not conflict with his survey of his
Senior grant made & running in 1716 —

Road   and over our property —

mesa   mesa
                                        our road above
                                1000 feet

. the canon is very steep and narrow below
the Hot Springs — . En 1908. Looking from
the Top of the mesa — I noticed clear running springs
close to the edge — but could not get down to them
I intended later to investigate — but something
or other interfered with my doing so — personally
I do not know whether they are hot or cold or
have any medicinal values — but whatever
they are they are on our property — X.
            which gives us two leagues frontage
to the Rio Grande — and the best
fishing in the State —
            If this is not quite
clear to you I will send you
the U.S. official survey which
shows how the Luceros grant
in part lapped on the Jarales grant
            very truly yrs
                    R. R. Manley

Note — under act of Congress how the boundary bound by
c land owners of grants are usually easily found .... copies
the survey — after the Lapse of 10 years [confirmed 1879] 1909
pat having from May 8, 1896;
March 3 1869 (15 stat 342) 2nd survey

again, engulfing him in a maelstrom of worry and anxiety. He awoke bathed in sweat, feeling the walls of his prison engulfing him; the pressure of his debts increasing; and beyond all this, the world closing in on him—the world that would soon be brought to a disastrous end after a War in the Air.

The certainty of this impending catastrophe did not prevent him, however, from observing that the town was crowded with automobiles from different parts of the country and the motels couldn't take care of them. "We are missing $50 a day," he complained to Thorne in July. He then came down to the brass tacks of immediate reality. The two paintings were still in the the vault at Philadelphia. He could not raise money to pay Farina for the necessary restoration, and Farina could not afford to do it on a contingency basis of being paid when the Van Dyck was sold. This was disastrous as Manby had been counting on the sale of one or both of the pictures to pay off his debts. Therefore he would be willing to give a note and chattel mortgage for $6,000 in order to pay his debt to Thorne and taxes and mortgage on the property next to his house which amounted to about $3,000. Failure to do so would result in the property being sold under foreclosure on August 11.

Thorne was never in a hurry. He simply returned the prospectus of the Don Fernando Inn, the name Manby had finally selected for his Taos hotel, and the sketch plans for the hot springs resort, with the practical suggestion that Manby erect an economical retaining wall at the river's edge and fix up the road a bit.

This gave Manby something to do. Every morning he hired a man to drive him out to the springs over the rutty dirt road that would require $1,500 to fix up, and pace off along the river's edge the extent of a retaining wall that could be built cheaply for $10,000. Then while the driver patiently waited a thousand feet above, eating his lunch, Manby would go into the little stone bathhouse, take off his clothes, and step gingerly into the pool of hot water. Immersed to his neck, he could feel the heat, the chemicals, and radioactivity soaking through his flesh into the very marrow of his bones. "We read of millions spent to rejuvenate men and women with monkey glands," he wrote later. "I maintain that removing calcerous deposits and building up healthy tissue by secretions of glands, the aged become restored. Of the secret glands controlling the genital organs, the stomach, brain, etc., little is known. These hot springs are good for this." So now he could feel the secret glands in his old, worn body being stimulated, coming to life. His jumpy nerves relaxed. His mind, that usually wound-up clock, ran down.

It was a strange place, this subterranean vault at the bottom of a river gorge deep below the surface of the mesa. There was no light save a faint diffusion of daylight through a hole in the wall above him, clouded by a veil of steam. Through the clear water he could glimpse his outhrust leg, an arm; they looked like pale fish-shapes, undersea monsters, that never came to surface. Listening closely, he believed he could hear the spring bubbling slowly up from the sand below, the wash of the river outside. Perhaps it was only his imagination. It was so quiet! An eerie silence like that of a tomb, of a mysterious labyrinth to which he had somehow found the key. How ancient it was, too. The steamy sides of the rock walls seemed to reflect the outlines, like faded mural paintings, of the generations of Aztecs and Pueblos who had come here to this sacred spring of eternal life.

And now he was beginning to lose perspective, and the heat was making him weak and dizzy. Laboriously he crawled out, dried himself with a towel, put on his clothes. Once outside again, he felt like a new man. Squatting down in the bright sunlight, he ate the lunch he had brought in a paper sack for strength to carry him up the steep trail.

Then came a morning in November when his driver did not show up. The sky was overcast with clouds; a storm was gathering. By night, snow fell. Winter was beginning, and his trips to the springs were over.

In December he wrote Thorne again. Farina was now of the opinion that the "St. Agnes" had been painted by Flinck, a Flemish painter born in 1615, and who had become Rembrandt's best pupil. Restoration work on both pictures would cost about $240, but Manby did not have the money to pay him.

Thorne, beset by troubles of his own and now in Toronto, Canada, did not reply. Still cautious, he referred the matter to H. E. Bishop of his Radium Company at 244 Madison Avenue, New York. Early in August Bishop wrote Thorne that he had seen Professor Farina who considered the "St. Catherine" a real Van Dyck. The "St. Agnes" was a beautiful and fine picture which he now believed had been painted by Flinck. Necessary restoration work would take two months and cost about three hundred and fifty dollars.

And now silence.

After proposing countless schemes, drawing up one prospectus after another, and writing letters almost every week for more than a year, Manby had encountered at last a friendly adversary he could neither hurry, persuade, confuse, or intimidate. He had reached the intangible perimeter of his last oubliette. The world was closing in on him, and its unbearable pressure was contracting the walls of a prison within which a strange and frightening but pitiful creature was now again raging to be freed.

Silence.

A deathly, ghastly silence that itself clamored to be broken.

8

It was then, in the winter of 1923-24, that a few people in Taos first became slowly aware, by whispered word-of-mouth, that there was being formed in town a secret organization vital to the safety and welfare of the entire country. Its name was the "United States Secret and Civil Service Society, Self-Supporting Branch," to which was appended the designation of the local auxiliary, "Grand House Service Number 10."[1]

Manby had organized it, Teracita was its president, and secret meetings were held in her house near the tourist camp. Trustworthy friends admitted to a meeting as prospective members were asked by Manby to sign the following oath of allegiance to the Society:

"I, ..., of precinct number . . . . . ., of the county of Taos, State of New Mexico, a citizen of the United States of America and of lawful age and being duly sworn according to oaths and provisions of the Secret Self-Supporting Branch, do hereby declare on my honor to do my best to serve God and my country, and to obey secret civil laws, to keep myself physically strong, mentally awake, and morally straight. So help me, God."

"The Society," Manby explained, "is a branch of the United States Intelligence Department in Washington, D.C., with

Western headquarters in Colorado, Wyoming, Arizona, and New
Mexico. Its work is highly important and necessarily secret. The
organization's detective work is amply financed by the government, and in due time each member will be handsomely rewarded. I am assured," he said earnestly after a pause, "that
the sum will be one million dollars apiece for each loyal member.
Meanwhile, of course, members are required to support their
own local auxiliary in discharge of their duties."

Manby gave the new members strange missions to perform.
One of them was required to stealthily follow a businessman in
town all day and make a detailed report of everything he did
and everyone he met. Another was instructed to saddle his horse
at daybreak and ride up a mountain canyon, waving a red flag
as a signal to invisible secret agents hiding on the slopes. No
one questioned these missions. Manby himself flashed signals
by raising and lowering the American flag he flew from the roof
of his house. Often at night he placed a lantern on the roof too.
This, he explained, was for the benefit of a strange new-style
air-ship, the *Garibaldi*, which periodically landed on his back
pasture with messages of international importance and disappeared before morning. It was understood that the *Garibaldi*
was flown from Italy.

Failure of the members in the performance of their duties
was punishable by death. Manby was not backward in showing
them how it might be performed. Leading them out into the
orchard, he would go through the motions of shooting a victim,
stamping on his body, and cutting off his head. It seemed more
than pantomime, even to Manby himself, for now in the pale
moonlight filtering through the apple trees the walls of an invisible prison cracked and the creature which had whimpered
so long burst out with shrieks of rage to possess him. In a black
and bloody hatred against the world, it shot, slashed with a
knife, stamped up and down until the old man, wheezing for
breath, dripping sweat, could shout and move no more.

Within the court lay the marker of the Society—a large white
stone underneath which were buried the officials and secret
agents who had died during the performance of their duties.
There were six of them, explained Teracita, patriots sacrificed
to protect the people, ideals, and property of their beloved
country.

If the members of the Society were yet somewhat mystified by the exact nature of the catastrophic dangers threatening them, Dr. Thorne was not. Manby broke his long silence that February with a letter explaining the matter fully:

"I am going to ask you something of a very confidential nature in regard to rumors circulating in financial circles in New York and Denver—in regard to lurid tales and happenings in this vicinity which outrivals the most tragic and lurid movies that were ever staged, in which Teracita and myself appear to hold the center of the stage, against the attacks instigated by wealthy business crooks to seize our properties.

"Teracita's father . . . owns the Mystic Mine which is not far from the Aztec from which it is estimated about fifty million in gold was taken. The Company operating the Aztec, after they had tested the property by drills without encountering further ore bodies, sold it out. In the meantime these experts reported that the great ore bodies lay under the Mystic. And then the trouble commenced. As regards myself, I am reputed to be the stumbling block to these interests getting possession of the Antonio Martinez Grant . . . and incidentally to the Aztec Hot Springs and the surrounding territory . . .

"It may seem incredible to you, yet I think you may be able to verify the facts in New York that not less than 121 bands of gunmen have been hurled against us—gunmen of wide celebrity both in the East and West—composed of nine to twelve in each band, with the exception of the Periot band in New York, and about a hundred in the last recruited from Colorado, Texas, and New Mexico points. But what mystifies the enemy who plan these raids is what becomes of all their gunmen—and what master mind and genius forestalls all their secret plans, and they have been filled with terror. Twice they have brought a million dollars beautifully done up in packages with the U.S. Treasury seal, to leave with me in settlement. Five times have they brought alike to Teracita, and as many times we refused to accept due to the fact they have committed the most dreadful acts and horrors against our other friends after giving a bond of two millions to cease hostilities and keep the peace. The enemy have been getting in deeper and deeper, and even should they succeed in bumping off Teracita and myself they will get nowhere—as the full history of the case is carefully preserved together with all happenings and testimonies of gunmen taken prisoner who have turned State's evidence.

"But what strikes the greatest terror to the enemy is the unseen forces that checkmate their plans and has swallowed up their army of gunmen . . . I should never have mustered the courage to tell you of these happenings, but I only do so now in order that you may more intelligently understand such queries as you may desire to make or that might come to your attention from certain rumors vague or otherwise which I am advised are pretty well discussed in New York banking circles and clubs.

"I am enclosing you a snap I took of little Teracita the other day when she was resting after strenuous house cleaning. It does not do her justice, however, and naturally omits her wonderful coloring and complexion . . . She is a devoted mother to her three little children and delights in helping the poor who adore her.

"So if you should hear of me being referred to as another Lenin of the West, and Teracita as a second Rosa, you will regard this as propaganda of the enemy attempting to justify their lawless actions."[2]

Just when and where the enemy's gunmen would strike, the Lenin of the West and his second Rosa did not know. They too were under orders from that unknown mastermind and genius who sent secret agents to direct all the Society's activities. The current directing agents were named Severino Gutierrez and Craig Kenneth. No one ever saw them. On the night of a meeting the members would gather with Manby in the front room of Teracita's house.

"Princess, will you please step into the back room and receive their orders?" Manby would ask.

Teracita would vanish for a consultation with the agents who had arrived that day, returning with their orders. One of the members was instructed to attend a certain funeral in Santa Fe and report the appearance and condition of the corpse in the casket. Another was ordered to inspect the ground around the Mystic mine up at E-town in order to ascertain if any of the enemy spies had left their footprints. Teracita often brought back orders in letter form which she read to the members:

President Teracita: You have my order to collect $300 from each member of the new branch at once. Notify me what you do.

                                        Craig Kenneth

Guard House Service: Why don't you make some ar-
rangements to get this $1,000 for Princess Teracita? She
has to have it by ten o'clock tomorrow morning. I will
send her right down to get it.

                                     Severino Gutierrez

Honorable Members: Your trustee certificate and application have gone to Washington. Teracita put up $5,000
last night. She has to have her money back at once.
Yours for service. S. G.

Instructions for individual members were handled in a more
delicate and private manner through the "Grapevine Messenger
Service." The messenger who delivered the letters was a young
man named Carmen Duran. Often called by his nickname Car-
mencito, he was suspected of having committed several highway
robberies and hence was quite capable of collecting the money
usually requested.

In the middle of August, Thorne broke his own long silence.
He had lost his wife after a protracted illness the past May,
leaving him with four children varying in age from nine to
seventeen. Also his Radium Company of Colorado had failed,
although there were enough assets to entirely liquidate the
company's indebtedness. Curiously enough after all this time,
he had forgotten the correct spelling of Manby's name, addressing him as "My dear friend Mamby."

His friendly letter called forth another frightening and yet
reassuring letter from Manby on August 17, 1924:

"The enemy have brought in their gunmen from nearly every
state in the Union—not to mention the small army from the
Mexican frontier, which was relieved when President Obregon
came through. . . . One of the wealthiest men in the United States
with a big force of gunmen . . . offered two millions to be turned
loose. Then three in settlements. Now I understand ten millions.
Teracita and I are willing to settle on the ground that this will
punish him for his wrongdoing. Our friends hold the view they
cannot compromise lawlessness."

He followed this several months later by writing: "Even though the enemy should succeed in wiping us out, I have filed in safe depositories where their influence cannot reach, a full history of the facts under seal to be published to the world in event of foul play—which will precipitate their destruction... They may say we cannot afford to be whipped by a girl and a man. True. But our answer is desist from wrongdoing."

It was true that these onslaughts of the enemy were repulsed so secretly that no one in town save the members of the Society knew of their danger. It was equally true that an uneasy air pervaded the whole valley—a vague feeling of something insidious, something evil, creeping through the streets and fields. Curiously enough, the Society grew so large that meetings were no longer held at Teracita's house. Members were contacted only by the "Grapevine Messenger Service" in the person of Carmen Duran.

The Society no longer restricted itself to collecting sums of cash from its members. It demanded first mortgages on houses, titles to real estate, possessions of the land itself. Just why all this money and property was needed, in view of the millions offered by the enemy as settlement, no one knew.

In fact, few of the members knew just who the other members of the Society were, although they included many prominent Anglo professional and businessmen as well as more simple Spanish neighbors. One of the former was Alvin Burch, a middle-aged man with five children. Moving to Taos from Las Vegas about fifteen years before, he had opened a butcher shop, buying and selling sheep on the side. Prospering from this, he established a large merchandise store on the north side of the plaza. Business was good; he was making and saving money; and his children were growing up and getting married.

Joining the Society, he was honored by being more and more frequently called upon for money. At any hour of the day or night Carmen Duran would bring him an urgent letter.

I will insist once more in asking your help for Princess Teracita, as I know the dangers. Can you raise $300 tonight? Just loan it to her until she sells the land. Please take action at once.

Serverino H. Gutierrez

Still another one read:

> I am asking this favor of you: to loan me $450, as I have
> several real estate men here looking at her car, just to
> stop business, unless overdue payment on it is made at
> once. Please do not fail me.
>
> S. G.

These loans Burch executed immediately, as he had many
others before. More and more letters, more and more demands
for money kept coming, until Burch was paying the Society
practically all he made from his large store. To make financial
matters worse in the family, his son Clyde also joined the
Society and became a regular contributor, receiving notes like
the following:

> Received of Hon. Clyde Burch $1200 for compensation
> retained by Mrs. Teracita Ferguson for the amount of
> $200,000. For rendered services and responsibility of
> trust.
>
> Officer S. Gutierrez, S. C. S.

> Outfit six cottages at Teracita's camp for 200 men coming
> in next week and want cottages ready by next week.
> So let me know if you can do this right away.
>
> S. G.

Cecil Ross, who had married Burch's daughter Ethel, became
alarmed. He suspected that the Society was only a bunco game
for fleecing money and property out of its members. So he too
joined with the hope of protecting his kind-hearted and easily
imposed-upon father-in-law from further attrition, signing the
following oath:[3]

> To the Fearless and Incorruptable (*sic*) Branch of the
> S. C. S.

> I, C. E. Ross, acknowledge the honor and responsibility
> placed upon me, by the transferring of the amount of
> twelve million dollars to my name, do hereby, on my oath,

accept the same.

I, C. E. Ross, of Precinct No. 1, County of Taos and State of New Mexico, a citizen of the United States of America, and of lawful age, being duly sworn according to the oath and provisions of the United States Secret Civil Service, Self-Supporting Branch. Hereby declare on my honor to do my best to serve God and my country, and to do faithfully all in my power to advance the principles of right and justice, as advanced by the Secret Civil Law. So help me God.

One of his important missions was to accompany George Ferguson, Carmen, and Juan Duran on a trip to the Mystic mine on Mt. Baldy. Manby and Teracita were waiting at the portal, sitting in front of a fire with a human skull and cross bones beside it. A few feet inside the portal he could see in the light of two candles a Navajo rug and a box of rattlesnakes. Upon Manby's demand, Ross delivered an envelope containing $2,500 cash which he had been ordered to bring. In return he was given a small bag of gold nuggets—which later, upon assay, turned out to be "fools gold" or iron pyrites.

Months later Ross began to get a clearer picture of what was going on when he was delivered the following unsigned letter:

Our plans to date are as follows. Buy the lodge and the M. Stearns place. Hold the place where Mrs. Ferguson now lives, through Carmen. Clear ownership on the Mc-Cabe place and obtain the Manby property, thus giving a connection between the Lodge and the town property through the Indian lands. Call for advice as to the best form of construction for protection of services.

The "M. Stearns place" was of course the large estate of Mrs. Mabel Luhan, formerly Mrs. Maurice Sterne, and the "Lodge" was the San Geronimo Lodge or guest ranch with its ample grounds. By obtaining these, with the other mentioned properties, the Society would control the whole sweep of land through the Indian reservation to the town plaza. But who was now in control of the Society and planning to obtain Manby's own estate?

Ross realized he was getting into something deeper than he knew. His father-in-law had been fleeced out of something between $25,000 and $60,000, Clyde and himself out of large sums themselves. Clearly it was time to get out.

Resolutely he informed President Teracita that he was resigning from the Society. That evening Special Messenger Duran came to see him. He was in an ugly mood. "You aren't getting out!" he said curtly. "Nobody leaves the Society once they're in. That means old Burch, Clyde, and you too. You know what you'll get if you try it! Manby showed you, and Teracita has appointed me to do it. Savvy?"

There was a great deal more to savvy than this. Ross had noticed that he could drive his car around the crowded plaza without making signals or obeying traffic laws, and that the town policeman never stopped him. Also that a few other members of the Society broke the town laws with impunity. Secret as the Society was, it was beginning to exert an influence. Townspeople, disturbed by rumors, were beginning to be careful to whom they talked, what they said. Everything was quiet on the surface, but underneath ran a current of fear and suspicion.

Once again, in June 1925, there began a flurry of correspondence between Thorne and Manby. Thorne happened to find in his safe deposit box two I.O.U. notes from Manby for $500 each—for money which Thorne had advanced to pay Manby's delinquent taxes. "Is it convenient to pay these off?" he asked.

Manby answered immediately: "The horrible fight here has assumed the proportions of a small civil war. Certain corporate interests with its allied branches feared I had the clearest proof which would destroy their title to some $60 billion of property. They concluded it was the safest policy to have me bumped off by their gun men ... But I am still here and holding my own ..." Then, in reference to the I.O.U.'s, he added a sentence that was a masterpiece of adroit evasion: "If I do not pay you before long, I must devise some plan of paying you."

The plan he devised was sent to Thorne exactly a week later. It concerned 96,000 acres on the Three Forks of the Black River in Missouri. The land was in the Ozarks and allegedly had been granted by Spain to one James Maxwell on November 27, 1816. On it were vast deposits of coal and iron. "Will this property interest you or your friends?" asked Manby.

Thorne ignored this for six months, then wrote on December 2: "I would like something more tangible than two I.O.U.'s. Can you make a payment and substitute a note for the balance? The Maxwell property is unattractive." He then asked innocently, "What happened to the Van Dyck?"

Manby hastened to reply. "Will try to pay loans. Regarding the Ozarks property: I had in view accepting of swamp lands in Louisiana in order to raise muskrats, as published returns show 6,000,000 were trapped last year at $1 per pelt."

To the busy, influential, and vastly wealthy financier, there must have seemed something at once magnificently courageous and ridiculously pitiful about this old man in a backwoods village in the mountains of New Mexico whom he had met only once. Land grants, hot springs, hotels, country inns, sheep, gold, iron, oil, coal—and now muskrats! What would he pull out of his hat next? The long diatribes about the Enemy—the vast armies of gunmen, the millions and billions offered for settlement— were of course ridiculous effluvia washed up by the writhings of an extraordinarily prolific and imaginative mind which could be considered, at best, not quite normal. Thorne was too preoccupied to waste too much time. He had fallen in love with a nurse from Toronto, Canada, and was busy commuting between there and his home in Greenwich, Connecticut, and his office in New York.[4] Still, being the man he was, he intended to collect what Manby owed him when he could get around to it.

9

The United States Secret and Civil Service Society, Self-Supporting Branch, was far from being only an imaginary fantasy spun by a prolific mind. It was a hard economic and social fact whose insidious ramifications, as it grew in importance, began to undermine the very foundations of the valley. The secrecy with which it was so successfully shrouded magnified its evil influence and at the same time created the humus of fear out of which it kept on growing. Like a form of witchcraft, the Society thrived on suspicion. No one knew whether his brother or neighbor, his grocer or butcher, was a member, but suspected them all.

Manby, the self-styled Lenin of the West, took on an aspect of suspected importance he had never before achieved. Nobody could pin anything on the old recluse, but then nobody dared to try. Not even Manby knew all the members of that strange organization he had set in motion, it had grown so far beyond him. But as he left his hacienda each morning to do his simple chores, he felt himself looking at some of the people he met with a suspicion he could not account for.

Down the road blacksmith Hinde put his hammer down on his anvil, and wiped his hands on his leather apron. "Tolerable weather, Mr. Manby!"

"Maybe so, maybe so," answered Manby walking slowly past with his cane.

Sunning himself in front of the artist Phillips' house stood Adolph Des Georges, whose brother was working his way up in politics to state senator. "Good morning, Mr. Manby!"

Manby gave the surly grunt of age to youth, and continued on to the post office. The place was crowded; the mail was still being put up. At the back of the line stood Captain William Frayne who carried the title due to having run a commercial or private fishing boat of some sort off the coast of Maine. Coming to New Mexico for his health, he had brought the anchor with him. Years before, he had served as Manby's cat's paw by redeeming the large Hadley tract of the Los Luceros Grant put up to sale for unpaid taxes, turning it over to Manby. He had then started an abstract company—the same company that Reverend Spotts was now taking over.

"Mr. Manby! I have no idear how things are going with you lately!" he said with his indestructible accent.

"About the same as with you!" growled Manby, noticing his white hair.

There was William Anderson who operated the mill down at Ranchitos, and two strange characters, Jack Bennett and Charles Weber, who batched together on a fair piece of land in Arroyo Seco Bajada. When they spoke Manby ignored them, glaring angrily through the wicket at the clerk still putting up the mail. The damned place of a morning was nothing but a country club where everybody came early and stood gossiping for an hour or more. Talk, talk, talk! Just when he was expecting a letter from Thorne, damn his stubborn hide. Manby flung around and stalked out.

On the doorstep stood Doc Martin. There was no escape for either. "Damned if it isn't Manby!" said Martin. "Thought you'd left town a year ago!"

Manby glared at him with bloodshot eyes.

"I wish, Manby, you'd tell those damned gardeners of yours to stop their everlastin' diggin' of a night! How the hell do you expect me to sleep? Tell 'em to pull up some weeds instead!"

"Mind your own business!" growled Manby, pushing past him.

Martin shrugged. He had been hearing some strange rumors of late, but put no stock in any of them. In his own, personal, private opinion his next door neighbor, the old coot, was suffering from paresis, brought on by syphillis.

In Burch's general merchandise store, Manby stalked up to the meat counter to dicker for a cheap piece of meat. Usually he came early in the morning before the fancy customers came for their shopping, in order to pick up an odd cut of yesterday's left-over beef. This morning Burch himself was behind the counter, talking to his butcher.

"Why, Mr. Manby! What can we do for you this morning? The best lamb I've seen in years has just come in. How about some nice little chops?"

"Beef!" growled Manby. "You never have it!"

"We'll find you a piece, Mr. Manby! Don't worry!"

When it came, neatly wrapped, Manby thrust it in the pocket of his frayed tweed jacket. "Charge it to my account!"

Then on the plaza, of course, he ran into Saca Muelas. The Tooth-Puller had been prospering mightily since he had made Manby's dentures, and his appearance showed it. He wore a new plaid suit of the latest fashion, pointed shoes, a bright necktie. With these he wore the air of the most popular man in town. Of all the people Manby had met, he was the only one who assumed toward him an unassailable attitude of deeply-rooted familiarity.

"Manby, my old friend! Are you getting a good cut on the deal?"

Manby scowled. There was a fatuous smile on Muller's face and he spoke in the jocular idiom of the day. Yet his sharp black eyes were wary and his greeting might be carrying a hidden meaning. Manby never knew quite how to take him.

"So you're buying another piece of property? Making false teeth on a sewing machine must be good business, Muller!"

As he walked back to the post office, it occured to him what a coincidence it was that both the blacksmith and the dentist were making money fast enough to afford frequent purchases of real estate while he, with Teracita behind him, could never scrape up enough money to pay Thorne. Moreover he was becoming uneasy about something he could not quite define.

There was no letter from Thorne waiting for him; Thorne had not written for months. This made Manby more uneasy. He went home and wrote Thorne that in order to repay his debt of $1,000, he would let him have the Van Dyck masterpiece worth

$50,000 for $5,000. That night in bed fear of the enemy began
to torment him. It was quite obvious to him now that secret
agents had been sent to spy upon him years ago. Why had he
not realized it before?

Jumping out of bed, he took down his favorite book, H. G.
Well's *The War in the Air*, and swiftly penned the following
note:[1]

> This book was presented to Victor Morawitz (*sic*) of 44
> Wall St., N. Y. C. by Fred Harvey of K. C. Mo. and given
> me by the former in 1922 when Mrs. Mabel Sterne
> insisted that he stay at my house.
> Was this part of the plan of the enemy to size me up?
>
> A. R. M.
> Taos. April 22, 1926

Summer dragged by, carrying the strange paradox of the
United States Secret and Civil Service Society, Self-Supporting
Branch, presumably raking in money and property from its
gullible members while its nominal head presumably became
poorer and more debt-ridden every day. Something was coming
to a verge.

Alvin Burch, for one thing, finally realized that he had been
duped and fleeced out of perhaps $60,000, and demanded some
return on his money. Yet there now came up something that
proved he was still unaccountably gullible enough to grasp at
a preposterous chance to recoup his losses.

On October 15 Teracita and Burch drew up one of the most
amazing contracts ever executed. According to its long text,
Teracita was about to have delivered to her the sum of $827,
000,000 which had been collected for her as damages by the
United States Secret and Civil Service Society, Self-Supporting
Branch. As Teracita did not have sufficient business experience to
handle a sum of this magnitude, she was reposing utmost
confidence in the honesty, integrity, and ability of Alvin Burch.

Hence she was authorizing the officers of the Self-Supporting
Branch of the Society to pay over the $827,000,000 to Burch,
"but to put in trust for her, her children, and heirs to invest in
securities approved by the officers of the Society."[2]

Burch agreed to manage the trust until Teracita's children

became of age. However, in the event Teracita should marry "such person as may meet with the approval of the officers of the Society, then her husband should become the trustee, and Alvin Burch be released."

Burch's compensation as trustee was specified as $1,000,000.

Burch duly signed the formal, notarized contract, then asked for his million dollars—or at least a good share of it. Where was it to come from?

That was a simple matter. Manby, on that same day, handed him a federal gold certificate for an even $1,000,000. All Burch had to do was to drive to the mint in Denver and cash it. Manby induced him to sign a receipt. Burch then drove off with his young son Elmer who later reported they were shot at twice while climbing up Palo Flechado pass, not far from Taos.

In Denver Burch presented the certificate to the office of the U. S. Treasury Department for payment. The certificate was obviously such a spurious forgery that the officials merely laughed, making no effort to arrest and prosecute him.[3] Teracita, upon his return, was enraged. She accused Burch of having received the million dollars and hidden it away for his own use.

Four days later Manby received welcome news that Thorne would have the two paintings restored at his own cost and taken to his home in Connecticut. Early in November Thorne wrote that he had received the paintings and, to tide Manby over, would advance him $300 provided Manby would give a legal lien on the "St. Catherine" for the total amount of his debt. The reason he gave for his insistence upon a lien betrayed for the first time a subtle humor. "In case anything happens to you, the enemy might on some pretext seize the picture and I would be left whistling for my money."

Manby at the time owed Thorne $1,750; so Thorne, on February 10, 1927, took a chattel mortgage to cover his loan on the painting.

That spring something began to happen. No one knew exactly what. On April 4 Manby wired Thorne that he must have $5,000 within three days, offering him the Manby Hot Springs with 1,500 acres as collateral. Thorne wired back that if Teracita would endorse Manby's note for $5,000 and he would include his own home property also, clear of all liens, he would wire that amount to the bank in Taos. Manby was forced to accept his terms and executed a note that same day. To secure Teracita's endorsement, he deeded to her the property held in the name of his Irish investor, Miss Margaret Higgins.[4]

By fall he was in hot water again, obtaining from Thorne three money orders for $100 each, and giving another note for the loan of $1,000. He then somewhat tardily informed Thorne that his home property was held in the name of the Colonial Bond and Security Company controlled by Teracita and himself. "During our wires last April, I couldn't go into all this. What suggestions now? It might be a good plan to sell the property to Teracita for $50,000 and take her note for six months."

A month later he hit up Thorne for another $5,000 loan, offering him as collateral Teracita's interest in the Mystic mine. He explained that Teracita's father, Columbus Ferguson, had located the Mystic and given his partners, Wilkerson and Stone, each one-fourth interest, intending ultimately to give them each one-third interest. Wilkerson died about 1917, and Teracita bought Stone's interest from his heirs. In 1918 a certain C. A. Probert entered into an agreement with Stone and Ferguson whereby he was to receive one-third interest, but Probert died in July 1918. "I took the position his contract died with him, but his widow claims his interest."

Confusing as this was, it was agreed that Teracita's interest comprised 1/3 of 2/9 of the mining property, plus another 2/9 acquired by purchase. Teracita and Manby acceded to the conditions laid down by Thorne that she give him all her interest in the Mystic as collateral for the loan.

Hence Thorne now held as collateral Manby's home estate, hot springs, and paintings, Teracita's Mystic mine, and several additional notes. Manby grew more and more uneasy. The enemy was closing in on him still tighter. Then suddenly came a message from secret agent Severino Gutierrez to the Society members of the Guard House Service, Number 10:

> Transmission No. 20685. Distress Signal 806. We lost two officers, our wonderful Craig Kenneth and his partner— both killed by the Lamar, Colorado bank robbers at Poniel Creek. We might bring the body of Kenneth over that way. His last word was to be brought to Teracita, dead or alive. So it is hard to keep her from knowing. He died in

full duty, under the stars and stripes of our country.[5]

The Society was beginning to come apart at the seams.

10

What had happened? Manby didn't know just when or how his suspicions had been aroused. Perhaps when old Ferguson had died and Teracita stopped coming to fix his supper each evening. He had thought then his Princess was kept too busy looking after her children, her tourist court, and the Society. But soon he began to notice she was too engrossed in the crucial business of the Society to give him any personal attention. Also he observed with alarm that Special Messenger Carmen Duran was assuming more and more responsibility. He was, in fact, delivering messages demanding money from members without Manby's directions, but on the authorization of the president, Teracita.

Manby knew now what was beginning to happen. He stormed and threatened, cajoled and begged, to avert the inevitable. To no avail. The hard granite streak in Teracita had come out. She told him, in effect, to mind his own business. And what was that without her? His loved and lovely Princess Teracita!

Nature took its course. Carmen Duran moved into the court to live with her as her common-law husband, and with an ugly sneer ordered the dirty old man to keep away.

Betrayed! By his adored Princess Teracita! By the Society! By Thorne! Had they all secretly gone over to the side of the enemy? Manby could not force himself to believe it, yet he had to admit that his misfortunes had reached their nadir. His great kingdom, the Martinez Grant, had fallen into enemy hands. So had his La Bajada tract with its Aztec Hot Springs, by which he had hoped to redeem the grant. And his Van Dyck master- piece, from whose sale he had hoped to develop the hot springs. And now his own home and estate

He was now sixty-nine years old. Wracked by jealousy, with no one to look after him, shunned and despised, he brooded alone in his weedy garden and in the dark cobwebbed rooms of his house. At twilight he paraded through the patios, shooting at stray cats, and seeing to his watchdogs. Then bolting gates and doors, he lighted a lamp and sat down to his desk.

It occurred to him that although everything he owned was tied up, he still might make something from Teracita's Mystic mine. The tactic he tried was an enthusiastic note to Thorne on June 1, 1928. Teracita had received a big offer for the Mystic, he wrote, but the parties wanted to do some work to see what was there before taking it over. This was an unnecessary pre- caution, Manby thought, unless they felt they ought to pay her more.

Three weeks later he reported that the prospective purchaser was more than satisfied with the Mystic, as its value far exceeded anything he had hoped for. This was good news, of course, for payment of the Colonial Bond and Security Company note, due July 5, was dependent on the sale.

On July 6 Thorne was informed by the bank that the note had gone to protest for non-payment. He wasted no time writing Manby curtly of his disappointment; he was counting on prompt payment in order to utilize the money for other purposes. Moreover, "as you have previously written me on numerous occasions that Mrs. Ferguson holds certain Certificates against the Treasury of the United States through Federal Reserve Banks for a large amount, I do not see why she cannot procure a loan of $12,000 on this security so that you can pay me promptly."

Manby had little to say in answer: Teracita had gone to Albuquerque with her little girl who had a bad case of neglected tonsils. "Teracita Ferguson," he added, "is very reticent in regard to her affairs when special interests have become mixed up."[1]

Everything was now coming to a head. It was quite obvious that Thorne in New York, fabulously wealthy as he was, and

after fifteen years of curious friendship with Manby, had got
from the old man all that was worth getting. Margaret Waddell
finally had obtained an attorney to renew her suit against Manby
for breach of promise and fraudulent securing of capital from
her. And Teracita, having replaced Manby with the younger
Carmen Duran, was ragingly angry.

She had not gone to Albuquerque to see about her daughter's
tonsils. She had gone to find a lawyer who would restore to her
the $827,000,000 entrusted to Alvin Burch. It was a miracle that
she found a reputable attorney to accept such a fabulous, almost
unbelievable case. Yet the legal firm of Downer and Keleher,
housed in the First National Bank Building, took it on. George
S. Downer of the firm selected D. T. Kingsbury to handle it.[2]

The grounds for Teracita's suit against Alvin Burch were
simple. On October 15, 1926 she had entered into a formal
contract with Burch, appointing him as her trustee to receive
a large amount of money. She did not know how much the
officers of the United States Secret and Civil Service Society,
Self-Supporting Branch, had given him that same day, but the
amount of $827,000,000 was covered in the contract. Undoubtedly
Kingsbury's eyes popped upon hearing the amount. Still he must
have retained enough sense of reason to doubt that the ex-
butcher and storekeeper was keeping such a sum hidden in an
old boot. For he induced Teracita to believe now that Burch
had actually received $817,000. For two years he had refused
to render an accounting of the money and accrued interest.
Hence Teracita was now bringing suit against Burch for that
amount.

Kingsbury filed the suit on August 24, 1928 in the District
Court of Taos County. Appended to the complaint were two
exhibits: one from Teracita giving Kingsbury the power of
attorney, and the other the previous contract she had made
with Burch.[3]

Manby had little time to brood upon this fortune about to be
wrung out of Burch's merchandise store. For two weeks later
he received from Thorne a very stiff letter reminding him that
the Colonial Bond and Security Company note was now nearly
two months overdue. "You wrote me early in June," Thorne
went on, "that parties were negotiating with Teracita Ferguson
in regard to the sale of her interest in the Mystic Mine and that

the price had already been agreed upon, and that the purchasers had already made a preliminary examination before absolutely closing. Later you told me that this investigation had been completed and that they were entirely satisfied. If all of this is so, I do not see why Teracita Ferguson has not been paid and the Colonial Bond and Security Co. note settled. I would appreciate a letter from Teracita Ferguson stating just how things stand in regard to the sale of her interest in the Mystic Mine..." He concluded by saying that if Teracita's sale of the Mystic was still hanging fire, his friend Jack Holmes of Boulder, Colorado, would be glad to look into it.

He then wrote Holmes that "on account of old friendships I do not wish to foreclose on the property, considering that the note is more than amply secured," but suggested he get in touch with Teracita as she really might have something worth investigating. "You will probably remember these claims adjoin the old Aztec Mine from which millions of dollars in gold are reported to have been extracted a good many years ago." He now, for the first time, revealed his appraisal of Manby. "You will remember that when you and Bunker saw Manby two years ago you both reached the conclusion that the old gentleman had marked delusions along certain lines, and in this I thoroughly agree as numerous letters from him show conclusively that he has well established delusions of persecutions."[4]

On September 20 Sheriff Antonio Gonzales served Alvin Burch the summons, ordering him to appear before H. A. Kiker, judge of the Eighth Judicial Court of Taos, within thirty days. A suit for $817,000! Actually filed by that Teracita Ferguson! Simple-minded old Burch, already duped, fleeced out of all he owned, and now running into debt, sat holding the papers with trembling hands. How was he to explain the undeniable fact that he had signed the contract with Teracita, and actually had gone to Denver to cash a forged million-dollar United States Treasury Certificate? The whole family was thrown into a turmoil of fear and confusion.

Ross, his son-in-law, hurried to Santa Fe to talk with attorney general M. A. Otero. Matters had got completely out of hand. An official investigation was necessary, perhaps by federal authorities. Otero was polite, but would do nothing.

On October 11 Burch appeared in court to answer the com-

plaint. He admitted having entered into the contract with
Teracita two years before, but denied that he had received the
money. A hearing on the case was set for the following year.

Few people saw Manby all that winter and spring. An ominous
silence held the town in its spell. It was the dark silence of a
theater waiting for the curtain to rise on the last act of that
tragi-comedy which as Manby had written, "outrivals the most
tragic and lurid movies ever staged, in which Teracita and myself
appear to hold the center of the stage."

The old man himself hid in the wings. Once again he took
to getting up while it was still dark and trudging to the lunch
counter on the plaza to drink his morning tea while watching
dawn break over the mountains.

In that crepuscular hour between darkness and silence, and
light and the beat of life, no worries scudded across his stilled
mind, no doubts gnawed at his frayed heartstrings. Everything
was translucently plain. Even the everlasting mystery of time
itself cleared before the greasy window pane. He saw it no longer
as a rushing stream carrying everything in its constantly acceler-
ated flow, but as a deep still pool embodying alike all that had
been and all that would be with the living now. The grant, the
dream, the folly—those monstrous passions of a misspent life!
—he saw now for what they were. In the depths of that great
still pool they gleamed nebulously real and entrancing as ever,
like white pearls beyond reach, sunken jewels forever immune
to a diver's grasp. The grant, the dream, the folly! Everything
had been one monstrous folly from the start—the triumphant
folly that attested to man's unobtainable but imperishable ideal
of beauty and power, at once his triumph and his despair. This
much was now clear as he sipped his tea from the thick-rimmed
coffee cup that still felt like a bit between his false teeth.

But clear to which Manby, he wondered as he sat facing the
bitter blue dawns breaking over the snow-white Sangres. The
old man in his ragged tweed coat and leather puttees did not
know—there had been so many Manbys playing their curious
roles throughout the years. Not to the one who embodied that
tyrannical, cold, rational, and prolific mind which like a con-
tinual wound-up clock had ticked out so many schemes
independent of him. No, not that one! This one, to whom
everything now was feelingly clear, seemed a secret self which

had underlain them all, but of which, for some reason, he had not been fully aware till now. This surprised him, for he could hear it speaking plainly now before day creaked open on its icy hinges.

"No official of the government may dispose of the property held in trust for the people, nor substitute his will or opinion for the law as declared by the Supreme Court again and again. The disposition of public lands is exclusively a matter calling for Congressional enactment under the Constitution. Neither can the United States Government be bound by the acts of its faithless or incompetent servants. The people of this country are all right, and they bled themselves white to win the war, a loyalty which was betrayed by official graft and corruption. This is what hurts and has destroyed the confidence of the people, and unless these things are cleaned up and the culprits punished we are liable to face the gravest consequences, and find history repeating itself."[5]

Manby cringed as the words rushed through his mind. He had written them himself, as if at the dictation of that secret self which now possessed him. Why, who could believe it! Not the young Manby who had rioted and killed to help steal the Maxwell Grant. Not the older Manby who had stolen the Martinez Grant from the public domain with the help of faithless and incompetent public servants. But legally! Oh yes, legally! As if that mattered to the quiet, secret self murmuring within him of his own graft and corruption, of the unavoidable punishment of all those innumerable culprit Manbys, and of the gravest consequences to us all.

No! Not he sitting here watching the sheen of the first light reflected from the hanging icicles had been at fault; he was absolved from all blame. The culprit was a shadow-creature imprisoned within him, alternately whimpering and raging to be freed. A damned nuisance with its perpetual cries! His awareness of it roused him into a temper. He banged on the table with his cane, rattling teapot, cup, and saucer.

"Look out there!" he shouted to the same slatternly girl in the same soiled gingham. "See that car coming!"

"Yes, Mr. Manby. Without no chains on this icy pavement, he's havin' a terrible time."

"God blast his terrible time! The sun's rising. You know I

want my tea in peace before the plaza is full of crazy people gossiping about me!"

"Yes, Mr. Manby. I'll bring you another pot right away!"

The succession of dawns was all one dawn. He watched the snowdrifts shrink into the shadows of the Columbian Hotel, then slink out of sight. A robin appeared, hopping across the portal of the court house as if on stilts; a miniscule spot of electric green on a bare limb multiplied into a canopy of leaves. Rain washed the faded letters "AIREHCNOL" painted on the window before him, only to have dust begrime them. The sun no longer emerged slowly and redly over the blurred white crests of the Sangre de Cristos; it burst forth white, hot, and blinding before he had finished his tea. A carful of tourists trooped into the *loncheria*: women in pants whining, "Y'all got a lil' cup of hot cawfee fo' us folks?"

Manby slammed down his cup and stamped out. He never came back.

The solstitial dawn of the year, like the dawn of day, had broken suddenly, as it always did on this highland plateau; as if a switch had been turned on, flooding the immense stage with a white-hot and glaring light. Manby, trying to hide in the wings of his dusty, cobwebbed hacienda, could not escape it.

It was June. Margaret Waddell had renewed her suit, and papers were soon to be served on him. Teracita's suit against Burch was soon to have a hearing which would uncover the manipulations of the United States and Civil Service Society. All of Manby's notes were long overdue. Thorne was about to foreclose on his hot springs, his house and estate.

It was June, and the rushing stream of time had caught him again in its inexorable current. The enemy was closing in from all sides. The War in the Air was about to begin, when great fleets of *drachenflieger* would rain death and destruction on an evil world already corrupted by Wall Street. Night and day Manby's ears rang with the enraged cries of a shadow-creature trying to break out of its prison. To break free at last! To tear down the walls, hurl bullets into soft flesh, slash off a head with a sharp knife, stamp the bloody mess into the ground! The time had come and Manby was ready for it.

On the morning of June 29 he went to the Indian trader, Ralph Meyers, and requested him to call at his house that

evening. Just after dark Meyers knocked on Manby's outer
gate. Manby unbolted it, led him to the front door and unlocked
it, then into a room which he locked behind them. Inside, he
took down a handsome silver-mounted rifle and handed it to
Meyers.

"You've been wanting this gun a long time."

"Thought I might find a collector who'd be interested in it,"
answered Meyers.

"Well, I'm going to let you have it!"

They began to dicker. Manby wanted a huge price for it; he
needed cash immediately. Meyers refused. Having no ready cash
for it, he wanted to take the gun on assignment. Manby became
angry and ordered him out of the house, locking the door and
gate behind him.[6]

Early next morning Manby called at the home of Ward
Lockwood, the artist. Lockwood's wife Clyde opened the door
to see him standing there in his grimy clothes and old leather
puttees.

"Where's your husband?" demanded Manby. "I want to see
him right away!"

"Ward's out fishing and won't be back till this afternoon, Mr.
Manby. Won't you come in?"

"No! I'll be back!" He walked nervously away.

That afternoon he pounded on the door again. "Where's your
husband?" he demanded of Clyde when she opened it.

"Fishing must be good, Mr. Manby! He hasn't come back
yet. Is there something I can do for you?"

"Yes! I want to breed that German shepherd of yours to my
dog Lobo here. I'll take her with me right now for a few days."

"I'm sure he wouldn't mind that, Mr. Manby, but he would
object to your taking our dog there. Perhaps you'd better see
Ward first, though."

Manby's face reddened with anger as he turned and stalked
away.[7]

He returned home and saddled his black horse, Nigger. Both
Doc Martin next door and blacksmith Hinde across the street
saw him riding past late that afternoon.

Manby rode up Canyon Road, past the large Byzantine-style
house built by the Russian painter Leon Gaspard, toward
Teracita's house. Between five and six o'clock two of her

neighbors, Juan and Jose Trujillo, saw Manby riding back. Down the road another couple, Mr. and Mrs. Ramon Garcia, fixed the time more exactly as five-thirty. Mrs. Garcia was putting supper on the table and Ramon, out in front of the house, called to the familiar old man to come in and have supper with them. Manby refused, setting spurs to Nigger and riding quickly away.[8]

Apparently he returned home, stabled his horse, and went into the house, bolting all gates and locking all doors behind him.

Of this no one would ever be sure.

The Mystery

1

For the first few days after Manby's body had been found and buried, it was assumed that he had died from natural causes and that his dog had chewed off his head. Hinde, the blacksmith who lived down the road, was appointed legal administrator of the estate. Teracita and her lover Carmen Duran moved into the house. No one questioned her right of occupancy; most of Manby's holdings had been transferred to the Colonial Bond and Security Company of which he had been president, and Teracita was still vice president. Joined by Teracita's nephew George, and Carmen's brother Juan, they began digging in the garden each night for Manby's hidden money.

Doc Martin next door could hear their voices and the sound of their picks and spades. "God Almighty! Ain't that diggin' ever goin' to stop!" he fumed.

Still, a few persons suspected that Manby's death was not altogether normal. Doc Martin insisted that the old man had not been mentally sound, that he was a paranoiac and deathly afraid of something. Undoubtedly his fear was not wholly a mental aberration. The old man had possessed a violent temper and had made a host of enemies. Conjectures spread that Manby had been murdered, probably poisoned; his house was known to be filled with patent medicines to which he was passionately addicted. Other assertions were made that the body found was not Manby's; he had been seen by several persons after his alleged death.

The stories spread rapidly and were picked up by newspapers in Santa Fe and Albuquerque. According to the *Santa Fe New Mexican*, everybody was agog with curiosity about the mysterious death of Arthur Rochford Manby except the authorities. Why didn't they do something about it?

Under pressure of growing public opinion, the attorney general of New Mexico, M. A. Otero, Jr., sent up a private detective from Santa Fe to investigate Manby's death. Herman Charles Martin—Bill Martin as he was generally known—was a small and wiry man thirty-four years old, with blond hair and hard blue eyes. Born in Sainte-Croix, Switzerland, he had come to America and taken out his first citizenship papers in 1921. Two years later he arrived in Santa Fe, setting up the Martin Detective Bureau and soon becoming the chief investigator for the state police. He was a particularly capable, fearless, and talented man. Within a period of eight years he investigated 174 murders, laying the groundwork for 160 convictions.[1]

He arrived in Taos on July 9, six days after Manby had been found dead, and was conducted to the house by Hinde, administrator of the Manby estate.[2] The big blacksmith was in his late forties or early fifties, with hair and mustache Saxon yellow, and eyes blue as cornflowers. With his English accent, and Martin's French accent, they were a peculiar pair.

The house itself, fronting the road, was as Deputy Marshal Martinez had described it: an enormous Spanish-style adobe hacienda of nineteen rooms built in the form of a square, its three wings, stables, and outer walls enclosing three patios. Detective Martin was a careful, methodical worker. He drew a map of the house, duly cataloguing and numbering each of its nineteen rooms.

He then began his investigation in room 6, in which Manby's body had been found. Curiously enough, Manby's usual bedroom lay toward the south end of the west wing. The cot on which Manby's torso had been found was still there and on the wall, at the height of the cot, Martin discovered bloodstains. There were no stains on the floor. If it seemed unlikely that the dog Lobo had chewed off his master's head, it seemed impossible that the dog could have carried it sixteen feet into the next room without leaving blood marks on the floor.

Accompanied by the big blacksmith, Martin went into this bedroom. There were no bloodstains, indicating that the head had been carried here and not disturbed afterward. He began to inspect the room carefully. Underneath a bureau in the southeast corner he found two vertebrae; they showed a sharp, clean cut. On the window sill lay Manby's false teeth, both the upper and lower sets, and on a shelf sat an empty glass that smelled of ether.

"Well, let's look through the other rooms down the hall," he suggested.

"There's nothing in them," answered Hinde. "We've already looked through all of them."

Martin shrugged. "We'll take a last look anyway."

The two men were now joined by Teracita and Mrs. Felix Archuleta. Princess Teracita was a small woman of about forty, with black hair and black eyes carrying a wary expression. Mrs. Archuleta, formerly married to a John Strongberg of Trinidad, was a large, well-dressed woman. While they were in room 10, a guest room, Martin noticed a large Mexican basket in the corner.

"There's nothing in that!" Teracita protested vehemently.

Her nervous manner aroused Martin's suspicions. Waiting until the two women had left the room, he lifted the lid of the basket. In it, underneath several pieces of clothing, were five towels which had been washed and ironed but still showed heavy stains of blood.

In a sunroom farther down the hall, room 13, Martin found still another piece of evidence—a small scythe whose blade was also stained with blood. He had no doubt now that Manby had been murdered, and that Lobo had been locked in the house by the murderer in the hope the dog would mutilate the body and thus supply false evidence.

"Where did the old man ever get that dog of his?" he casually asked Hinde.

"Lobo? I believe Carmen Duran gave it to him," answered the blacksmith casually.

Martin gathered up all the articles he had found to present as evidence to District Attorney Fred Stringfellow and Probate Judge Henry A. Kiker, both in Raton. Then he began to talk with everyone he could find who could tell him something about

Manby.

After interviewing the Trujillos and the Garcias who had seen him riding back from Teracita's court, Martin could find no one who had seen him after that. He accordingly fixed the time of Manby's death as that evening or night of June 30th.

Continuing his investigation, he talked with Ernie Brandt, a roving, bow-legged cowpuncher. Brandt on July 3, the day when Manby's body was discovered, had been asked by Spotts, the county commissioner, to serve as a guard around Manby's house to keep out all curious townspeople. Carmen Duran was also named a guard, and he in turn had appointed John Strongberg, the former husband of Teracita's friend, Mrs. Felix Archuleta. For several nights these guards had patrolled the grounds. One night while sitting around a bottle of bourbon and talking about Manby's strange death, Brandt's tongue loosened.

"I don't think the old man's dead at all!" he conjectured. "That isn't his body buried out in back!"

"Whose is it then?" asked Strongberg.

"This is the way I figure it," continued Brandt. "You know old man Brooks—the J. B. Brooks who lived down the road in that funny two-story frame house? He died just ten days before Manby. Well, Manby had been fixing for a get-away and this came in real handy. That night he went to the cemetery, dug up Brooks' body, cut off the head, and carried them back to plant in his house here. Then he skipped out for Mexico."

Teracita's lover, Carmen Duran, related Brandt later, sat there during the conversation without saying a word. Later that night he began a violent quarrel with Brandt, demanding they shoot it out in the garden. Brandt assured Detective Martin that he saved his life only through a "clever trick."

A town butcher, A. A. Cummings, held the same opinion. Manby once had borrowed $500 from him, offering a jar of gold dust as security. According to Cummings, Manby had possessed $17,000 several months before his disappearance; and only a month before, he had deposited $5,000 in the local bank which he had drawn out in small amounts. Moreover he had netted $9,000 from the household and Indian items he had been selling for months. There seemed no doubt that Manby had been preparing to leave.

Brandt's and Cummings' conjecture sounded plausible to

Martin, considering the fact that Manby had tried to raise cash and to secure the Lockwood dog so that it would look as if the dog had attacked and mutilated Brooks' body beyond recognition. But when Martin went to the cemetery he found that Brooks' grave apparently had not been disturbed since the burial.

Interviewing more people who had known Manby, he met a man named Eugene Risner who took him to see Marguerita Tafoya in the small village of Arroyo Hondo nearby. Something had been preying on her mind for eight years and she was glad to talk about it. She then related how she had discovered the murdered body of Wilkerson in her room at Teracita's house. Frightened by the incident, Marguerita soon left her job, returned to her home in Arroyo Hondo, and had never mentioned the occurrence since.

Detective Martin and Risner drove back to Taos and enlisted the help of Bill Jenkins who knew the Moreno Valley mining area well. At dawn on July 17 the three men drove out of Taos on a sixty-mile trip into the mountains. The road led up over the high pass of Palo Flechado, down into the great mountain-rimmed Moreno Valley, and then climbed steeply up the mountain range that marked the head-waters of Red River.

Leaving the car near the top of the range, the three men struck out on foot up the side of Mt. Baldy, nearly thirteen thousand feet high. At eleven o'clock, about a mile from the summit, Jenkins let out a shout. Martin and Risner hurried up to see lying at his feet the skeleton of a man. Scattered around it were the decaying fragments of a gray hat, part of a coat, a pair of high shoes, a pipe, and a case for eyeglasses.

"This is it!" said Jenkins.

"But where's the skull?" asked Martin quietly.

The three men continued their search. A mile and a half farther lay the portal of the Mystic Mine, now abandoned, and near it they discovered the skull. Carefully packing the remains back to the car, they drove down to Elizabethtown. A few old-timers still living in its log cabins and wooden shanties identified the articles as Wilkerson's. One of them was an old prospector named Thomas Brankfort, a nephew of William Brankfort who once had been Stone's partner.

"Sure I know those Miller half-length boots!" he maintained.

"I saw them on Wilkerson the day he bought them. It was in the fall of 1921 when he was dressing up to go to Taos. And if you ask me, you'll find some more stuff up on the hill if you poke around some more."

Martin was convinced the skeleton was that of Wilkerson who had been murdered at the Ferguson home and whose body had been driven up to Mt. Baldy for disposal. He drove to Raton and turned over the remains to District Attorney Fred Stringfellow and Judge Henry A. Kiker. A few days later when Judge Kiker came to Taos, Martin induced Marguerita Tafoya to tell him under oath her story of finding Wilkerson's body after his murder on the night of September 28, 1921.

A week or more later Martin drove back alone to Mt. Baldy, taking Brankfort's advice to poke around some more. Here, as he recorded in his personal notes, he found a heap of bones and skulls, with their owners' remnants of clothes and belongings, that turned out to be skeletons of seven other men. Taking them back to Elizabethtown, he found a man who identified them. He was an elderly man named McIntyre who in the mining camp's prosperous days had run a hotel and livery stable, a saloon and a store, staking prospectors and selling them their outfits. According to him, all seven men had been associated with Manby in some way.

One of them he remembered by the name of Griffin, a relative of the Dan Griffin whom Manby had killed in Vermejo Park. McIntyre believed Manby had killed him when he found out who he was. Another was a Mexican cowhand named Varos who had worked for Manby. One morning the two of them had ridden horses up into the mountains. That night Manby came back alone, saying that Varos' horse had killed him—kicked his head off. Brunner had disappeared, his claim being taken over by Manby. So had the prospector Gallegos. Serverino Gutierrez had worked in the mines for Manby. So had a fellow named Kenneth. They had suddenly and mysteriously disappeared too. Like old Stone, they most likely had been done away with by Manby. What the reason was, nobody in Elizabethtown knew. It didn't pay to be too nosey.

Martin, still perplexed, drove back to town. *The Santa Fe New Mexican* every day for ten days had been running stories on the case, listing ten rumors speculating that Manby was alive

Hunches and Tenuous Trails Led the Searchers Up the Slopes of Mount Baldy Where They Made a Startling Discovery — A Private Cemetery. Each Skull Had Been Neatly Severed From Its Skeleton and Lay Half Buried Nearby.

Illustration from the feature article, "The Strange Death of Mysterious Mr. Manby," *The American Weekly*, August 1, 1943.

or dead, alleging the "great hermit" had possessed huge jars of gold dust and boxes of gold nuggets, and insisting that, while his only cash assets were two nickels found in his trousers pocket, his estate was worth a fortune. On July 25, three weeks after Manby's alleged death, it broke out with a story headlined:

THE GREATEST MYSTERY OF THE SOUTHWEST

An editorial two days later further insisted, "*The New Mexican* is convinced that here is a real mystery, worthy of the talents of Sherlock Holmes, a Lecoq, or the pen of Edgar Allen Poe, or E. Phillips Oppenheim . . . One cannot help believing something has been going on in Taos which when revealed will astound the world."

Sharply critical of the authorities, it demanded that officials open up the grave, identify the contents, and clear the mystery. The excitement was not restricted to New Mexico. Dispatching a reporter to Taos, the *Kansas City Star* began to run a series of lurid special feature articles on the case.

Governor R. C. Dillon of New Mexico squirmed uneasily in his executive chair. His annoyance changed to worry when on August 2 he received a letter from Eardley B. Manby, now in Woodhall Spa, Lines, England, and from Alfred V. Manby in Cluny, Alta, Canada, asking what investigation was being made into the "cruel and brutal assassination" of their brother. This was followed on August 12 by an official letter from S. W. Barnes of the British Consulate in Galveston, Texas. Attached was a letter written to him on July 31 by Jocelyn Manby from Mt. Massive Ranch, Malta, Colorado, the third brother, advising the consulate of the unexplained death of Manby. The consulate, accordingly, requested a complete investigation into Manby's death.[3]

So on August 21, nine days later, Manby's remains were dug up from the back garden. The group disinterring the body comprised District Attorney Fred Stringfellow from Raton; W. H. Roberts, an undertaker from Santa Fe; Saca Muelas, the dentist, Dr. Fred Muller; crusty Doc Martin; blacksmith Hinde; and Detective Martin.

Doc Martin identified the body as Manby's. The dentist Dr. Muller identified the dentures as those he had made. Hinde

also was satisfied the body was that of Manby from a diamond
stickpin still pinned to his underwear and three rings, one of
iron made in Germany and which Manby had believed to possess
medical properties.

All now inspected the body closely. Detective Martin observed
that while it had seemed to be in bad shape when it was buried
on July 3, now on August 21 the flesh was still firm. They all
saw that the top of the torso had been cleanly cut near the
collar bone, which was broken. Two ribs had been shattered.
There were seven shot holes on the left side of the chest, and
the right side of the face and lower jaw had been shot away.
All this seemed to prove conclusively that the body was Manby's
and that he had been brutally murdered. Doc Martin and
Roberts then opened up the body, removing the stomach, liver,
and left lung to send with the skull to a laboratory in Albuquerque for chemical analysis.

That afternoon after finishing their gruesome job, Detective
Martin and Stringfellow were met in the plaza by a disheveled
and wildly angry Teracita. She had just come from a street
fight with Carmen and Juan Duran, and insisted on swearing out
warrants for the arrest of the two men on charges of assault
and battery. Warrants were made out and the two men arrested.

Stringfellow and Martin took the opportunity to question
them closely. Neither one of them could furnish an alibi for
the nights of June 30 and July 1, Carmen saying that he had
been out fishing. Then unaccountably Teracita appeared with
bonds for both men and they were released.

The following night an unsigned letter was slipped under the
door of Detective Martin's hotel room. "Keep out of Taos
and the Manby affair or we will fix you. Orders." Martin
ignored it.

Sending in his first report to Governor Dillon, he reviewed his
findings which indicated the case had many ramifications still
to be uncovered. It was impossible for him to continue his
investigations without funds, however, for he already had spent
$375 of his own money which had not been reimbursed. Nor
had he been paid for the services he had rendered on the
authorization of Attorney General Otero.

2

All that fall the squabble continued over Martin's investigation.

On September 18 Martin submitted to Attorney General Otero a bill of $750 for his services to date. Otero appealed to Governor Dillon. He had paid Martin $93.81. The district attorney of Taos County had promised to pay $250 but had no funds to meet the obligation. If and when Taos County did make the payment, the state still owed Martin $406.

The governor was embarrassed. Under pressure from the British Consulate and the three Manby brothers, he instructed Otero to continue working on the case, assuring him that $1,500 would be made available from state funds.

The attorney general was embarrassed. No money would be available, for according to law no money could be taken from the state treasury without a special appropriation by the legislature for this specific purpose. Nor was he satisfied with Martin's conclusions. The charges mentioned in the detective's reports could not be substantiated. The detective could not produce sufficient evidence for the issuance of warrants, and Otero believed that with so much publicity given the case it would be impossible to get evidence. He accordingly prepared on November 26 a synopsis of his work on the case for the United States government at the request of the Department of Justice operative Harry C. Leslie. He concluded that a trained crimin-

227

ologist was needed.

United States District Attorney Hugh Woodward then requested the Department of Justice to call in one of its special
operatives. His conclusion was that, as there had been no
counterfeiting, the United States government was not interested
in the case. He suggested that Otero get in touch with the chief
of police in Berkeley, California. The chief in turn referred Otero
to Edward Oscar Heinrich, a consulting expert on legal chemistry
and microscopy, in San Francisco. Heinrich was willing to under-
take the investigation for a fee of $500 plus $100 for every extra
day after the initial three days. Otero submitted the bid to the
governor who rejected it on grounds the state had no money to
finance such an investigation.[1]

Apparently the Manby case was dropped. But not the publicity
about it. On November 10 the *Denver Post* came out with a
double-page story headlined:

HEADLESS BODY NUMBER 5 IN THE MYSTERY OF THE SPANISH MANSION

The spread was profusely illustrated with photos of Manby,
Princess Teracita, old man Ferguson before he began to see
visions of headless bodies and was sent to the insane asylum,
and a close-up of Manby's front door with three different kinds
of locks mounted on it. According to the article, "Manby was
the fifth man of a small group to die as he had, mysteriously,
and to be found head and body separated... In the days
when the Aztec and Mystic mines were going full blast, old
residents recall at least three other 'decapitation slayings' in the
neighborhood. All were miners, and it is rumored that all
three had been connected, in ways not clear, with either the
Mystic or Aztec." Of the five, only Manby, Stone, and Wilkerson
were identified.

This was followed by an AP dispatch reporting that "Manby's
death is a matter of international note because of the intervention of the United States Department of Justice at the
request of the British Embassy."

The *Kansas City Star* gave more details. "At the request
of the British Embassy, the American Government through the
Department of Justice has launched an investigation. The State

Department communicated with the Attorney General who ordered an investigation by the El Paso office of the Bureau of Investigation." Two days later the *Star* came out with a double page, illustrated spread—thirteen full columns—on the case.

Governor Dillon had indeed sent the case to the British Consulate in Galveston, which in turn had forwarded it to the British Embassy in Washington, D. C. The assumption behind the intervention of Her Majesty's government in the case was that Manby was a British subject. Jocelyn B. Manby affirmed this with a public statement headed, "Manby Never U.S. Citizen, Says Brother," stating that Manby had taken out first naturalization papers in 1883 but had let the application go by default, as he had returned to England for a visit in the nineties. His application of 1899 was but a renewal of the first. This was denied by a Santa Fe attorney who asserted Manby had been admitted to citizenship in the district court of Taos County on December 4, 1899.

While this international controversy was going on, another state argument got under way as reflected in the *Santa Fe New Mexican* front page headline:

DILLON SCORES KIKER;
CALLS MANBY MURDER DISGRACE

Governor Dillon had testily written Henry A. Kiker, judge of the eighth judicial district, inquiring why he had not sent in a report on his investigation. Judge Kiker was a southern gentleman, thin to emaciation, whose soft voice had an edge which could cut like a razor. He was not a man to be intimidated by a governor. He replied curtly that as he was without funds he had made no investigation. Moreover, he refused to make a report under any conditions, saying that the public press was not a place for trial cases—an outright rebuke to the governor for the statements he had made to the press.

"HANDS OFF MANBY CASE" KIKER TELLS DILLON

Finally needled into action, Dillon requested the state board of finance to approve use of $1,500 from his own contingency fund to prosecute the Manby investigation. Apparently Kiker did not acknowledge receipt of the funds, and made no investigation.

As a postscript to the whole affair, Doc Martin crustily refused to deliver to the authorities a report of the autopsy he had made on Manby's exhumed body because no one would pay him for it.

Meanwhile another threatening note was slipped under the door of Detective Martin's hotel room during the first week of January. "You let Teracita alone. Severino will kill you." Martin ignored it and continued nosing around. Evidence turned up indicating that the United States Secret Service Society, Self-Supporting Branch organized by Manby, was a bunco game for obtaining land by fraudulent means and for fleecing its members of large sums of money.

More important was the discovery of Manby's diary. There were many peculiar things about it. Manby had kept a diary for more than thirty years in the form of letters addressed to "Hon. D. M." Names of persons were never written out; only the initial of their first or last names were used, and he usually referred to himself as "A. M." or "A. R. M." The diary revealed his engrossing interest in criminology. A bank robbery at La Mar, Colorado fascinated him. He discussed the Saint Valentine's Day massacre in Chicago at length. And of the $167,000 Hartford, Connecticut swindle by Roger Watkins, an English,-man, he wrote: "Roger Watkins was an English gentleman of intelligence and ability to defraud and make money from the imbecile American public. Watkins is safe because of the untrained tactics of detection employed by American detectives." Martin also noticed in Manby's library a well-thumbed history of the Vendetta and the Mafia, and several volumes on poison.

Manby's entries in his diary for the last few days before his death or disappearance were confusing; not only because of his use of initials, but because of his frequent use of dashes instead of filling out sentences.

Under the date of June 28 he had written: "Later called at Canyon and T cut loose on me—that I ought to have been retired years ago as I was feeble, old, deaf, and blind etc. Some truth in this as I told her, after being gassed and poisoned so often in her service and defense—but poor taste for her to throw this up to me ..."

The entry for June 30, his last, was a long letter addressed to "Hon. D. M.":

"Have been under the weather all week—no appetite— shortness of breath and exhaustion following the least exercise— possibly result of last attempts to gas and poison me from T. P.'s side. T denies this—but this does not change my belief. Looks like T. P. after trying to qualify as a boy is a double crosser etc. —after years of struggle and practice along these lines may at last by the aid and council of higher ups carry out the orders for J.D., W.P., et al in the absence of S. P."

Along the margin of this paragraph was scrawled: "Note— Nearly six times while writing this sheet have had to snap awake???

"Referring to the different incidents of June 28—It would not surprise me that a dangerous combination existed between McH, S.D. et al to poison T's mind against S.G. and A.R.M.— due to delays etc.—on which they are held responsible—that both ought to have been retired long ago.

"In the meantime P.P. stands high ace with McH, so T tells me with modest pride."[2]

The phrase "ought to have been retired" meant, of course, that Manby ought to have died years ago. Most of the initials Martin could easily identify. A.R.M. was Manby himself; T. was Teracita; A. was Mrs. Felix Archuleta; G.F. stood for George Ferguson; W.P. for William (Guillermo) Pacheco; and S.G. for Severino Gutierrez. After a time the meaning of "T.P.'s side" became clear. T.P. stood for Dr. T. Paul Martin whose house adjoined Manby's, thus being on the other side of the common wall separating them. McH referred to George McHorse and S.D. to Sam Davis who had been members not only of the Society but of a stolen car ring. Cars stolen in west Texas and eastern New Mexico were taken to Davis in Clovis or Tucumcari who then brought them up to McHorse in Taos to be doctored up and sold. McHorse's base of operation was up Canyon, opposite Teracita's house. Shortly after Manby's death both men had been caught, convicted, and were now serving time in the federal penitentiary at Leavenworth.

Into what pattern were all these ramifications woven? Was it possible that Doc Martin had been allied with the Society and had tried to poison and gas Manby, although Teracita denied it? Clearly McHorse and Sam Davis were allied with Teracita within the Society. But who were the "higher ups" who had taken over control of the Society when Manby began to fail? Too, there were coincidences of names that puzzled Martin, if they were coincidences. Craig Kennedy was the name of a popular fiction detective. Craig Kenneth, one of the invisible directors of the secret society, was suspiciously like it. But Kenneth also had been the name of one of Manby's miners in Moreno Valley who had mysteriously disappeared. So had the name of Severino Gutierrez, the leader of the Society, been taken from another miner who had disappeared. Francisca Ferguson, Teracita's sister, had been married to a man named Varos or de Varos. Teracita also claimed she had been married once, briefly, to a Varos, although she still obdurately used the name of Ferguson herself and had given it to her children. Were these the same man, by whom Teracita possibly had had an illegitimate child? And had he been the cowhand named Varos whom Manby had killed out of jealousy—saying that Varos' horse had kicked his head off?

Martin had no definite proofs in answer to these many questions, but in his report to Governor Dillon, he reconstructed the case as he now saw it:

During the old man's latter years, "Manby's faculties began to grow feebler day by day, the fear of death hovered over him and was such that he was always fearful some unknown enemies were about to strike him down . . . It is striking that in all Manby's wandering diary, the night of 'September 28, 1921' (the night that Wilkerson was murdered in Teracita's house) cannot be forgotten; it appears again and again as a nightmare.

"His conscience apparently hurt him, and certain Psalms of the Bible are quoted in his diary. Also many warnings to his love, 'Princess Teracita,' were uttered by him—he mentioned the sufferings he had endured *since the night of September 28, 1921!* Manby's hallucinations came to the point where mental telepathy was working; he knew death was not far off.

"The murder of September 28, 1921 was weighing heavily upon him and Manby did never go out at night except the night of July first, 1929, when a message was sent to him by the supposed 'S.G.' that Teracita was very ill. Manby was urged to go to her at once. Manby responded to the call; he went to Teracita's home in Canyon.[3] There Manby received some poisoned whiskey—he became delirious and his hallucinations of previous years worked so hard upon him that Manby put up a fight for his life. He was knocked down by a woman and a man. Then the reaction of the poisoned whiskey, in addition to the blows, caused Manby to lose consciousness.

"Manby's enemies, knowing that poison could be easily detected, and realizing that Manby might have been seen going to that place that night, decided to get rid of his body. Four people went into conference over the matter and decided it best to cut Manby's head off so as to bring a *quicker decomposition of the body* and thus *conceal the cause of death*—poison or blows on the head—or both.

"A woman and a man then took charge of Manby's body and cut his head off. During the night of July 1st and early in the morning of July 2nd, this man and that woman, with the help of another man, loaded the body into a truck, head wrapped up in towels, and brought it back to the Manby residence. There it was placed on the little Army cot. . . .

"They unwrapped the head, took the towels away—towels which bore the name 'Manby.' They placed the body in a natural position, resting it on its left side. They placed the head on the trunk.

"In undressing Manby's body, they placed Manby's shoes and socks in a room thirty-six feet from where the body lay. They took the towels back to Canyon to be washed and ironed, but the job was done so quickly that the blood stains were not thoroughly removed in the wash. On the night of July 2nd those towels were brought back to the Manby house by a man and a woman who knew the place well, who had keys to gain admittance, and who were well acquainted with the police dog and other dogs.

"They put the towels back in an old fashioned Mexican basket in a corner of a bedroom situated in the southwest corner of the house. They put those towels mixed up with quilts and blankets, making sure that everything was well concealed, as every criminal will do. They went back to where the body was lying to see if it was in proper position. Manby's police dog, which had been alone in the house with the body of its dead master, did naturally try to lick his face. In doing so, the head rolled off and leaned against the wall, and left blood stains on the wall. Realizing the situation, the murderers took Manby's head in the adjoining bedroom and later the dog, hungry and thirsty, started to chew on it.

"On July 3rd, at 12:30 in the afternoon, one of the murderers gave the alarm of Manby's death. He told the authorities that Manby had died. How did this man know it? There was no way for any human being to know it, or to see into the hall through a locked and bolted door.

"The authorities were notified and a deputy sheriff arrived at the house. Keys were sought to gain admittance.

"Preparations were made to battle with ferocious dogs concealed within the house. Then suddenly the house was found opened; one of the murderers kindly had unlocked the doors and taken the police dog out into the yard, chaining the animal to a kennel.

"A coroner's jury was formed; it came to the conclusion, after NO investigation, that A. R. Manby died of 'natural causes'."

Martin, in his last report to Governor Dillon on February 25, 1930, summarized all his findings and stated that Manby had been murdered. He took pains to list all the motives: robbery, jealousy, fear, and vengeance. He suspected Carmen and George Duran, Teracita and George Ferguson. In conclusion he stated flatly, "I do not see any mystery to the A. R. Manby case. If less publicity, less talk, and more work was done, the guilty party could be brought to justice without much time."

The report was unheeded and Martin was taken off the case. Teracita's suit against Burch, and Miss Waddell's suit against Manby, were dropped.

The next day there occurred something that focused still more attention on the Manby case.

On the night of February 26, Juan Vasquez, the caretaker of artist John Young-Hunter's home, noticed smoke coming from the house. Rushing inside, he found a mattress and a pile of newspapers ablaze on the floor. Putting out the fire, he found the house had been robbed. It was quite obvious that whoever had broken in had set fire to the house in an attempt to conceal the robbery.

Jack and Eve Young-Hunter, then at their New York apartment at 130 West 57th Street, were notified at once and caught the first train back. They found the house almost completely gutted of clothes, silverware, blankets, linens, art treasures, and furnishings with several fine paintings blackened by smoke. Reporting the thefts, Young-Hunter engaged Herbert Cheetam, a former Secret Service operator and the son of attorney H. J. Cheetam, a long resident in town, to trace the missing articles.[4]

A *New York Tribune* story headed "PAINT BRUSH TRAIL" reported Cheetam's successful search. The trail was easy to follow. Underneath the barbed wire fence on the edge of the property, Cheetam found one of Jack's paint brushes and Eve's Japanese parasol. Down the road lay more paint brushes and a pair of bridle bits, and just inside the gate of Teracita's court lay still more paint brushes.

Obtaining a search warrant for the Ferguson home, he found Teracita dyeing two of Young-Hunter's monogrammed silk shirts. Other pieces of clothing, silverware, and dishes were strewn throughout the house District Attorney Stringfellow immediately arrested Teracita, admitting her to $500 bond. This was soon raised to $1,200 and she was bound to district court under charge of concealing stolen property. Her nephew, George Ferguson, was also arrested. As he was already under bond for holding up a town policeman, Palemon Martinez, and robbing him of money, he was held in jail under Judge Kiker's instructions that he was not to be admitted to bail nor allowed to see anyone. During questioning he implicated Carmen Duran in the robbery, who was then arrested for arson and burglary, and placed under $2,000 bond.

The *New York Telegram* broke the story with the headline:

ARTIST TAMES WILD WEST,
JAILS EXTORTION THEFT GANG

and the sub-head:

Wanted: A modern Kit Carson to break the power of
of a sinister secret society in the Pueblo
country of New Mexico.

It and Associated Press dispatches revealed for the first time
the existence of "a secret band that had held the region in a
state of mild terrorism," the mysterious United States Secret
and Civil Service Society. It reported the discovery of many
letters from Manby to Ceferino Gutierrez, a secret agent. One of
the papers found was reported to be a letter from Manby to
Teracita advising her on August 8, 1926 what to do with the
$827,000,000 she was to receive from the Society. Among the
items, he advised her to invest $5 million in government bonds
which would give her an income of $200,000 annually—enough
to live on comfortably; an investment of $5 million for her
children; the establishment of a home for girls; and a colony in
South America for races like the Armenians trying to escape
religious persecution.[5]

Stringfellow and Cheetam continued their search of Teracita's
home. Under the front porch they found four of Young-Hunter's
silver bridles valued at $100 each, and boxes, trunks, and gunny
sacks filled with other stolen articles buried in the garden. They
also found a supply of goods stolen from Alvin Burch's general
merchandise store ten days before, and articles stolen from the
home of Mrs. Felix Archuleta.

Bonds for Teracita were set at $1,200 for concealing the
Young-Hunter loot and $600 for the Archuleta robbery; and for
Carmen Duran, $2,000 for burglary and $2,500 for arson at
the Young-Hunter home, and $600 for larceny at the Archuleta
home. George Ferguson had waived preliminary examination
and was left in jail at Raton.

Going to Manby's house, Stringfellow and Cheetam found it
almost bare. Evidently Teracita, Duran, and George Ferguson
had stripped it of all furnishings, paintings, and silverware.[6]
Where had it all gone? There was one clue, at least. Shortly after
Manby's alleged death, B. F. Meyer of Santa Fe had bought
from Teracita a painting by the noted Taos artist, Ernest L.
Blumenschein, which he had then sold to Judge E. R. Wright.[7]

During his examination of the house, Cheetam reported finding
several Number 2 buckshot in the cracks of the floor of the
bedroom facing the garden. When he tapped the window sill,
more buckshot rolled out. These indicated to him that Manby
had been shot by someone outside. In a pile of rubbish he found
more tablets of Manby's diary, and still more evidence of the

United States Secret Service Society.

Four Taos attorneys, embarrassed now at all the goings-on, passed a resolution saying that the district court and district attorney had been duly diligent in probing the Manby murder.

The *Santa Fe New Mexican* promptly let out an editorial horse-laugh: "Is anyone in the state really ignorant of the fact that the Manby case has become the big wheeze of the year?" And on March 11 it indignantly declaimed, "The limit has been reached if no state action is taken now in view of the *Kansas City Star* publicity, the intervention of the federal government, and the arrests in Taos. The failure of justice to move so far has done incalculable damage to the reputation of New Mexico in the United States and abroad."

Next day another aspect of the "big wheeze" came to light when Teracita was taken to federal court in Albuquerque. Dr. Thorne, hearing of Manby's murder, had come to foreclose on the mortgage he held on Manby's property.

Hearing on the case was conducted before Judge Colin Neblett. Dr. Thorne was present with his attorneys, E. R. Wright of Santa Fe, and James L. Goree of the Denver firm of Hodges, Wilson, and Rogers. Teracita and the Colonial Bond and Security Company were represented by J. H. Crist of Pojoaque and Pacheco of Santa Fe. Behind these lawyers sat Teracita. The *Albuquerque Journal* took pains to describe her.[8]

"The Princess Teracita sat at the rear of her counsels' table. A black felt hat, which resembled nothing so much as some sort of a straight-sided pot, adorned with figures in another shade of black, sat on the back of her head. Her plush coat and serge dress also were black.

"The gray hose which she wore, wrinkled at the ankles just before they disappeared into light brown oxfords.

"Her black eyes were piercing, and gave a look of cunning to the face which was marked by spots of rouge on either cheek. Occasionally her head was bent as she stared at the floor, and wrinkles under her chin were plainly evident. She is about forty years old."

What the observant reporter did not notice was that she was pregnant—the reason for her loose-fitting serge dress.

The courtroom was full of curious spectators due to the case "which has taken on an international tinge because of its

relationship to Manby's death, which Great Britain has asked
the United States to investigate." Detective Martin sat in the
front row.

The case seemed simple enough. Dr. Thorne was instituting a
foreclosure suit on Manby's property for loan on a promissory
note for $11,547.30. The property was held in the name of the
Colonial Bond and Security Company, of which Manby had been
president and Teracita vice president. The company, according
to its reports, had been chartered in 1909 to deal in lands,
minerals, and general real estate business. Of its total stock of
50,000 shares, Manby owned 49,990 shares. In 1922 Manby had
transferred all his property to the company; this was confirmed
by the company's annual report for 1928, listing Manby as
president and Teracita as vice president. The annual report
for 1929 had not been filed yet, although it was eight months
delinquent. What was the status of the company now?

J. H. Crist, attorney for Teracita, spoke up. "Teracita
Ferguson and I control the Colonial Bond and Security Company. Together we own 33,000 shares of the company's stock,
and Fidel Cordova owns 1,990 shares. Mrs. Ferguson is
president and I am secretary."

As Cordova was his assistant, and Crist was also defending
Teracita against the Young-Hunter charges against her, it was
quite evident that Teracita was paying him for his services with
a large share of the company stock.

Dr. Thorne was put on the stand to identify a number of
letters which he had written to Manby. Questions then came
up regarding the background of Manby, his mysterious death,
and consideration for the loan. This was suddenly stopped
when Teracita and Crist agreed to allow in full Thorne's claim
against the estate.

Judge Neblett accordingly entered a decree granting Thorne
$13,071.30. The foreclosure sale was to be held January 12, 1931
and any balance left after this amount was to revert to the
Colonial Bond and Security Company.

Reported the Associated Press:[9]

MANBY ESTATE PAYS $13,000 TO STOP SUIT

Asked why he suddenly capitulated, Crist replied in brief

that the contest of Thorne's suit was principally to gain time
so a just price could be received for the property.

As Thorne left the courthouse, a reporter caught him for an
interview. Thorne mentioned he once had paid Manby $5,000
for an oil painting represented to be an original old master,
but which had turned out to be false.

"What did you do with it?" asked the reporter.

"I still have it; it's a pretty picture," replied Thorne.

Presumably the painting alluded to was Van Dyck's "St.
Catherine." Yet Bill Martin, standing by, was not so sure. In
his perusal of the countless letters which comprised Manby's
diary, he had found that Manby had persuaded Farina to make
copies of the "St. Agnes" to place on the market in New York,
Chicago, and Philadelphia at prices ranging from $15,000 to
$20,000. Manby had not paid Farina for making the copies,
so Farina still retained possession of the original. But also,
wondered Martin, had Farina palmed off on Thorne a copy of
the "St. Agnes" instead of the original "St. Catherine"?

Teracita was rushed back to Taos for the preliminary hearing
on the Young-Hunter robbery. It began on the morning of
March 15. The case had attracted so much attention that a
virtual holiday was observed in town so that everyone could
attend it. The only building large enough to hold the spectators
was the dance hall of the Sociedad Filantropica. Long before
the doors were opened, a crowd of more than five hundred people
—artist friends of Jack Young-Hunter, Spanish *paisanos* in
overalls or black *rebozos*, Anglo ranchers in Stetson hats and
Levis, businessmen in suits and shined shoes, *políticos* and
townspeople—were milling around the horses, wagons, and
automobiles outside.

One noted member of the art-and-literary colony was missing:
D. H. Lawrence who had died in Nice, France two weeks before.
A newspaper heralded his passing: "Prophet D. H. Lawrence
Slips Into Oblivion."

At last, like a breaking tide, the crowd rushed inside to fill
the seats and aisles.

The dance hall was still in its usual gala attire. Streamers
of red, white, and blue paper hung from the *vigas* in the ceiling
and stretched across the walls. The piano and trap drums still
stood on the orchestra platform. All the principals were present:

District Attorney Stringfellow and attorney H. J. Cheetham opposing J. H. Crist, defending Teracita and Carmen Duran; Jack and Eve Young-Hunter seated opposite the accused; Mrs. Felix Archuleta, John Strongberg, a host of witnesses, and the omnipresent Detective Martin.

All the stolen property had been recovered, reported String-fellow; most of it had been found buried in the back garden of the Ferguson home. The judge asked to see it.

Stringfellow smiled. "It would fill the platform here, Your Honor. There were more than one hundred fifty articles. Allow me to submit an itemized list."

At the conclusion of the preliminary hearing it was obvious to everyone that Crist did not have a leg to stand on. The case was moved to Raton on a change of venue, and the trial before Judge Kiker was set for July 14. On July 7, a week before it was to begin, it was announced that Teracita might not go to trial; the preceding Friday she had given birth to a new son— her fourth child—in the Manby home at Taos. Her request for postponement was denied and news of the trial proceedings was featured in all newspapers for two weeks.

The trial ended on July 31. All defendants were adjudged guilty. Teracita was sentenced to prison for a term of from four to six years, and Carmen Duran was given from seven to ten years. George Ferguson was not tried for participation in the Young-Hunter robbery, but sentenced to from four to six years on conviction of assault with intent to kill in his previous stabbing affair. Juan Duran was also given the same sentence for participation in the same fight. Due to the untimely birth of her new son, Teracita was not committed to the penitentiary until January 12, 1931 when her previous three children—two boys and a girl—were made wards of the court.

The convictions, however, did not clear up the Manby mystery. Repercussions and criticisms kept pouring in to Governor Dillon.

Jocelyn B. Manby wrote from Edgewater, Colorado to declaim, "The murder of my brother is a disgrace to New Mexico."

On September 2 Miss Margaret Waddell, whom the lawyer Renehan had characterized as a "Scotch lassie, strong of mind and body," wrote a long letter to Governor Dillon in her fine handwriting, recapitulating her troubles with crooked lawyers in New Mexico. Despite Manby's criminal act, his murder was a disgrace to the state. Now "this woman sentenced to the penitentiary and living in the murdered man's home as a matter of right, with a man she is not married to, is selling a piece of the murdered man's property to the sister of the Probate Judge." Something was wrong with New Mexico, with its judges and lawyers. She herself was now in absolute destitution, without a roof over her head. She was ill and had no money . . ."[10]

Another letter came from Mrs. Violet Manby Edmunds, Leigh on the Sea, Essex, England, identifying herself as "the daughter of Lydia Manby before her marriage," and saying she was now 79 years old.

Still another came from E. T. Manby, an officer of the Colonial Trust Company in Pittsburg, Pennsylvania and the treasurer of the Layman's Missionary League in the diocese of Pittsburg. He had heard that Manby was still alive and wished all late information on the investigation. The governor had none to give him.[11]

Earlier that year, however, the *New Mexican* had published reports that Manby was in Italy and had sent back a photograph of himself to show how he had improved in health. Newspapers in Los Angles had picked up the story and were trying to trace its source.

Also the governor himself had received a telegram on April 28, and a letter on May 2, 1930, from Miles Plemmons, a detective in Bentonville, Arkansas, stating that he possessed evidence that Manby had checked out of the United States on July 8, 1929, a week after he had been reported murdered. Plemmons asserted he could produce photographs of Manby taken from his passport, and would be glad to assist in returning him to this country.[12]

Governor Dillon did nothing about it. Nor did anyone else. Yet over all hung the darkening shadow of the belief that Manby was still alive.

3

Dead or alive, Manby had stirred up all the resentments and rivalries between the three racial elements in the valley. Any one of them, Indian, Spanish, or Anglo, it was asserted, could have killed him.

The Pueblo Lands Board in a bill sent to Congress shortly after his alleged death recognized that many settlers had encroached upon Indian land, and offered to buy back their land for the Indians to the amount of $14,064. It proposed to restore to the Pueblo that portion of the Martinez Grant known as the Tenorio Tract which had been awarded to Manby. Furthermore it offered the Pueblo monetary payments for all rights to the townsite of Taos itself which had been located on the Pueblo Grant.

But Manby's appropriation of the Tenorio Tract and his claim to the waters of the Lucero had aroused among the Indians a fear and hatred not to be dispelled so easily. They stubbornly refused the total Congressional offer of $297,684.67, demanding instead clear title to the mountain headwaters of the Lucero and Pueblo rivers, the area surrounding their sacred Blue Lake.

The result was that Congress finally passed on May 31, 1933 an act giving the Pueblo a fifty-year tenure of their sacred area, their "church,"[1] and restoring to it the Tenorio Tract which extended the Reservation boundary to the Arroyo Seco.

Manby's acquisition of the Martinez Grant, the hot springs, and town property had aroused the Spanish element against him as well as the Indian. Its spearpoint was the strange sect of Penitentes which long had dominated the Rio Arriba country. The *Hermanos Penitentes*, Penitent Brothers, or *Hermanos de la Luz*, Brothers of Light, practiced self-flagellation and each Easter hung one of their members on a cross in emulation of the crucifixion of Christ. Deriving from the Third Order of St. Francis, their rites had been brought to New Mexico in 1598. Later outlawed by the Catholic Church, the sect perished except in the mountains of northern New Mexico. Here it flourished, Taos being its headquarters.

Its membership, although secret, was known to be large, controlling affairs in villages and exercising force in state politics. There was reason for its influence. Incoming Anglos were gradually taking over control of the eastern and southern parts of the state. Only the Rio Arriba remained as the last stronghold of Spanish-Catholic domination. Now it too was being menaced by Anglo-Protestants eager to acquire land and dominate politics. Chief among them was, of course, Manby. He had not only obtained the Martinez Grant, but he had organized a secret society said to include many Anglo-Protestants and Masons who had joined in order to oppose the secret sect of the Spanish Penitentes. If Manby had not been murdered by the Indians, the talk ran, he could very well have been killed by the Penitentes.

The Anglo element was not excluded from the honor of having put the finishing touch on Manby's unpopularity. Among it too were dozens of persons whose motivations for murder could have been easily understood. Even his own Society, which had grown corrupt and evil, might have done away with him if it had not been Teracita and Duran themselves.

In brief, it could not reasonably be said that a soul in town —Indian, Spanish, or Anglo—missed him. Perhaps because almost everyone had the uneasy feeling that the mysterious old recluse was peeking out at them from behind some bush. If there were those who believed he had been murdered, their voices were muted by the constant buzz of conversation proclaiming he was still alive.

Manby obviously had been quite aware of the animosity

against him. Ralph Meyers was certain Manby wanted to sell his treasured rifle for cash in order to make a quick get-away before papers could be served on him by Margaret Waddell and before Teracita's suit against Burch came up. The Lockwoods were equally sure Manby wanted to plant their German shepherd in his home as false evidence.

To be sure, the body had been dug up for identification by four men. But Stringfellow from Raton and Roberts from Santa Fe had not known Manby and certainly could not identify a mutilated body. Doc Martin didn't give a damn, and destroyed his autopsy report the minute he found out he was not to be paid for it. Of the four, only Saca Muelas positively identified the body as Manby's from his dentures. But Detective Martin had found both the upper and lower plates in Manby's house and had turned them in to Stringfellow and Kiker in Raton. Just whose dentures and whose body had been found in the grave no one knew, although most people believed it was that of Brooks, a neighbor who had died a few days before. If the Brooks family believed this, it did nothing to confirm or deny the rumor.

Victor Higgins, the watercolor painter, also held the opinion that Manby had killed and mutilated another man to leave in his place. Higgins believed he knew who it was. He had quarrelled with Manby, telling him never to set foot on his property. A few days later when he was under his car, he saw what looked like Manby approaching—similar boots, puttees, riding trousers, shirt. Crawling out from under his car, Higgins now saw the man's face. The man was not Manby, but an itinerant who said he wanted a job as a gardener. Higgins promptly sent him to Manby.[2]

Three weeks later Manby was reported murdered and the gardener had disappeared. When Manby's alleged body and head were exhumed, a friend of Higgins who had found the gardener's hat, casually dropped the hat on the severed head. It was so large that it covered the head completely, proving to Higgins at least that the buried body was not the gardener's.[3]

Joseph Sharp, the noted painter of Indians, returned to town after a long voyage with his wife. The couple was greatly disturbed upon hearing the wild conjectures about Manby's alleged murder. In Italy both of them had seen Manby on a street in Florence and had quickly walked over to greet him. Manby, however, had ducked into a store and escaped through the back door.[4]

More evidence that Manby had fled was given by runty Doughbelly Price, the colorful real estate agent whose "Goddamn it, my word's as good as my dollar!" had established his reputation for veracity. He positively had seen Manby furtively slouching past his office two days after his alleged death.[5] Elmer, the son of Alvin Burch, reported that a friend of his in Mexico who knew Manby well, Jesus Mares y Maesta, had seen him in Ojinaga, Chihuahua two years after his reported death. All these statements seemed to be confirmed by the telegram and letter received by Governor Dillon from Miles Plemmons stating that Manby had checked out of the country a week after he had been reported murdered, and offering to produce a passport photograph of him. Dillon still did nothing about this.

If all this was assuming the proportions of a pulp-paper mystery, indignation was running higher than could be expected from a public that had not lost what could be considered a favorite citizen. Why had Detective Martin's investigations been stopped by Attorney General Otero and Governor Dillon? Why had Her Majesty's government, the British Embassy in Washington, and the British Consulate in Galveston dropped the case? Why had Manby's three brothers, just as unaccountably, washed their hands of the affair, refusing to aid in the continuance of the investigation or even to buy a marker for his grave?

Apparently the only answer was the fact that Manby was still alive, and for some strange reason they all wanted to ignore the case. Why?

Dr. Thorne, somewhat irked at finding out that Manby's original Van Dyck painting was false, now requested the law firm of Hodges, Wilson, and Vidal in Denver to investigate the title of Manby's Hot Springs. This was also confusing, as the Colonial Bond and Security Company on the authorization of Teracita and Crist had given a mortgage on it to Crist to pay his attorney's fees, even though Manby previously had given it to Thorne as collateral.

In due time the answer came back. The Hot Springs property had never belonged to Manby. A rancher named Short had bought the tract from one Emilio Martinez, had paid up in full all the taxes on it, and did not want to sell it at any price.[6]

That old rascal, Manby.

In 1935 Doc Martin died and his widow converted his house into the Martin Hotel. The following year there arrived a stranger to take over Manby's house for Dr. Thorne. She was a middle-aged woman named Miss Helen Williams, very sharp, capable, and close-mouthed, whom everyone assumed had been Thorne's private secretary in Canada. Within a week she had employed three full-time gardeners to put the weedy garden and the big park in shape. Then came crews of plumbers, electricians, masons, carpenters, and workmen to completely rebuild and modernize the nineteen-room house. A corps of engineers from Denver arrived with the first central heating plant to be installed in town. Not in its entire 315-year history had Taos witnessed such a spending spree.

"Don't stint money. Don't ask what anything costs. Just send me the bills," Thorne had told Miss Williams.

For months the work went on. When the house was finished, decorated, and completely furnished, a housekeeper, a maid, and a cook moved in. Then Miss Williams threw open the front door. "Thorne House" was open for business.

"The purpose of Thorne House," she announced, "is to serve the community." Once or twice a week dinners were served to small groups in town. Organizations were invited to discuss their affairs. Bedrooms were offered to visiting artists and young people for short periods until they could establish themselves. For the first time the town had a community center. The only guest it lacked was the mysterious Dr. Thorne who never showed up at all.[7]

The whole thing was viewed by the town as quite unreasonable. No one except Manby had seen Thorne on his brief visit years before. The few who knew of his existence wondered why he had taken over the property instead of merely collecting the $13,000 judgment on it awarded by court. All regarded it as preposterous that a man in New York and Canada was spending such a mint of money to benefit a town he did not know, never came to, and in which he had no friends. The only possible explanation was that the mysterious Dr. Thorne was Manby with a new name, a fistful of money, and a bad conscience.

Miss Williams was of little help. She said nothing, but she

Manby's home restored as Thorne House between 1937-1940. Front gate seen from the road. *Photo by Paul Juley.*

Front gate viewed from inside the grounds, Thorne House, 1937-1940. *Photo by Paul Juley.*

Front entrance, Thorne House, 1937-1940. *Photo by Paul Juley.*

Inner patio, Thorne House, 1937-1940. *Photo by Paul Juley.*

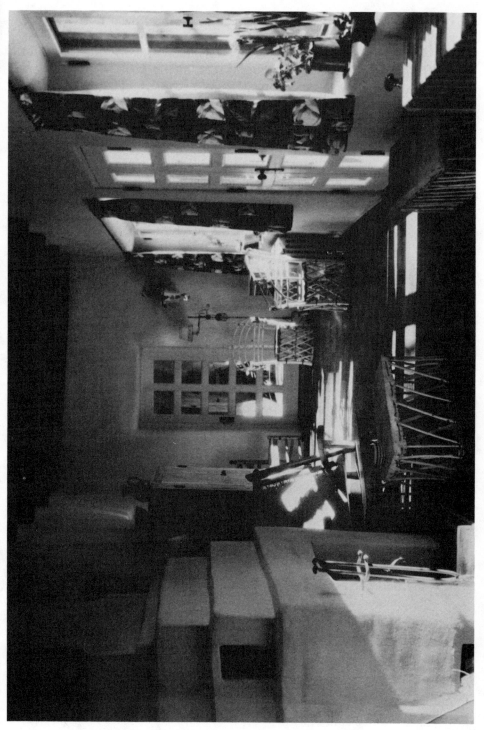

Sun room, Thorne House, 1937-1940. *Photo by Paul Juley.*

was extremely sensitive about anyone speaking the name "Manby" or referring to the old man in the house.

A few years after Thorne House had been opened, Mabel and Tony Lujan and a couple of other Taos friends were spending the winter in New York. Mabel happened to run into Miss Williams on the street and invited her to dinner that night.

"I can't come. Dr. Thorne is in town to discuss some business with me."

"So much the better!" said Mabel. "Bring him along!"

That evening Mabel and her guests were sitting in the living room of her apartment in the tower of One Fifth Avenue, talking as usual about Manby and the mysterious Dr. Thorne.

"Of course Manby's Dr. Thorne," said one. "So naturally he won't show up."

"Well if he doesn't, we'll know for sure."

At that moment Dr. Thorne, without ringing the bell or knocking at the door, stepped in with Miss Williams at his heels. Making a little bow, he said humorously, "Well, you can see I'm not Mr. Manby!"

Indeed, he wasn't. He was years younger, shorter, more lightly built, and with a sharp mind and quick humor. Everyone laughed and settled down to an enjoyable evening. Thorne made no explanation of his purpose in creating and maintaining Thorne House or why he never went to see it. But just the same, he seemed to have been provided with a *dossier* on everyone in town. There was not a person mentioned, not a rumor nor shred of gossip, he did not know fully and intimately.[8] This fact struck everyone as peculiar after he had gone. The consensus was that if he were not Manby, he was a close associate of the old man and acting as his agent.

Years later Miss Williams explained the nature of her association with him. She herself had been a professional interior decorator of high repute in London and in New York where she had been under contract to Macy's department store, and independently wealthy. One of her friends in Toronto, Canada was the nurse whom Thorne was then courting and later married. When Manby was murdered, Thorne requested her to investigate the property in Taos as he had heart trouble, and could not stand the high altitude. This led to her restoration of Thorne House.

In 1948 Dr. Thorne suddenly dropped dead in church. It had been expected that he would leave a trust fund to finance continued operation of Thorne House, as he had intended. It was then discovered that he had not amended his eleven-year-old will to this effect. Thorne House, accordingly, was sold for $45,000 to the Taos Art Association.

He had left, however, a trust fund of $100,000 for Miss Williams to manage for the benefit of the community as the Taos Foundation. More was added to it from time to time, enabling the foundation to donate $125,000 to the Embudo Hospital, downriver from Taos, for the purpose of adding a new wing. Its activities still reflected, in some measure, the eccentricities of both Thorne and Manby. It not only loaned money to medical and business school students, but it made donations to needy persons needing false teeth. It would not pay for extracting the old ones, but bought the new dentures. Every Christmas it also supplied at cost to school children hundreds of shirts, jeans, and galoshes.[9]

All this was strange too. A man who had poured a half-million dollars at least into a small, remote town he'd never been in but once! No one was ever convinced that there hadn't been a closer relationship between Thorne and Manby than was known.

Teracita was paroled as a model prisoner after serving five months in the penitentiary. Returning home, she moved into a small house and took up fortune-telling. She read from cards, palms, or a crystal ball. She was considered excellent and had a large clientele. Affable but close-mouthed, she took pains to give the impression of a woman who had suffered much and unjustly from false rumors. She admitted having sued Burch for a large sum of money, hoping for a return on several loans Ferguson had made to him, but she knew nothing about the existence of the United States Secret and Civil Service Society. As for Manby, he was a fine, misunderstood man who had been like a grandfather, an uncle, to her. A certain gang of crooks had ruined him, and tried to kill him for his money. Shortly afterward the gang had burned the courthouse in order to destroy all the records of his and their activities. Now no one would ever know anything about him. . . . This was all anyone could get out of her.[10]

There was a great deal to be known besides what had happened to Manby. The old man had been poor for years, little by little losing everything he had. Yet time and again, in every pinch, he had raised from somewhere all the money he needed. In that somewhere he had cached a great deal of money. Had it been buried in his garden—that weedy garden in which, to Doc Martin's disgust, he had been interminably digging, only to be followed by Teracita and Duran? And that fabulous collection of free gold in his immense safe, from which for years he had kept drawing as if from a safe deposit box. Who had got that?

On the surface, continuous gossip, rumors, and conjectures. But underneath, a silence impregnated with fear. It wasn't healthy to poke into such matters.

In 1938 the dentist, Dr. Fred Muller, secured a new assistant who remained with him for nine years. She was Mrs. Dolores Montoya, whose mother, Mrs. Jesusita Perrault, came from one of the old, noble families of Chihuahua and who in 1929 had been elected Secretary of State under Governor Dillon. Mrs. Montoya was a capable assistant and an understanding woman with good judgment. She had to be, for Saca Muelas was riding the peak of prosperity and popularity.

He had been elected mayor of Taos that year, was president of the New Mexico Dental Society after having served as its secretary for many years, a prominent member of the Masonic Lodge, and a busy politician who attended every Republican convention. Hence Mrs. Montoya's duties were not restricted to handing him a clean towel when necessary. She helped him to write his speeches, rehearse Masonic rituals, and secure votes.

One evening he abruptly confessed, "That wasn't Manby's body we exhumed and which I positively identified from his dentures. I lied. I made Manby's dentures and remembered them well; we had a little argument over them. Those shown me were not his."

"Why did you say they were, then?" Mrs. Montoya asked.

He hesitated a moment. "The talk was that it was old Brooks' body, and I didn't want to cause Mrs. Brooks any suffering over it."

One of Saca Muelas' best friends was Hinde. He called often and in Saca Muelas' private office the two men talked of odd subjects with impassioned intensity: of a gang in town headed by Pete Nolan, and of the activities of the Leighton or Layton Brothers, a band of train robbers in Colorado prominently in the news. Also, constantly, of Manby.

She then discovered that Saca Muelas kept in his personal file all the records of the United States Secret and Civil Service Society. He was constantly referring to them and often showed them to Hinde. She never saw them, never asked questions; it was a dangerous subject. What happened to the files when Muller died in 1947 is not known.[11]

There grew in town the feeling that the Society constituted the core of the Manby mystery. Manby, with his fertile imagination, had established it to fleece gullible members out of cash and property. It had then become too large and profitable to be dominated by a crazy old man, an unlearned Spanish woman, and her outlaw lover. A small, sharp and ruthless group within the Society took it over, branching out into other activities like the stolen car ring and possibly the Colorado train robbers. Undoubtedly this was the gang to which Teracita had alluded.

Of all persons who had known Manby, Hinde was probably the closest to him. What was his opinion regarding the murder or mysterious disappearance of Manby? But Hinde too died without talking.[12]

Ex-governor Dillon, running a little country store on a dirt road beside the railroad tracks at Encino, could not give a reason why the state couldn't afford the few hundred dollars necessary to clear up the case. He blamed Judge Kiker for refusing to make a report, his only excuse for stopping the investigation.[13] Kiker died without telling what he knew. Detective Martin died, leaving voluminous notes on the case which had never been admitted in court as evidence by M. A. Otero, then attorney general. "How could I?" asked Mr. Otero years later. "One can't build a case on suspicions and imaginations. They have to be substantiated. And who cared?"[14]

Carmen Duran, so intimately associated with the case, moved away from Taos soon after Manby's death. In 1971 he returned, dying there on May 14. His death again revived in the press speculations about the case.[15]

So the mystery continues to live and prosper.

4

With the large trunk of the Tenorio Tract knocked off, Manby's Lost Kingdom dwindled rapidly. The Watson Land Company sold pieces quickly and cheaply, disposing of most of the remainder to a local attorney, Esquipula Martinez, who continued the process of attrition. Today, a horde of real estate agents, as ruthless as Manby, are avidly acquiring the land for resale in a booming market.

Manby's Folly!

As yet there is no Rochford-town or Manbyville-on-the-Seco, no towns or cities on the area of the grant. But with the rampant commercialization of once backward Taos, the town is rapidly expanding his way. A country club and nine-hole golf course has sprung up in the sagebrush where the Indians held their rabbit hunts. Near Manby Springs a spectacular bridge spans the deep gorge of the Rio Grande. To reach it there is a new paved highway, part of Manby's proposed Boulevard. Up Hondo Canyon modern cabins fill the aspen glades at Amizette; and on the site of the old mining camp of Twining a large ski resort has mushroomed with hotels, Swiss-style chalets, and A-frame lodges. In town there stands a million-and-a-half dollar motel not far from the resort hotel Manby envisioned. The Martin Hotel, Doc Martin's former residence, has been enlarged and renamed the Taos Inn. Manby's own home, later Thorne House, has been bought by the Taos Art Association which converted

Manby's grave marker, Taos.

his stables into the Stables Art Gallery. Behind it stands a new theater. His great English-style park has been bulldozed and made part of the Kit Carson Memorial State Park. It may well be that Manby's long Avenue and circular Boulevard will finally be achieved to meet tourist demands. There is no assurance that his great dream will not come true.

The Dream—the obverse side of the Folly!

Manby must be given his devil's due. On Arbor Day, a scarce three years after his departure, an editorial in the weekly paper appeared, headed: "MANBY GREAT TOWN BENEFACTOR." It stated:

"A. R. Manby was probably the greatest benefactor Taos ever had. He planted hundreds of trees and shrubs on his property years ago; many of those which make up our most priceless possession, the cottonwoods lining Pueblo Road."

His faults and sins, his avid greed, unrestrained ambition, and violence are amply recorded. Yet one cannot doubt that he loved the raw and tempestuous land which reflected his every mood; he had a quick eye for the beauty of line and texture everywhere. More than most men, he strove mightily and unscrupulously to build a mortal foundation for a nebulous dream —and watched it collapse ignominiously upon him. Perhaps his one great fault was that he lived before his time, and failed to leave a monument as a Founding Father to hoodwink us into believing he had a noble motive for getting too rich too quickly.

No mortal judgment can be made on a man like Manby. For in him we must recognize the same illuminating vision and dark shadow cast by the dual nature of every man. Only a hairline, too fine to detect, separates them. The Dream and the Folly are but opposite sides of the same cosmic die from which all human coins are stamped. Perhaps the mystery of the sacred mountain which overlooks his Lost Kingdom is that, serene and immutable, it reconciles, as we cannot, these conflicting opposites.

Below it stands the gravestone of Taos' reportedly greatest scoundrel, erected by the state scarcely a dozen steps from that of Taos' reportedly greatest hero, Kit Carson. The lettering on it reads:

Arthur R. Manby
Born 1860
England
Died 1929
Taos
He planted the trees in
this park and on Pueblo Road

The date of his birth is wrong, and perhaps the date and place
of this death, and all the great cottonwoods have been cut down.

Notes

THE DREAM

Chapter 1

1. Commonly misspelled "Rockfort."

2. The London General Register Office also supplies birth certificates for four children: Eardley Blois, January 17, 1851; boy (not named), March 15, 1853; girl (not named), March 6, 1854; boy (not named), December 30, 1855.

   The family genealogy, in disagreement, lists nine children: Emily (no date given); Clara, 1849; Eardley, 1851; Charles, 1852; Edith, 1853; Earnest (no date given); Alfred, 1858; Arthur, 1859; Jocelyn, 1862. This material and family background was obtained from Mrs. Edith Kearney whose grandmother Edith was Manby's sister; and from Steve Peters.

   The Manby family tree was compiled by Alfred Manby in 1929. Captain Cook made three Pacific voyages: 1768-1771, during which he discovered Australia; 1772-1775; and 1776-1779. Peters does not find Dr. Edward Manby listed in the roster of doctors on any of these three voyages. Kearney asserts that he accompanied Cook on the third voyage when he finally reached Alaska.

4. The *Santa Fe New Mexican*, July 25, 1929, reports this statement by Eardley Manby.

5. From personal interview with Edith Kearney and Steve Peters. The estate was finally settle in June 1950 and divided among twenty-one heirs in seven families.

6. Maxwell Grant history from William A. Keleher, *The Maxwell Land Grant;* Jim Berry Pearson, *Maxwell Land Grant;* and Herbert O. Prayer, *William Blackmore;* Harold H. Dunham, "New Mexico Land Grants"; Leroy R. Hafen, "Mexican Land Grants in Colorado"; W. A. Keleher, "Law of the New Mexico Land Grant."

Chapter 2

1. William A. Keleher, *The Maxwell Land Grant.*

2. From personal interview with Edith Kearney and Steve Peters.

3. Background material on 'Cassel" or Castle Rock, Griffin, Brackett from personal interview with Frank "Bunny" Alpers, Cimarron, New Mexico; F. Stanley, *The Grant That Maxwell Bought; Springer Stockman,* June 29, 1883; *Raton Comet,* July 13, 1923.

4. From personal interview with Kearney.

5. There seems to be a discrepancy in the reported dates for the killing. The *Las Vegas Daily Optic* of May 14, 1884 reports it occurred on May 11, the hearing taking place on May 14 as reported by the *Raton Register.* The District Court of Raton in its Bill 809, Criminal Docket of September 20, reports the killing on July 20.

While I have adhered to the *Raton Register's* report of official testimony given at the hearing, another, contradictory version of the killing was given by Jocelyn to Edith Kearney. Steve Peters reports this other version in *Headless in Taos:* Jocelyn was in the kitchen and Alfred was in the barn when the argument between Manby and Griffin began. Jocelyn grabbed up his rifle and shot Griffin. Alfred, running from the barn, caught a stray slug, presumably Griffin's. The bullet hit his front pants button, deflected enough to travel around his body to one side, then dropped into his boot. It was a freak happening, and he carried the scar across his side the rest of his life. Peters also mentions a supposed payoff of $3,000 by the three Manby brothers to a "high official of the law" to secure Manby's dismissal, but this has never been substantiated.

6. William A. Keleher, *The Maxwell Land Grant.*

Chapter 3

1. Steve Peters, *Headless in Taos.*

2. Ibid.; *Livestock Journal; Raton Comet.*

3. Frank Waters, *The Earp Brothers of Tombstone.*

4. February 28 hearing at Blossburg from Peters, *Headless in Taos.*

5. This version of the riot is largely based on George Curry's eyewitness account from *An Autobiography, 1861-1947*, with additional details from Jim Berry Pearson, *Maxwell Land Grant;* Steve Peters, *Headless in Taos;* and the *Raton Comet.*

6. For the killing of Dick Rogers, Tom Wheaton, and John Curry in Springer, ibid.

Chapter 4

1. Springer and Catron backgrounds from William A. Keleher, *The Maxwell Land Grant.*

2. Save for Manby's statement at his preliminary hearing, details of the Griffin feud and killing are lacking. They were presented in full by the defendants and many witness during the trial, but the records have mysteriously vanished from the files of the Colfax County Courthouse. Frank Brookshire, a personal friend, managed to unearth for me the original sixty-page transcript of the case, Criminal Docket No. 1110, taken down in early Pitman shorthand. After five years' search I have been unable to find anyone to transcribe it, including the Shorthand Reporters Association in Madison, Wisconsin. If it is ever transcribed, it will undoubtedly reveal sidelights unknown to us now.

3. Civil Docket No. 701, 837, and 839, District Court, Raton.

4. From personal interview with Edith Kearney.

5. Civil Docket No. 1058 and 1059, District Court, Raton.

6. Deed No. 808, 925, and 935, Colfax County Records. Located for me by Mr. Frank Gumm of the Box Cattle Company in Raton. Mr. Gumm was formerly custodian of the Maxwell Grant Papers.

Chapter 5

1. History of Martinez Grant from Abstract of Title, File No. 111, U.S. Court of Private Land Claims, Taos County Records.

2. History of Sangre de Cristo Grant, ibid. This history is most involved. The grant was made in 1847 to Narciso

Beaubien and Luis Lee, both of whom were killed in the Taos Massacre. Charles Beaubien inherited his son's share and bought Lee's share. In 1853 he sold for $500 a quit-claim for one-half of the grant to Maxwell, Play, and Quinn. In 1858 Play, his wife and the wife of Stephen Luis Lee sold all their interests to Ceran St. Vrian for $1,000. The United States Congress in 1860 confirmed the grant which was later established at 998,780 acres. St. Vrain two years later sold 1/6 of the grant to William Gilpin for $20,000. All the heirs of Charles Beaubien (his wife, six children, and two sons-in-law) sold their shares in 1864 to Gilpin for $15,000. This makes Gilpin's total investment of $35,000 which the text mentions. In 1865 Gilpin sold 1/6 of the grant to Fisher for $252,000.

3. Marshal Sprague, *Newport in the Rockies.*

Chapter 6

1. Steve Peters, *Headless in Taos.*

2. Thorne Letter File.

3. From personal interviews with Teracita Ferguson and Francisca Ferguson.

4. The Ferguson-Wilkerson-Stone-Manby business has never been satisfactorily cleared up. Almost every commentator has a different version. The simple summation given here is more fully developed in later chapters.

5. Detective Martin's report to Governor Dillon states that Manby sent telegrams to the Mexican government regarding mining leases and claims; and cablegrams on the same subject to English capitalists. Martin further reports that Manby obtained $85,000 specifically for development of the Marble Mine in Mexico. Location of the mine is unknown, and there are no records of its development.

6. Abstract of Title, Valley Abstract Company, Taos.

Chapter 7

1. Warranty Deeds, Taos County Records.

2. From personal interview with Teracita Ferguson.

3. Warranty Deeds, Taos County Records. With these pieces of property and the seven acquired in April, Manby had by now bought up nineteen pieces of land. Section and page numbers from the records, names and locations of these nineteen purchases are too voluminous to be detailed here.

4. Promissory Note, Taos County Records.

5. Mortgage Deed for $1.00, August 17, 1898, Taos County Records.

6. Manby had taken out his first citizenship papers in Raton on September 12, 1883, as described in Chapter 1, but had let that application go by default. His admission now to United States citizenship was the result of a successful renewal of his application.

Chapter 8

1. The following incidents have been related to me by my neighbors of twenty-five years in Arroyo Seco, New Mexico. While these incidents cannot be specifically attributed to Manby, they are typical examples of the way unscrupulous Anglos have obtained land from them. There is no doubt, from his long record, that Manby used the same methods.

2. Judge N. B. Laughlin Papers, State Archives, New Mexico Records Center, Santa Fe, New Mexico.

3. Manby to Laughlin, Judge N. B. Laughlin Papers, State Archives.

4. Where Manby was in Mexico is not known. All his alleged trips to that country are a mystery. Presumably he had mining interests there. From several later sources, one might suppose that he went to Ojinaga, not far from the Texas border. There was a mountain, the Cerro de Santo Cruz, where it was said the devil once lived, but apparently no mines in the vicinity. Edith Kearney, a member of the Manby family, doubts that he ever had mining interests in Mexico, saying that he was in Colorado at this time visiting Jocelyn and investigating opportunities there. Yet from this letter to Laughlin and other records, it certainly seems he was in Mexico—where, and for what purpose, no one knows.

5. Taos County Records.

Chapter 9

1. Personal interview with Aloysius Liebert; Rebecca James, *Eighteen Ladies and Gentlemen and Taos, New Mexico, 1885-1939.*

2. Santistevan-Manby business deals from Judge N. B. Laughlin Papers, State Archives, New Mexico Records Center, Santa Fe, New Mexico; Taos County Records.

3. *Santa Fe New Mexican*, July 25, 1929.

4. Articles of Incorporation, Taos County Records.

5. Judge N. B. Laughlin Papers, State Archives.

6. Taos County Records.

Chapter 10

1. According to *Headless in Taos* by Steve Peters, the Manby couple had briefly two visitors, Edith's teenage brother and Charles Manby's nineteen-year-old son who had a tubercular hip.

2. Judge N. B. Laughlin Papers, State Archives, New Mexico Records Center, Santa Fe, New Mexico.

3. Taos County District Court.

4. Register of Births, Taos County. Dr. Martin at the time was delivering a baby to Delfina Tafoya, wife of Earalino Barcela, a laborer.

5. Judge N. B. Laughlin Papers, State Archives.

6. Marshall Sprague, *Newport in the Rockies: The Life and Good Times of Colorado Springs*.

7. Articles of Incorporation, Taos County Records.

8. Laura was Jocelyn's daughter.

9. *Santa Fe New Mexican*, March 14, 1930; State Archives, Santa Fe, New Mexico.

10. Articles of Incorporation, Taos County Records.

11. Ibid.

12. Deeds, Taos County Records.

Chapter 11

1. Taos County Records.

2. Ibid.

3. This is a conjectured incident based on a reported brief scrawl in Manby's diary saying how upset he was but giving no reason. A number of authenticated entries in his diary will be quoted later, but, as will be described, the diary has disappeared.

4. Sworn statement, April 29, 1910, Taos County Records.

5. From personal interview with Teracita Ferguson.

6. From personal interview with M. A. Otero, Jr., former attorney general. Manby's feelings about this political excursion are quite clear; once home, he foreswore and denounced the whole business.

Chapter 12

1. Taos County Records.

THE FOLLY

Chapter 1

1. Taos County Records.

2. Blanche C. Grant, *When Old Trails Were New.*

3. Governor R. C. Dillon Letter File, State Archives, New Mexico Records Center, Santa Fe, New Mexico.

4. Detective Martin Files.

5. Thorne Letter File.

6. Detective Martin Files.

7. From personal interview with Teracita Ferguson.

8. Detective Martin Files.

9. Letter dated October 28, 1913, Taos County Records.

10. All this regarding the St. Agnes painting from the Thorne Letter File.

11. Waddell letters from Detective Martin Files and Governor R. C. Dillon Letter File, State Archives.

12. According to the Detective Martin Files, suit was filed July 14, 1914.

Chapter 2

1. Taos County Records.

2. Ibid.

3. Vine House and its characters from Rebecca James, *Eighteen Ladies and Gentlemen and Taos, New Mexico 1885-1939.*

4. Taos County Records.

Chapter 3

1. October 11, 1916, Taos County Records.

2. November 22, 1916, Taos County Records.

3. Warranty Deed, Lot 2, December 5, 1916, Taos County Records.

4. December 28, 1916, Taos County Records.

5. February 10, 1917, Taos County Records.

6. Taos County Records.

7. Judge N. B. Laughlin Papers, State Archives, New Mexico Records Center, Santa Fe, New Mexico.

8. Ibid.

9. Ibid.

10. Was the alleged purchase price of the grant sold by the TVLC to the TLC separate from or included in the $320,000 in claims against Manby? Was his total indebtedness a quarter- or a half-million dollars? I can make out these figures no better than the half-dozen lawyers who were concerned.

11. Receiver's Deed, Taos County Records.

12. Quit Claim Deed, Taos County Records.

Chapter 4

1. From personal interview with Edith Kearney.

2. Mabel Dodge Luhan, *Edge of Taos Desert*, vol. 4.

3. From personal interview with Mabel Dodge Luhan.

4. This letter was published in *Lorenzo in Taos* by Mabel Dodge Luhan.

5. Incident related to me by Mabel Dodge Luhan.

6. From personal interview with Andrew Dasburg.

Chapter 5

1. Thorne Letter File.

2. This letter and all following letters and material relating to Manby's paintings and to his relationship with Dr.

Thorne on other matters are taken from their voluminous correspondence contained in the Thorne Letter File.

3. Thorne background from personal interview with Helen Williams.

4. From personal interview with Teracita Ferguson.

5. Background and incident from personal interview with Captain Milton Arthur Spotts.

6. From personal interview with Mrs. Demetrio Rodriguez.

7. Articles of Incorporation, Taos County Records.

Chapter 6

1. From Detective Martin's official report to Governor Dillon. In a personal interview, Francisca Ferguson denies the facts. She asserts that Wilkerson, one January 1, left E-town to carry supplies to another worker in the Mystic Mine. A blizzard came up, and Wilkerson stopped at a miner's cabin to get warm. The miner asked him to stay all night. Wilkerson refused, went on, and perished in the blizzard. Ferguson in Taos read of his death in the newspaper the next day, and was very upset. I have found no record of his death in any newspaper to substantiate this. Both Francisca Ferguson and Detective Martin use the spelling "Wilkinson." I have adhered to "Wilkerson," the spelling most commonly used by other sources.

2. Manby to Thorne, October 17, 1921, Thorne Letter File.

3. From personal interview with Mrs. Fechin.

4. Background and following incident from Rebecca James, *Eighteen Ladies and Gentlemen and Taos, New Mexico 1885-1939.*

5. From personal interview with Dolores Montoya.

6. Governor R. C. Dillon Letter File, State Archives, New Mexico Records Center, Santa Fe, New Mexico.

7. This "Quo Warranto" case filed in District Court on February 7, 1935.

Chapter 7

Thorne Letter File. Manby wrote eighteen letters to Thorne between December 8, 1921 and December 7, 1922, many of which are quoted in this chapter.

Chapter 8

1. Existence, operation, and membership of this secret society from reports of Detective Martin and former Secret Service operator Herbert Cheetam; from the Thorne Letter File; from personal interviews with Cecil Ross; and from wide press reportage specified in the text.

2. Thorne Letter File. The seven-page letter from which this excerpt is quoted is dated February 25, 1924.

3. This oath, the following incidents, and Burch family background from personal interview with Cecil Ross.

4. From personal interview with Helen Williams.

Chapter 9

1. This book was, and presumably still is, in the Harwood Foundation Library, Taos, New Mexico.

2. Contract dated October 15, 1926, Taos County Records.

3. Related by Elmer Burch to press, to Detective Martin, and later to me.

4. This property comprised the tract of 1,500 acres deeded on February 2, 1921 to Margaret Higgins, Rosganna, County of Antrim, Ireland, but Manby still held her full power of attorney. This property he now deeded to Teracita on April 5.

5. Detective Martin Files.

Chapter 10

1. Thorne Letter File.

2. From personal interview with W. A. Keleher.

3. Taos County Records.

4. Thorne Letter File.

5. This surprising letter was written to Thorne in 1924.

6. From personal interview with Ralph Meyers.

7. From personal interview with Mrs. Ward Lockwood.

8. Detective Martin Files.

THE MYSTERY

Chapter 1

1. From personal interview with Mrs. C. O. Ward, widow of Detective Martin and author of his biography.

2. This account of Martin's investigations taken from his reports to Governor Dillon and from his widow's extensive collection of his personal files.

3. Governor R. C. Dillon Letter File, State Archives, New Mexico Records Center, Santa Fe, New Mexico.

Chapter 2

1. Governor R. C. Dillon Letter File, State Archives, New Mexico Records Center, Santa Fe, New Mexico.

2. Manby's diary included not only notebooks with notations and letters addressed to himself, but letters of all kinds described by Detective Martin as "embracing the movements of the universe, with maps, counterfeit money, medals and badges, signed and sent out by him to Teracita and also 'S.G.' Among the letters found in Manby's house and in his diary were shown all his transactions in land, irrigation projects, hotel projects, gold, silver, and marble mines, architectural projects of all kinds, as well as his transactions regarding the St. Agnes painting. Evidently his diary was a complete record of thirty years.

On the evening of Martin's examination of the murdered body, Hinde delivered to Martin the last letter Manby wrote in his diary, dated June 30, 1929. This letter Martin included in his first report to Governor Dillon, and it is quoted in this text. Martin also recorded the various entries quoted in this chapter. Portions of the diary were also seen and reported by Herbert Cheetam, former Secret Service operator who was called into the case, and other persons.

What became of this voluminous diary of such signal importance is a mystery. It is commonly believed that it was turned over to Attorney General Otero. However, he now denies any knowledge of its existence, the case having been droppd. As the diary comprised a great file of letters, much of it was probably left in Manby's house upon his murder, pending disposition with all his personal effects. Teracita and George Ferguson, and Carmen Duran who moved into the house, promptly stripped it clean. This no doubt included the diary which, according to Martin, implicated them in Manby's murder.

3. This is in variance with Martin's earlier report that the Garcias had seen Manby riding away from Teracita's house about 5:30 P.M.

4. From personal interview with Jack and Eve Young-Hunter.

5. This is one of the letters embodied in Manby's diary and found by Herbert Cheetam.

6. According to Edith Kearney, Jocelyn Manby, upon learning of his brother's death, rushed down to Taos only a day or two afterward. He found Manby's house already stripped.

7. The *Santa Fe New Mexican* of March 17, 1930 reports that a man had disposed in Santa Fe of a Blumenschien painting twenty years old and worth $11,000, and a portrait of Kit Carson, missing from the Manby house in Taos. Later Meyer said he purchased the Blumenschien painting from Teracita and sold it to Judge Wright. He added it was not worth $1,000.

8. March 12, 1930.

9. March 13, 1930.

10. Governor R. C. Dillon Letter File, State Archives.

11. Ibid.

12. Ibid.

Chapter 3

1. Ownership of this area was granted to Taos Pueblo on December 15, 1970 after a national controversy and prolonged debate in both houses of Congress.

2. From a personal interview with Victor Higgins.

3. There is another version of this related by Teracita Ferguson. Manby wore a size 7½ hat, and one of these was in her possession. Shortly after Manby's death, one of his brothers, presumably Jocelyn, and a lawyer, borrowed this hat to try on the skull. The hat didn't fit and this convinced Teracita that it was not Manby's body which was buried.

4. Quoted from Joseph Sharp by many printed sources.

5. From personal interview with Doughbelly Price.

6. Hodges, Wilson, and Vidal of Denver to Thorne, May 12, 1936, Thorne Letter File.

7. From personal interview with Helen Williams.

8. I was one of the guests of Mabel and Tony Lujan present on this evening.—F. W.

9. From personal interview with Helen Williams.

10. From personal interview with Teracita Ferguson.

11. From personal interview with Dolores Montoya.

12. From personal interview with Doris H. Brink, his daughter.

13. From personal interview with ex-governor Dillon.

14. From personal interview with ex-attorney general Otero.

15. *Santa Fe New Mexican,* June 1, 1971.

Sources and Acknowledgments

Due to the strange secrecy still surrounding Manby and his activities more than forty years after his mysterious death, little based on documented fact has been written about him until this present book. Therefore an attempt has been made here to substantiate every basic fact about him by thorough research into primary source records which were commonly believed did not exist and by interviews with innumerable persons who could give first-hand information about Manby's personal life and involved affairs.

ARCHIVES AND COLLECTIONS

Colfax County Records. Raton District Court criminal and civil court dockets, deeds. For exhuming a complete court record of Manby's and Jocelyn's trial for murder (not yet transcribed from Pitman shorthand), I am indebted to Frank Brookshire of Maxwell, New Mexico.

Taos County Records. Patents, warranty deeds, mortgage deeds, receivers' deeds, quit claim deeds, titles, certificates of incorporation, public notices, receipts, powers of attorney, promissory notes, contracts, marriage licenses, and registrations of births and deaths. For permission to unearth these innumerable entries transcribed in ink in great leatherbound books of official records kept in the vaults of the old Taos County courthouse, in Taos, New Mexico, thanks must be given to Mrs. Ursula Trujillo, county clerk, and her assistants. Without the help of Mr. Robert Montoya, an accomplished abstractor, it would have been impossible to trace these old records.

New Mexico State Archives. Judge N. B. Laughlin Papers; Governor R. C. Dillon Letter File; William Blackmore Papers, London File; Detective W. H. Martin's Reports to Governor Dillon. Dr. Myra Ellen Jenkins, senior archivist, kindly allowed me to peruse this material at the New Mexico Records Center in Santa Fe.

Abstracts of Title. Abstracts of the Antonio Martinez or Lucero de Godoi Grant, Sangre de Cristo Grant, and the Costella Estate, comprising the southern half of the Sangre de Cristo Grant, were provided me by Milton A. Spotts of the Valley Abstract Company, Taos, New Mexico.

Detective W. H. Martin's Personal File and Reports. Mrs. C. O. Ward of Santa Fe, widow of Detective Martin, kindly unearthed this extensive collection of papers for my use.

Thorne Letter File. A collection of more than fifty letters exchanged between Dr. V. C. Thorne and A. R. Manby, never before made public. For the privilege of inspecting and quoting from this intimate correspondence, I am grateful to Miss Helen Williams and Mr. Spud Johnson, former custodians of the collection and both old friends of many years.

Manby Family Records. Marriage and birth certificates were obtained for me from England by the artist Don Perceval of Santa Barbara, California. In addition, Mr. Steve Peters of Santa Fe gave me his own research notes on the Manby family history, and generously introduced me to Mrs. Edith Kearney whose grandmother, Edith, was the sister of Manby. Mrs. Kearney provided me with her own personal recollections.

Personal Interviews. Of the dozens of persons interviewed, I am especially indebted to ex-governor R. C. Dillon, ex-attorney general M. A. Otero, Mrs. C. O. Ward, Mrs. Dolores Montoya, Mr. W. A. Keleher, Mrs. Demetrio Rodriguez, Mr. and Mrs. Cecil Ross, Miss Helen Williams, Mr. Spud Johnson, Captain A. M. Spotts, Mr. Louis Wengert, Mr. Brice Sewell, Mrs. Rowena Martinez, Mrs. Doris Brink, Mr. Aloysius Liebert, Mr. Andrew Dasburg, Mr. Saul Harburg, Mr. Bill McGaw, Mrs. Mabel Dodge Luhan, Mr. Ralph Meyers, Mr. and Mrs. John Young-Hunter, Mr. Frank Gumm, Mr. Steve Peters, Mrs. Edith Kearney, Mr. and Mrs. Ward Lockwood, Mr. Victor Higgins, Mr. Robert Edmond Jones, Mr. Herbert Cheetam, Mrs. Teracita Ferguson, Mrs. Francisca Ferguson, and any others whom I may have inadvertently omitted.

* * *

Further acknowledgment and thanks are due to:

Mr. Jack Boyer, director of the Kit Carson Museum, to Mrs. Toni Tarleton and Mrs. Richard Dicus of the Harwood Foundation Library, Taos, for obtaining materials for me, saving me many trips out of town.

Mrs. Edith Kearney, Taos Art Association, Kit Carson Memorial Foundation, and Taos County Chamber of Commerce for kindly supplying photographs.

The Bureau of Land Management, Department of the Interior, Santa Fe, for furnishing copies of the original plat of the Antonio Martinez or Lucero de Godoi Grant made from the Walker survey, 1894, and of the Antoine Leroux or Los Luceros Grant made from the Walker survey of 1905.

Lastly and belatedly I must acknowledge here the devotion of my late sister, Mrs. Naomi Arnell of Sedona, Arizona, expressed in the secretarial and research assistance she has given me on this, as on all my previous books. Without her unstinting encouragement and assistance it could never have been prepared.

BOOKS

Curry, George. *An Autobiography, 1861-1947.* Albuquerque: University of New Mexico Press, 1958.

Ferguson, Erna. *Murder and Mystery in New Mexico.* Albuquerque: Merle Armitage Editions, 1948.

Grant, Blanche C. *When Old Trails Were New.* New York: Press of the Pioneers, 1934.

James, Rebecca Salisbury. *Eighteen Ladies and Gentlemen and Taos, New Mexico, 1885-1939* (Privately printed), 1953.

Keleher, William A. *The Maxwell Land Grant.* Santa Fe: The Rydal Press, 1942.

Luhan, Mabel Dodge. *Edge of Taos Desert.* New York: Harcourt, Brace & Co., 1937.

——————— *Lorenzo in Taos.* New York: Alfred Knopf, 1932.

Martin, Bill and Molly Radford Martin. *Bill Martin, American.* Caldwell, Idaho: The Caxton Printers, Ltd., 1959.

Pearson, Jim Berry. *Maxwell Land Grant.* Norman: University of Oklahoma Press, 1961.

Peters, Steve. *Headless in Taos: Arthur Rochford Manby.* Santa Fe (privately printed), 1972.

——————— *Incident on Red River,* Santa Fe (privately printed), 1972.

Prayer, Herbert O. *William Blackmore: The Spanish and Mexican Land Grants.* Vol. 1. Denver: Bradford-Robinson, 1949.

Sprague, Marshall. *Newport in the Rockies: The Life and Good Times of Colorado Springs.* Denver: Alan Swallow, 1961.

Stanley, F. *The Grant That Maxwell Bought.* Denver: World Press Publishing Co., 1952.

PERIODICALS

Dunham, Harold H. "New Mexico Land Grants, With Special Reference to Title Papers of the Maxwell Grant." *New Mexico Historical Review*, vol. XXX, no. 1.
Hafen, Leroy R. "Mexican Land Grants in Colorado." *Colorado Magazine*, vol. IV, no. 3.
Keleher, W. A. "Law of the New Mexico Land Grant." *New Mexico Historical Review*, vol. IV, no. 4.
de Mendoza, Gaspar Domingo. "Antoine Leroux Grant, August 12, 1742." *New Mexico Historical Review*, vol. XVI, no. 4.
Nunn, A. D. "Taos Terror." *True Detective Magazine*, August 1950.
Peters, Steve. "Three Lives in Taos." *Esperanza Magazine*, 1972.
Von Diest, Edmond C. "Early History of Costilla County." *Colorado Magazine*, vol. V, no. 4.

NEWPAPERS

McGaw, Bill. Series of articles on the Manby mystery. *The Southwesterner* (Columbus, New Mexico), August, September, October 1963.
Also consulted were *Taos Valley News, Taos Valley Cresset, La Revista de Taos*, and the *Taos El Crepusculo; Santa Fe New Mexican, Albuquerque Journal, Denver Post, Kansas City Star, St. Louis Post-Dispatch, New York Times, New York Telegram, New York Herald Tribune*, and Associated Press dispatches.

Index